WHY WOMEN *Cheat*

CONFESSIONS OF A PICKUP ARTIST

DANIEL GRAY

© 2014 by Itonia Press, Brooklyn New York.

TABLE OF CONTENTS

PART 1

EMOTIONAL COMBINATIONS:
THE KEY TO UNLOCKING A WOMAN'S HEART

Introduction/Instructions 11
    Introduction of Myself (Chan) 13
    Introduction/Introductions (Lola Key) 18
    Introduction and Background (Claudia) 19
The Truth and Nothing but the Truth 24
    Chan 25
    Lola Key 27
    Claudia 29
I Absolutely Do not Understand Women! 33
    Chan 39
    Lola Key 41
    Claudia 43
How to Make a Woman Fall In Love with You 48
    Meeting Future 48
        Chan 53
        Lola Key 54
        Claudia 57
    How a Woman Processes Information 60
        Chan 61
        Lola Key 62
        Claudia 63
    The Top Three Things Woman Said after Debriefing Me 64
        Chan 66
        Lola Key 68

Claudia 70
Lovers versus Husbands 75
Chan 76
Lola Key 77
Claudia 79

Safety First 81
Physical Safety 81
Chan 82
Lola Key 83
Claudia 84
Emotional Safety 88
Chan 89
Lola Key 90
Claudia 92

Lead an Interesting Life 94
Step One 94
Chan 95
Lola Key 96
Claudia 97
Why be Interesting? 98
Lola Key 100
Contrast 101
Lola Key 102
Claudia 103
Set your Goals 104
Lola Key 104
Claudia 107
Does She find <u>You</u> Attractive? 107
Chan 109
Lola Key 109

Create your own Necklace 111
Step two Involve her in your Dream 111
Chan 112
Lola Key 112

Be the Boss of your Dream 113
    Chan 114
    Lola Key 115
Be Involved in What Makes Her Special 116
    Lola Key 116
    Claudia 117
Example of My Friend Popeye 117
    Chan 122
    Lola Key 122

The Pearl Catalyst 124

Don't be a Dick! 124
    Chan 124
    Lola Key 125
Step Three – Share your Vulnerabilities 125
    Lola Key 126
Why are Vulnerabilities so Powerful? 127
    Chan 128
    Lola Key 129
    Claudia 130

The Death of the Neg 132

What's a Neg? 132
    Chan 133
    Claudia 135
RIP Neg… 135
    Lola Key 136
The Essence of the Neg 136
    Lola Key 137
A Personal Example 137
    Lola Key 139
    Claudia 141
Step Four – Throwing Down the Gauntlet 143
    Lola Key 143
Step Five – Neg her Hard! 143
    Chan 144

Lola Key..145

Assess the Situation 146
   Step six – Give her space and Just Chill 146
      Chan 146
      Lola Key..148
   Step seven – Let her Go..149
      Lola Key..149
      Claudia 149

How to Have Sex with Different women Every Day............................152
   Logistical problems...152
      Lola Key..153
   Sometimes Women Need Sex..153
      Chan 155
      Lola Key..156
      Claudia 157
   You Don't Need Anything Special 158
      Chan 160
      Lola Key..165
      Claudia 166
   Consider Ethiopia 169
      Lola Key..170
      Claudia 171
   Men are too Sensitive 172
      Chan 173
      Lola Key..175

My First Combination..176
   Letter to Rose (Excerpt) 176
      Chan 181
      Lola Key..183
   A Difficult Journey 184
      Chan 186
      Lola Key..187
      Claudia 189

Some Personal Combinations 191
   Please don't try this at home!..191
      Chan 192
      Lola Key...193
   A trip to Barnes & Noble 194
      Chan 197
      Lola Key...198
      Claudia..200
   Introducing my Penis 200
      Chan 204
      Lola Key...205
      Claudia..206
   I reiterate. Don't try these!! 206
      Chan 207
      Lola Key...207

Conclusion..209
      Chan 209
      Lola Key...216
      Claudia..217

PART 2

GUYS, IT'S ALL YOUR FAULT!

Discovering The 'Inner Woman' 221
   All the Parts that make a Human..221
      The Conscious Selves..221
      The Inner Selves..223
      The Greater Self...228
   The Woman's State 229
   Defending the 'Inner Woman' 231
   Introduction to Your 'Inner Woman' 233
   How the Professionals Engage the 'Inner Woman'...................234

    Ross Jeffries 235
    David Deangelo 241
    The Venus Butterfly Technique 243
    Mystery 245
  Why did I write this book? 248

What is a Man? 250
  I hate stupid lists! 250
  Men are Mission Focused 256
  Men aren't born Sexy 259
  The Origin of "Women's Words" or Ending my PUA Mission 263
  I don't understand women! 265

The Education of Mr. Crying Arab 269

A Worthy Mission 290

Note to Daddy Chan 292

Final Conclusion 298

Part 1

Emotional Combinations:
THE KEY TO UNLOCKING A WOMAN'S HEART

Answering the question 'Why do women cheat?' is quite simple. The most obvious reason is that she is being mistreated or abused. This makes sense to everyone. What perplexes both men and women are the times when the woman isn't being mistreated or abused. These instances when a woman has everything she could ask for in a man, yet she still cheats, seem hard to understand, but are actually just as simple.

The answer is the "Inner Woman" takes over and then leaves the woman to figure out and rationalize what took place. People use the term 'Inner Woman' loosely, so I need to clarify who this part of a woman is. The 'Inner Woman' is the subconscious part of a woman, who is in control of all of her lady parts. To be clear, this "Inner Woman" can chose to represent itself as young or old, male or female, or human or nonhuman. This is something that we'll discuss later. I use the term "Inner Woman" so that we can all understand what I'm talking about. If that term offends you, feel free to refer to that part in a different way.

The original title of this book was "Emotional Combinations." I changed it to add clarity for the female readers. An emotional combination is just what it sounds like. It is nothing more than a series of emotional states or outcomes. The 'Inner Woman' likes emotional stimuli, like cats enjoy catnip.

For the first part of this book, I hired three female writers from around the world to comment on the techniques to make women fall in love with you, and how to have lots of random sex with women. While these techniques may have merit, they are useless to me. There are literally an unlimited amount of techniques out there. Guys may learn something from the techniques that I wrote about. But if this is all that you notice then you've missed out on the ultimate purpose of this part of this book, which is to connect to the 'Inner Woman' of three random women.

"Emotional Combinations: The Key to Unlocking a Woman's Heart" was written to connect with the 'Inner Woman' of three women I'd never met, and who live hundreds of miles away from me and each other. Ultimately, I didn't get what I expected. I wanted them to notice what I'd done at the end. Only one noticed, and it was unforgivably lackluster. I'm not attempting to impress you with my abilities. But I do want to impress upon you that I created a unique and interesting experience for three different women, which lasted for about three weeks. I'd never done this remotely before and the results even surprised me.

There are two ways to approach the 'Inner Woman', either being super direct or by walking backwards and focusing on something totally unrelated. In the second part we will focus on being direct. If men and women want to understand why women cheat, they will first have to understand how players somehow connect with the 'Inner Woman', while talking about something else.

INTRODUCTION/ INSTRUCTIONS

My name is Daniel Gray. I am 36 years old, I have a degree in Mathematics from Vassar College and I taught chess all around the U.S. for about twelve years. I spent a few years playing poker professionally and was most recently deep into real estate. However, for the last two years I've all but sabotaged my entire real estate business, and wrote incessantly.

It would be nice to say that this book came from my years as a superstar player and the ladies can't get enough of me. Even if there is a sliver of truth in that statement, I have actually spent most of my life struggling with panic attacks and being emotionally unavailable especially with women. Two years ago, I reached a breaking point and the only answer I could find was to put in writing everything that was going on in my world and in my head.

I wrote and cried, I neglected my business and I became blind to everything else in my life. When I finally finished my book, no agents were interested so I self-published it on Amazon. It's titled "Violent Tremors: Journey to Overcome the Legacy of Slavery."

I'm proud of my accomplishment, and feel particularly liberated, although the book kind of sucks. It's far too long, and honestly it was not written particularly well. The biggest issue though is the multiple themes running through the book. I could potentially write individual books on each of those themes.

This book is based on just one of those themes. I mentioned "Emotional Combinations" only twice in an almost five hundred page book. I copied and pasted both of those instances in this book for your reference. I chose this theme because it seemed to be the most sellable of all the ideas I wrote about. I know it is not a terribly sexy reason to write, but I like honesty.

Feeling the need to have the opposite sex's opinion I decided to write this book with three random female writers from the internet. I posed ideas and situations all throughout this book, and it is my hope that the three female writers can shed their own personal light on anything that I've asserted in the book. Sometimes she'll give her opinion, share stories, share her thoughts, or share her feelings. She can be as anonymous as she wants to be and I will vigorously protect her identity.

The instructions to the female writers were: Ladies, you are free to write whatever you wish. I am deeply interested in what is happening with you. I want to know how you feel and what you are thinking. It would be kind of annoying if you just gave your advice. I'm not interested in lists or female advice. I say this because over the years I have interacted with many women and no offense, but their advice usually goes in one ear and out the other. Please understand that I'm not trying to diminish who you are. I'm just saying that a woman declaring what makes sense only to other women is totally useless to men. If you do have advice please explain the hell out of it.

I am enthralled by what women have to say, but what they say also frustrates me to no end. Please be aware that I'm a man and probably will not instantly understand the message you are trying to get across. Please feel free to introduce yourselves here. If you intend to use your real names and locations, please don't use the real names of anyone that you will be writing about. You are free to type whatever you wish and I will add it to this work. I just ask that you are honest. After you finish introducing yourself, would you mind explaining to a man what a woman is?

Introduction of Myself (Chan)

I am a 37-year old (probably 38 by the time you publish) newly married, recently unemployed, honest and I will admit often an irrational woman. (Aren't we all?) God help my husband. My current address, our first house, is my twenty-first address in 15 years. I have lived in one-stoplight towns and in downtown San Francisco. I feel like I have a fairly good grasp on suburban versus urban life and it certainly feels to me like I have interactions with every type of person under the sun, including the men that I have dated.

I was very excited to read this book and get a view into how the other half thinks. More importantly though I was touched and happy Daniel thought it was important to have the female reaction to his words. To me this shows the desire he has to change his approach and understanding of women. This shows a move towards courage and overcoming any previous lessons learned the hard way.

Before my unexpected unemployment status I was in the business of development. For the layperson that means fundraising or even more simply asking folks for money. I spent 10+ years becoming what the client needed me to sell. Not too different than a pick-up artist actually, since what I was normally selling ran close to people's ticket into heaven. I gave people the opportunity to give money that soothed their consciences and gave them bragging rights.

As I understand it pick-up artists (PUA) are given the tools to overcome their emotional/social hurdles and then they get bragging rights when they successfully get a woman into bed. I am a bit unnerved by that analogy but I digress. The strongest point being that anyone in sales or development has utilized some form of what is generally considered PUA behaviors. As you will see later on, when and how you use these behaviors makes all the difference in the world.

I started my dating life early. I had my first boyfriend in sixth grade although we did not even hold hands. He wrote me love notes (some of which I still have believe it or not) folded into origami-like shapes and our song was "Every Rose Has Its Thorn". As depressing as that song seems it is certainly not worse than my eighth grade boyfriend's suggestion that our song be "Janie's got a Gun." My early dating life was clean and pure as it should be just trying to harness all the hormones in.

As I grew up one thing become clear I was always going to be a one-man woman and I have never technically cheated on anyone. Remember the Ross and Rachel break thing from Friends? Yeah it went like that. I thought we were on a break and relapsed to an old boyfriend but the guy was only taking a few days off to think things through. It was only once and I truly never meant to hurt him. Unfortunately to this day he still does not even want to friend me on Facebook. A lesson was learned the hard way.

I lost my virginity at 16 to my high school love. The actual act of sex was not as important as finding the time and places to do it without our parents finding out. I always thought we would get married even if we broke up and lived our lives only to come back together years later, like it was our destiny. That was until one day I asked while fighting, "Don't you love me?" And he bluntly said, "I don't think so." Still makes my heart sad all these years later.

I have romantically truly loved three men and cared deeply for several more. That sentence was harder to write than I thought it would be. If I were to have worded it to illustrate the number of men I have told I loved them, the number would increase significantly. (Yes, women do that too because we do not want to hurt your feelings.) So I really had to buckle down and sift through years of relationship baggage to find out who really captured my heart. Those three men will forever have a special place in my heart and they have influenced every relationship I have had since them.

I have dated jocks, nerds, pretty boys, bad boys, musicians, older guys, younger guys, dicks and nice guys. I always had a particular thing for musicians. They were usually good in bed but horrible in a relationship. It sounds like I dated a lot and I certainly had my fair share of relationships but I never felt like I was dating more than my friends.

I was always very selective in my choice of sexual partners, even when I would seek out a no strings attached fling. Physical attraction was never enough for me, there had to be another redeeming quality (addressed later) to make them attractive enough for me to want to go to bed with them. I always looked for a man with kind eyes, a wicked sense of humor and the ability to hold his own in argument (which I have a tendency to start often). I was not easily swayed into bed and I always made the guy work for it. Sex is a powerful tool in a women's arsenal and I for one made sure I used it to the best of its ability.

Of course I do not have to make any of those choices now because I have found the one man that checks all the boxes. I would be lying if I said I miss dating. When I listen to my single friends tell me horror story after horror story (especially with Internet dating) I turn to my husband and realize just how lucky I am to be out of that scene.

What Is a Woman?

A woman is generous and confusing. She is capable of unconditional love while being able to hold a tremendous grudge for decades. Every woman is beautiful in her own way. Women can be strangely sentimental creatures. A woman is strong. We may not be able to bench press 200lbs but we can handle emotional turmoil like a champ. That is not to say that we always do handle every emotional situation with style and grace, but that strength is present in each one of us.

I have a girlfriend who lost her second child when he was two. She had two other small children, a full-time job and a grieving husband. She showed immeasurable strength as she somehow got back up and continued living their lives. She made sure the laundry was done, the kids were fed and continued to be active and she made sure her husband was drinking more water than beer. Recently, she had a miscarriage (the fetus was 3 mos. old) and after a medical mistake the doctors had to give her a hysterectomy. Their initial plan was to have 4 children in total, so they were still in discussions about at least one more child. I know of no man that could physically or emotionally continue on with his life, let alone support and run the lives of their entire family after the setbacks she endured. She went back to work 2 weeks after the surgery and planned and executed a child's birthday party with homemade cupcakes for her daughter. She is a gladiator.

Women honestly do not know where this strength comes from or why it chooses sometimes but not others to appear. We accept it as a burden, a blessing and ours alone.

A woman is generous. Do you ever hear of a man doing too much for everyone but himself? Is society telling men to make sure they get some "me time"? I get the "I work so hard to provide for my family" normal man response, but what I am talking about is something that plagues women everywhere. It is our innate need to take care of everyone else before ourselves.

I have another friend that has two children (one with a medical condition that is not critical but can go bad if not carefully watched), a high-pressure finance job, a husband who has good intentions but is not especially helpful when it comes to the daily life stuff and she is completely OCD when it comes to cleanliness and making sure her children have access to homemade organic snacks. She runs several miles a day, has a white couch and dresses like a J Crew model. This woman has let massage gift certificates expire because she is too busy doing everything for everyone else to stop and take care of herself.

The whole family was visiting a few months ago and the kids brought their sickness with them (daycare strikes again). She obviously was fighting a cold or sinus infection and the husband, who also seemed to have a touch of a cold, was milking his sniffles for all they were worth. Yet who made sure the kids were properly fed, medicated and comfortable? She did in spite of her own fever and constant headache. Now mind you my husband and I were there and so was her mother. All of us completely capable of taking care of two kids. It is not that she just has energy to burn, even though she actually does, but it is because she embodies what all woman feel whether we give in to it or not.

We are guilty of forgetting that in order to take care of others properly, we have to be healthy and happy ourselves. I do not blame men for this. They are merely taking an opportunity that women provide. Sometimes generosity is not the most attractive quality. A double-edged sword if you will.

A woman is a confusing creature saying one thing and doing another. All women are guilty of expecting men to understand the difference. You'll learn more about the difference further in the book. I will be the first to admit that what I say and do is often confusing and when a man does not respond or react appropriately, I often fall into an irrational mindset. Instead of communicating the fact that we wanted you to read our minds or translate all the non-verbal signs we gave you, we fly off the handle which strains the contact even more. Every man reading this last paragraph is nodding his head in agreement.

There is no way for us to turn this off fellas. Deep breathing, walking away, understanding you cannot read our minds, or any other of the logical solutions you have for this particular quality are of no use to us. Some women adapt to their irrational state and some feed on it and continue to allow it to run and ruin their lives. We all know those women but before you turn your back on them remember that they are acting on a natural instinct. If you find yourself with this type of woman make sure you do not take these irrational outbursts personally. She is just working through her process, which you will learn about soon enough in this book.

It would take years to write the entire definition of what a woman is and it still would never be finished. A woman has a great talent of becoming what she needs to be when she needs to be it. This makes us complicated to explain and wondrous to study. There will never be a *day when you wake up and come to the realization that you understand women. Just learn all you can and appreciate the differences between us. However if you show us all respect and equality there is a good chance we will let you in on few more of our secrets!*

Introduction/Introductions (Lola Key)

I choose not to introduce myself. I don't know why this was my primary instinct when I started writing this to you, or with you. I guess we still have this inhibition upon ourselves. The inhibition telling us that the questions of our heart and especially our bodies are the questions that are supposed to remain unanswered.

Or at least, this is the case in the part of the world I live in, Eastern Europe. I won't specify the country either. It is not the country that affects these cultural differences; it is the part of the world, the heritage in our genes. I mention this issue at the very beginning since I think this is very important.

We know you Americans. We always have been surrounded by you in one way or the other. We listen to your music, watch your films, read your authors, and watch your documentaries. We have a pretty clear idea about what kind of life you lead. So this means that I am ahead of you. I guess you don't know a lot about people from here.

I am not implying any positive or negative connotations; I am just saying that there are differences. And what do you Americans know about us? Have you ever watched a Croatian movie? Have you read any beautiful love poem written by any Serbian poet? Have you ever wondered how people manage to survive with the average salary of $500 a month? And finally, how do all these things affect our emotional lives? Do we know how to have fun the way you do? What do you think?

So for now, I choose not to introduce myself and I choose not to tell where I am from. I may change my mind during the course of my writing.

My instinct is for you and your readers to be surprised how different we are, or how similar we are.

I am 32 years old. This is very important for the course of this writing. Now that I am 32, I have completely different opinions than when I was twenty-something. I grew up. I matured. I took a deep look into myself. I have become aware of myself. I am satisfied with myself.

Don't worry, this is not going to be some social criticism about how we live difficult, burdened lives, how we are all mature because of that. Me and the people around me lead normal lives, have a lot of Sex and the City discussions, and contemplate a lot about the relationship between a man and a woman. Let me just comment on what you have written. Get ready, you!

Introduction and Background (Claudia)

My name is Claudia and I am a forty-nine year old Argentine female. I've been together with my partner, Horacio, for 13 years (although we are not married), and have an eight-year old daughter. Until I met the father of my only child, when I was close to turning 37, I thought I would never have a "normal" relationship. By "normal" I mean whatever relationship I saw around me that lasted more than just a few weeks or months. I was starting to believe that I would always be a witness of love stories but never a main character. I felt like an outsider, watching movies develop around my so-called life.

Of course, I rarely blamed myself but rather I would blame guys or fate (never God, as I'm an agnostic). I started dating when I was pretty young, only 14 years old. Until I turned 20, I guessed that my relationships were always casual because at the time I used to meet most of these guys at discos. I had always attended all-girl schools and was kind of shy; therefore, going dancing was my way to hide (or disguise) my shyness and almost the only place to meet members of the opposite sex.

After 20, I stopped going to discos. I believed I was over that phase. However, my romantic situation didn't seem to change much. I met guys whom I dated for a few weeks, or ever months, but that was that. I was aiming at a more permanent type of relationship, but I didn't seem to know how to keep a man interested. Of course, those who did remain interested in me really sucked, and I ended up dumping them.

At 23, I moved to the U.S. There, I hoped, EVERYTHING about my life would do a 180. I would live in a totally different place, with no parental control, make new friends, study something else, teach at university, and all this in what for me was a second language. Often times, I felt like I was immersed in a movie with no subtitles. American movies are big around the world, so as an Argentine I had been deeply influenced by the American culture seen in movies. Now, I was in one of them, like in "The Purple Rose of Cairo." However, my baggage was heavy and some things remained the same: my love life continued going (what I perceived as) "the wrong way". When I talked about this with someone else (friends in Argentina when I visited, or my therapist in the States), they said to me: "Well, of course, you're living on a university campus; everyone is there temporary, people come from different states and different countries, and it is hard to build a permanent relationship in that situation".

Well, it just seemed that everybody else around me could "get away with murder", so to speak, except me! I had three other female Argentine roommates who seemed to have traveled to the States with an agenda, which was: get a fellowship...then, a fellow! The natural consequence of this was marriage, and either a green card or a ticket to a European country where the guy was originally from. People used to call the house where I lived with these girls "the Argentine sorority". And they imagined that my agenda was similar to theirs...

As a matter of fact, I wasn't that smart. Although I always gave the impression of being controlled by my brain, I tend to be much more foolish than that and follow what my heart tells me to do. Therefore, I had no plan, no agenda, and just kept wondering why "life" seemed to happen to everyone else but me.

My ten years in the U.S. were full of wonderful experiences: I studied literature (which I've always loved), taught university undergrads and prep school students, got the chance to travel around the U.S. and other countries as well, and met lots of great people I can still call my friends. But finding love remained elusive.

I had this idea in my mind about what kind of person I thought would be right for me. However, after many disappointments, I just started paying attention to whatever guy I liked and seemed to be interested in having "something" (whatever) with me. As you can well imagine, this was the beginning of a series of even shorter and shorter ...relationships? encounters? one-night stands? What to call them? Until I decided to follow a (male) friend's advice: "If you know those kinds of relationships are doomed from the very beginning, just wait for the right guy. Don't start seeing people just because you 'have to' see someone".

Following this advice meant not dating anybody for many years. Seven years, to be exact. And turning 30 didn't help my self-esteem at all...

When I made the decision to go back to my country, there was not one single reason to do it. Actually, I remember making a list of reasons why I wanted to leave the States, and a list of aspects where my life would make great improvements if I decided to go back home.

One of those aspects was my romantic life. I felt that I had grown, I had "seen the world", so to speak, and now that I understood life better (??), I would enjoy more having a partner that spoke my language and had my same cultural background.

Unfortunately, it was not so easy to find "my place in the world" after ten years abroad. Some of my Argentine friends had also moved to other countries (to Italy, Spain, or the U.S.). Others had families of their own, and I hated feeling like "the single aunt". And I found that with some of them it was rather difficult to communicate, given that they didn't seem to understand or even be slightly interested in my experiences abroad. Again, I felt like I was coming from a different planet.

Somehow, I started reinventing myself. Although it was depressing to be doing the same kind of job I had been doing before my departure (teaching English in companies), there was a different dimension now as

I was also teaching Spanish for foreigners (which was almost not done at all until the nineties in Argentina). My job wasn't great but I could afford renting my own apartment downtown, I took photography courses my first year back here, and a year after that I registered in Journalism school, which had been a longtime dream of mine. I was still alone, but started feeling something close to happiness.

2001 was a dreadful year for Argentinians. The financial, political crisis hit rock-bottom and it felt like a big revolution was coming. After many of us lost most of our savings, experienced having 5 presidents in a week and shouted "Go home, everyone" to every and each politician responsible for this disaster, things started going back to (some kind of) normal. In the midst of all this chaos, I met Horacio.

I had started taking salsa classes at a place just down the street from where I was living. I'm not going to lie to you: I had ulterior motives. Of course it was a good excuse to meet guys. But in a way I ended up following the advice of a therapist I hadn't seen for years now. And it was this: "Instead of 'being looking' all the time, obsessively, just do something you enjoy, something you find interesting, and you'll meet other people (among them guys) with your same interests". So, dancing was fun, it kept me in good shape, and...yes, I could eventually meet guys there. And yes, I have always believed what they say about guys who can dance: there's a lot of other stuff they can do well too!

And just when I was not even looking, not even paying attention and just enjoying dancing salsa and swing, Horacio and I met.

That night I had been dancing with a guy that I had danced with before. He was a good dancer, and that was all. I didn't have my designs on him. So it wasn't heartbreaking when, in the middle of the class, he decided to go home; but it was a little frustrating because I did feel like dancing some more...and my partner was leaving!

I had to find someone else fast. The class was moving on, and I was just standing there, in the middle of the dance floor, partner-less. For dancing, I didn't need the guy to be cute: but he had to be tall. Otherwise, it became difficult for me to dance, as I am quite tall for an Argentine woman and dancing with shorter guys can be really awkward.

It was then when, looking around the dancing floor for someone my height or higher, I saw Horacio. He was taller than me, blond as I like them (although at the time this was irrelevant to me), and wore old-fashioned kind of glasses. Without realizing, I was choosing my daughter's father.

I will say more about this relationship later on. I don't want this introduction to be too long, and it's gotten long enough already. I wanted to summarize my love life and probably have failed already, as this is not the right size for a mere introduction!

Suffice it to say, for now, that Horacio and I have been together since that turmoiled 2001, have had our ups-and-downs but somehow managed to stay together. That has made me a different kind of person. And becoming a mother completed that transformation. Still, as I spent so many years by myself, jumping from one guy to the other or having no contact with men at all for years-on-end, I can sympathize with the way single people feel; much more, at least, than women who have always been involved with one man, or who have always had long-time relationships and have taken for granted sex, love, company.

Reading your book, Daniel, made me go back to that time. I tried to imagine how I would react to your strategies. And I also tried to figure out why the women you mention in your book reacted the way they did. I will make my attempt at trying to give you my own interpretations on their behavior, as well as telling you what I would do if I were in their shoes.

THE TRUTH AND NOTHING BUT THE TRUTH

I've been to many pick-up artist meetings, watched videos, attended seminars, and read books and articles on the subject of women. It's an almost universal truth in the PUA (pickup artist) community that *"you fake it until you make it."* They would say to practice your lines until you become believable. They would say that every failure is a learning experience. I wholeheartedly disagree. **Don't lie to women!!**

I can tell you from experience that lying is unnecessary. I've never once been caught in a lie because I always told the truth. I never needed a cover story and never needed anyone to back me up. Women are incredibly flexible and love the truth. Even if the truth hurts, they appreciate the honesty and will respect you even more.

It is beyond important to start this book off by getting you to commit to the truth. Women are incredibly complex; lies do nothing but shut the doors that you never knew could be opened. In addition, women are natural bullshit detectors. This is a fatal flaw in the reasoning behind a majority of the PUA information that I have picked up over the years.

Let's say you perfect a series of lines well enough to fool a woman. The first thing that has transpired is that you have desensitized yourself from the very nature of what a woman is. In doing so you may never experience the true gift a woman can give you. Secondly, no matter how hard you try the woman will eventually discovery your deceit. Then you are stuck in a giant hole attempting to dig yourself out. I've known many successful PUA's and that moment is the hardest part of doing what they do. If a woman knows that you can deceive her senses, then it's all but over.

This may come as a shock to guys who regularly read books about women. The difference between me and the rest is that I am not concerned about immediate results. Also, I'm not interested in making boot camps or private training sessions. If you pay thousands of dollars for a product or service, then surely you have a right to demand immediate results. Mastery, on the other hand, takes time and cannot be learned over a single weekend.

Some of you might be happy with your success from lying. If so, I'm happy for you and you should continue on to your heart's content. But realize, at the core, you are admitting to yourself that you never wish to understand or appreciate a woman. And I'm not talking about marriage either. There are too many patzers that get married and then get played. But to study and learn, only to lie is like eating bran cereal on the toilet. If you are going to do that, just dump all you know in the toilet and just flush.

Chan

Lying is not only unnecessary but also detrimental to any and all interactions you have with a woman. Women appreciate a man's honesty, even if it leads to a night of crying and the consumption of an entire pint of Ben and Jerry's.

For example, I once dated a guy who happened to work at a restaurant with a bar attached (nothing but trouble FYI). He would come over after work and I would leave the door unlocked so he could come in if I was already asleep. One morning I woke up alone even though the plan was that he was going to stop by. I called his house phone and cell phone and there was no answer. I got ready for work and decided I would just stop by there on the way. I was concerned since he could be a heavy drinker and sometimes chose to drive when he clearly should not be driving. My mind obviously went to jail, hospital and morgue.

When I pulled up to his house there were two cars parked in his driveway. I walked up to the front door and it was open to the screen door. It was a studio apartment so everything was in view and I could clearly see him in bed with another woman. I was feeling angry more than hurt, which surprised me. I must have made a noise because he noticed me standing there and came (buck-naked mind you) to the door. "I'm sorry," he said. "It just happened. It was a dumb mistake but I obviously slept with her and I apologize."

There was no begging or pleading. No excuses or fabricated stories; just straight honesty. Believe me when I tell you that I have been with guys that thought they were so smooth they would try to get out of what was a pretty obvious scenario. I held on to some of the anger but over time realized that while his honesty did not make his actions any better; it made my strange reaction ok. We stopped seeing each other until a few months later when I ran into him and he asked if we could get together (aka have sex).

He was very good in bed and surprisingly I did not have any residual romantic feelings for him. So I said yes and agreed to try out a new arrangement. So for about 3 months we had a friends with benefits relationship with the agreement that if either one of us found someone else we were to be upfront and honest with one another and it we would end smoothly. When I told my friends about the new arrangement they were shocked at my behavior. Not because we were choosing to sleep together without a romantic relationship, but because all they were stuck on the fact that he cheated on me.

Oddly, once I explained to them how I was processing his honesty (he did not try to cover up his cheating or beg to come back) they saw it my way. (Example of that secret woman's language later in the book.) I never worried about him lying to me and he did meet someone that he thought he could like romantically and he wanted to try to date her, which meant we had to stop seeing each other. Again honesty. We said our goodbyes and that was that. No leftover anger and no unnecessary hurt. Honesty allowed for a clean cut. Later on in this book you will see that some comments from me regarding how women feel about sex. So to cover myself I should mention that every time we slept together after the cheating incident I did make the choice to disregard that in my thought process. I still thought about everything that brought us to that point but chose to sleep with him in spite of it.

Women let men lie and get away with it, which is why a lot of PUA information gets through and allegedly works on women. I am considered a smart woman but even I have stayed with a guy much longer than I should have letting him spin his lies. Sometimes it's because I was lonely, or I enjoyed one single part of the relationship or the man (he was eye candy, good in bed, knows everyone, etc.). Sometimes we do not consciously see the lies but it will inevitably come to light and we will not bat an eyelash using it against you in a most revengeful way. Did I mention women can hold a grudge?

Daniel-I can tell you that you have hit the nail right on the head with this one. Honesty is always at the top of a woman's "must have" list. I do not know any women that would choose to be with a man who continuously lies to her or those around her. If you have something to lie about then you need to take a step back and evaluate your own behavior to see what the problem is. There is nothing more cowardly than a man who blames a woman for his lying. You chose to lie so man up and face the music.

Lola Key

It has always sounded to me a little bit lame when a person speaks about 'the truth'. A person does not talk about the general moral values; he or she lives their life accordingly. The same goes for the emotions of the deepest *sorrow and the most ecstatic joy. You simply cannot put them into words, they lose their true strength.*

The same goes with the truth. Live accordingly, don't talk about how you comply with the laws of the truth.

But, anyways, let me explain what I think when it comes to truth. "The truth" and our relationship to it is something that grows up and matures with our own age. When I was younger, the only truth I was interested in when it came to relationship with guys is the one that would make me compatible for him. I would change myself in order to fit the ideal version of a girl he would like to be with. Not being honest to myself, not being the true, genuine me. When you start realizing that being true to yourself is so liberating, that you can be loved, ohm, how you can be loved for what you really are, this is the moment when you really embrace the truth.

Yes, I have a lot of flaws. I don't say I should love them. I say that we should simply be aware of them and not hide them in ourselves. For, whatever we hide deep down in ourselves is a time ticking bomb, waiting to explode. Or, rather, implode; which is a lot worse.

So, ok, we are true to ourselves now. We are true to our partners as well. But what happens when our partner is not true to us. I had two boyfriends of such kind. When I was twenty-something, I was pissed-off because of that. I had an eight-year long relationship from my age of 16 to the age of 24. We started off as kids. As we grew older, the differences between us became more obvious and the first instinct to deal with them is to pretend you are what the other person wanted you to be. I don't remember, I might have lied to him probably in the same way he had lied to me, and for the same reason. We were quarrelling all the time about that. I simply couldn't understand why he would be lying to me.

What do I mean by lying? I don't want to say that we were lying to each other on daily basis and about some unimportant things. I want to say that we didn't express our needs, our opinions, and our true selves. We broke up, of course. I fell in love with somebody else, he did too. He got married after a few months, divorced after a few years. He wanted us to get back together; never ever.

The second time, I was with a great man, N, who wanted to make the world perfect. N wanted everybody around him to be living perfect lives; great idea. It had its benefits. N believed in it so much that a lot of times he managed to achieve almost impossible things simply by believing and acting and smiling.

A perfect world is difficult to be achieved. Yes, it hurts more for me to know that you would rather spend your days off with your mother than with me. But, on the long run, I wish I had known that from the very start since I would have had enough time to come to terms with that. I wish I had known the truth. But no. He used to have a perfect explanation for everything, and not a single one hurt me. Pink glasses were on. But in a number of cases, this does not comply with the TRUTH.

So, don't talk about the truth. Embrace it, find it in yourself. Accept its flaws, accept its beauty, enjoy in its simplicity. Getting rid of your insecurities is something that will follow the way.

Claudia

THE CONCEPT OF A "PICKUP ARTIST"

First of all, I have a confession to make: maybe because I'm not American (even though I lived in the U.S. for ten years), the concept of a "pickup artist" escaped me until I came across your book. Of course I saw "Hitch" with Will Smith. And I have read about Argentine men who have opened "seduction schools" (that's what they are called here), where they supposedly teach other men how to make a woman fall in love with them. I guess the difference is that here, men like the Will Smith character in "Hitch" are considered crooks who just want to make money opening sleazy kind of schools, whereas the men who enroll in these "seduction" classes are seen as losers who should get a life...and get it soon.

In any case, I did a little research to get more information, which today is easier than ever thanks to the Internet. And I am still struggling to understand why a man would want to follow instructions from another man in order to pick up a girl. This is a little hard to do, but understanding men has never been one of my skills (just as understanding women is still a major challenge for you!). And maybe understanding is beyond the point. I read some graffiti on a wall the other day. "You live your life or you understand it. You can't do both".

THE TRUTH...

I see why lying was necessary years ago. Women didn't use to jump into bed with men so easily; also, they all wanted to have exclusive relationships. But that's not the case nowadays. There are many women who are not looking for "a boyfriend", a husband, a steady relationship, and are open about their intentions. "A good girl's reputation" stopped being an issue long ago.

Therefore, what's the point of lying for a man? Still, I found that many men still do so in order to catch a girl's attention or even to try and make them fall in love with them. Later on in the relationship, they start being themselves. But they've already fooled the girl, who thought she was falling in love with the man he was during the first few weeks or months of their relationship.

I'll tell you about a guy who was trying to cheat on someone else with me. We met online, where he could have contacted any kind of girl he wanted, for whatever end he had in mind. However, he wanted to "play the boyfriend game" with me. After chatting online, we spoke on the phone. He spoke as if we had some kind of mental, emotional connection, playing the "we're soul mates" game. He started telling me about his difficult personal situation. He had married a few years before, but he and his wife had grown apart. However, they continued living under the same roof for "practical reasons". Fine, I told myself. Let's see how he handles this if he asks me out for a date.

Not surprisingly, he asked me to meet on a Wednesday for lunch. Typical cheating date, at least here in my country. A guy who wants to play the game of sharing a mental connection and stuff like that would ask you out on a date for Saturday night.

Anyhow, I went to that coffee shop downtown. It was a time when it was not customary to exchange pictures on the Internet. Digital cameras were still expensive and scanners not so common. Or maybe we were both kind of old-fashioned and believed in keeping the mystery until we actually met face to face.

There were no butterflies in my stomach, nothing special at all, when I finally saw him. The conversation was Ok, and that was it. When we said good-bye, he pointed out that he liked my skin. Here people say something like "I have skin with someone" meaning there's good chemistry; that is what he wanted to say.

Just like I had done many other times before, I thought I should try giving this guy "one more chance". Later on in life I learned that it's useless to force yourself to try to like someone. Things happen naturally when they have to, and if you make a big effort maybe that story should never take place at all.

But I thought: "I'll ask him to see me on a Saturday night." If what he's doing is cheating on his wife with me, he'll refuse. And I was not interested in dating a married man. Of course, I was right: the mere mention of "Saturday night" made him recoil: "Well, uh, you know, that could be a little awkward". "Why?" I asked. "Didn't you say you are separated, and you only continue living in the same house for practical reasons?" "Yeah," he conceded. "Still, she would find it odd that I go out by myself on a Saturday night. I don't want to hurt her feelings. I'm sure you can understand that." Well, no, I couldn't, and wouldn't. That was the end of it for me. I told him before hanging up that nowadays it wasn't necessary at all to tell lies to have a lover. The Internet is a new resource, but even if it didn't exist, there are so many places these days where you can meet women that do not mind being just lovers, having a one-night stand, or being told upfront that you are a married man who is looking for an affair.

Still, men continue lying. It might pay off for some of them. But I still don't get it. I hate to be treated like a fool. I don't want a man to insult my intelligence.

"Women are natural bullshit detectors," you wrote. You got that right! It may take us more or less time, but eventually we realize whatever a guy did to seduce us was just an act. Sometimes there are women who appreciate a little deceit ("tell me lies / tell me sweet, little lies", as the song goes) when they see it just as a gigantic effort the guy made during courtship. But if the bullshit lingers on...it stops being fun and cute.

Through the years, I also learned that a woman can always win an argument. I remember that when I had my first American boyfriend, I thought: "Oh, no. It's the first time I have a relationship entirely conducted in English. It's not my first language...He'll probably win all our arguments! Will I be able to handle that?" Easy, girl: that never happened! In spite of my inferiority complex regarding the language issue, I won each and every argument. The most he said was "I don't know", "I don't know what to tell you." Other times he just remained silent or evaded confrontations. When faced with the truth, in my humble opinion, men tend to run away. Women prefer to be completely devastated, but be given the truth...and nothing but the truth.

I guess I understand, nevertheless, why many men would rather lie when they meet a woman. It seems that their urgency for sex is so pressing, that they would just blurt out anything to get into a woman's panties. As this is a short-term goal, they don't care if lying doesn't get them very far. As long as the lie lasts for one night or even a week, they are happy. Then, they move on. I understand, then, why lying is not what you want, Daniel, if your goals are long-term.

I ABSOLUTELY DO NOT UNDERSTAND WOMEN!

I told you that I am going to be honest, and I am not ashamed to admit that women baffle me. It is incredibly humbling to admit to myself that there is something that I don't understand and will likely never understand. I recently just finished writing and self-publishing my memoir, "Violent Tremors: Journey to Overcome the Legacy of Slavery." It took me close to two years to write and was incredibly liberating.

In it, I mentioned a process called "Emotional Combinations." As a chess player, this process is how I attempted to express the complexity of a woman. Other guys, with a lot of experience with women, have different ways of expressing similar ideas. I chose what makes sense to me. I would like to share with you what I have learned because it's a little depressing how clueless the vast majority of guys are.

The first steps towards the "Emotional Combinations" I discuss are for you to have a come to Jesus moment yourself and realize the infinite chasm between yourself and the nature of a woman. Since, most of you may never experience that moment yourselves, I'll tell you of the day I realized that women are totally not men.

Before I continue, I want you to know that I am somewhat retired from the game. It's been over two years since I have been with a woman.

This is by choice. Having sex with a different woman every day might seem impressive, until you are living that life. If that is what you want, I will tell you how to get that life later, but that life will limit you to only part of what a woman is.

A few years ago outside of a store in Manhattan, I met a gorgeous Puerto Rican woman. After we talked for a while, I had to go and she gave me her work email address. When I saw the address I knew immediately that she was married.

We exchanged email for a while and she sent me pictures of herself. When we met it was the dead of winter and she wanted to show me how good she looked when she was made-up. She was so amazingly beautiful. In time, we started talking in the phone and making plans to meet during a 'ladies night out.' The last time that she tried to organize a ladies night out with her girlfriends, she became remorseful. I remember that she took a deep breath and somberly said.

Perfecta: "What am I doing?"

Me: "Organizing a ladies night out with your coworkers."

Perfecta: "No what am I doing with you! I don't understand. Why am I talking to you? Why am I trying to meet up with you? Why? I don't get it." I quietly listened. "I have a wonderful family and a perfect husband. What am I doing? Why am I risking ten years of marriage? Why? My husband is so perfect! I'm so lucky to have a perfect man like him. Why am I trying to throw all that away?"

Me: "What do you mean 'perfect'?"

Perfecta: "He's perfect! He treats me like a queen. He's always there for me. He takes care of me. The other day while pmsing he went out, in the middle of the night and looked for three hours to get my favorite ice cream. He's the man that other women wish they had! He's a perfect father to my kids and he's a perfect husband to me. He's perfect!"

I had become overwhelmed with emotion at that point. At that time, it was rare for me to experience anything emotional, but as she described her husband I became sad, jealous, and afraid. It felt like I could be Mr. Perfect. It felt like I was seducing my own future wife. Even though, at the time, I was emotionally unavailable. I had high hopes that I would be the man that she was describing. So I cut her off.

Me: "Okay. That's enough. You're confused, and I understand that. I'm a player and I have a process. You feel the way you do because you are going through my process. I'm going to tell you what would've happened. I would have sex with you for a few weeks, and then I'd tire of you and move on. Let me tell you something. I've been with a lot of women, and you are the only one who described her man as perfect. Women always have something bad to say about their man. There is no way that I'd allow you to mess that up. We are never going to have sex; ever. Even if you magically appeared in my bed butt naked. It ain't gonna happen. Also, we are never going to go out on a date. If you have a perfect husband then you need to stay with him. One thing though, you are very intelligent and I enjoy talking to you. I told you that I'm a player, and I have between eight and ten hours of material that I say to women. I'd like to run my routines by you because I'd like to have your opinion."

Perfecta: "Okay!" She said in a cheery and upbeat way.

During that period, I was enamored with a pick-up artist named Mystery and the "Mystery Method." His method for getting women was especially technical and I liked that. The Mystery Method basically was a series of routines that would lead to sex with a woman if done properly. Since I am all about honesty, I did not use any of his pre-written routines. I made my own routines and placed them in an orderly way that I believed would be effective. Also, I spent at least an hour every day practicing my routines at home and a few hours per day practicing in public.

In addition to my routines, I regularly practiced what I called 'Women's Words.' I've had a lot of experiences with women, and they would share stories and/or say things that simply did not make any sense to me. I was in the habit of writing down what these women would share with me and then I would bring it up to other women. For some reason beyond my understanding, women loved the things other women would tell me.

Because the 'Woman's Words' I would say clearly came from another woman, it's like it qualified me as someone who other women like. Some of the things women would say were upsetting and I argued with them about it. They would just conclude that I did not understand. During that time that I was talking with Perfecta, I was in the midst of randomly arguing with women about who was the one that caused me to pick them up. It came to the point where I would hit on a woman, and after she gave me her number I would tell her "I'm a player, and the only reason that I stopped to talk to you was to prove that it was me who was the one who set this all up." One by one they all said that it was in fact them who made me come and talk to them.

Me: "Okay Perfecta. I'm glad we settled that. But there is just one thing I think we need to agree on before we go on."

Perfecta: "Sure what is it?"

Me: "Well, I told you that I do this all of the time and I spend a great deal of effort to get the results that I do. I was just wondering. Who do you think caused us to meet?"

Perfecta: "I did."

Me:	"What? How can you say that? I was the one who initiated I contact, I was the one who smiled first, and I was the one walked over to you and smiled. There's no way that you can say that you did any of that."
Perfecta:	"It doesn't matter. I was the one who made you come over."
Me:	"Even though you know that I'm a player and will help me with my routines?"
Perfecta:	"Yes."
Me:	"Okay. I'm going to strip away all of the reasoning other women gave me to why they caused me to approach them, then I want you to tell me how exactly you caused us to meet."
Perfecta:	"Okay."
Me:	"First you weren't dressed up at all. You were wearing layered sweatpants, sneakers, a bubble jacket and a puffy hat." It was December. "You weren't wearing any makeup, or any special eye catching items. Nothing about you said come talk to me. Also, let's not forget I'm an admitted player who does this all the time, and I mean all the time! Please tell me how you caused me to talk to you?" I was completely unprepared for her answer.
Perfecta:	"I was wearing sexy underwear that day."
Me:	"What? But I never saw your underwear!"
Perfecta:	"That doesn't matter."
Me:	"It doesn't matter? You think that I was drawn to you because of sexy underwear that I did not even see? You can't be serious?"
Perfecta:	"You don't understand. It makes a difference."

I was furious after that last sentence. I said goodbye to Perfecta and planned to never talk to her again. Fortunately for me I was going through my 'Women's Words' phase. I went out to talk with more women and relayed the entire story. One by one they all said the same thing unprovoked "You don't understand. It makes a difference."

I like to think myself a genius. I like to think that given enough time and information that I can solve any problem. This moment in my life is extremely frustrating for a person like me. I literally get a headache every time I think about this story. I never saw the underwear! I cannot understand why women actually believe that sexy underwear makes any difference at all. You see! I'm getting a headache now just thinking about it.

It is incredibly humbling and annoying to know that there is no way that I can understand a woman's logic. I can't even write; this is giving me such a headache. When all the women that I spoke to said the same thing, it was like I realized that women are an alien species hiding in plain sight! The chasm between what a woman thinks and what a man thinks is so wide that it's eye opening to stare directly into the abyss known as woman.

Most guys, when confronted with the complexity of a woman, do everything possible to avoid what she is or attempt to cover the woman she is up. That is when I totally scrapped all of my routines. I realized that the Mystery Method was nothing more than one man's interpretation of the complexity known as woman.

I spent the following months picking Perfecta's brain. When I realized how different she was from me I had to study her. I did, in the beginning, talk to her about some of my routines. After hearing her feedback I began to create new routines to see how she would react. In time, I had no routines. All I would do was emotional combinations.

For those of you wondering whatever happened to Perfecta, I'll tell you. She broke it off with me. Even though I promised to never meet with her and to never have sex with her. Even though we never even talked about sex, she sent me an email saying simply "This is too much for me. I love my husband and want to be a good wife for him. Please delete my number and email address and never contact me again."

When she said that, I was sad and furious. I wanted to debate with her about her reasoning. All we were doing was going over things that I would say to other women and getting her response. She was the best teacher that I had and wanted to keep her. The fact that I couldn't understand why she was cutting me off gave me pause. I don't think that I'm supposed to understand. I emailed her back and said, "I understand." We never spoke again.

Some of you still might not get it. It seems innocuous and silly. But you need to understand how different women really are to us or you will never learn. I've shared the moment I realized this, but it's not enough for you to read it, you must do it yourself.

What I want you to do is to relay this story to a woman you know. If you don't know any women just go on the street and talk with one. If you have a hard time talking, print this story out and ask her to read it. Be sure to do your best to pick her brain. The most important part of that story is the words "You don't understand. It makes a difference." I get upset and get a mean headache thinking about that. I hope the experience is the same for you.

Chan

On Perfecta: The truth is that women do not always believe that they deserve the perfect man. Societal history dictates that women are "lesser" in some way, shape or form. For examples see glass ceiling, right to vote, women in the military, etc. I realize that is a very broad statement but a lot of women feel these restraints on a daily basis and it affects their self-esteem. Even those women that seem to have their shit together are always questioning whether they are good enough and whether they deserve to live the life they are living. Then there are the women that were given the bumpy road in life who do not understand what they did to deserve this pain and suffering while at the same time do not believe that they deserve more. Confusing as it is, your example of Perfecta clearly said to me that she loved her husband and the problem was within her and with her self-esteem.

The PUA routines work because women as a norm are always somewhat insecure. The PUA tactics feed on these insecurities and instead of reducing them, it intensifies them when they actually come to terms with the fact that you will not be calling again. Slippery slope I would say.

A women's self-esteem is a fragile and complicated part of the real her. If you are ever given complete access to a woman's self-esteem and the baggage it carries consider yourself in the inner circle. We hold it so close to ourselves because it is the reason why we bloom into a gorgeous flower or wither to the ground. Tread lightly here men and really think when doing PUA routines or emotional combinations because your actions could be the straw that breaks the camel's back.

Moving on to the "Mystery Method". I know these practices exist but I would be wrong if I did not say that I find them insulting and disturbing. The part that creeps me out the most is that you practiced them like they were a job or acting gig, not actually an event in a woman's life. Explaining the PUA routines to me is like watching a "how to" reap crops video where the end result is a cut down field of corn. Strange analogy? Think about how the routines go step-by-step teaching men how to get a woman into bed, or how to reap a crop. Unfortunately all these routines do is teach the men to cut down the crop not build it back up. The future is bleak for those that rely on these routines. Needless to say at this point I do not appreciate nor find the good in these routines.

My favorite line is "You don't understand. It makes a difference." This makes your book and your point in two sentences. Men do not understand and even when they take the time to try, the chances are very slim they will actually get it. Men and women are genetically made up differently and therefore our thought processes will always continue to be different. What is truly important to us rarely even crosses your mind. I am not saying this in collaboration with a "men suck" attitude. Rather, I am stating a fact that our priorities are different whether a woman externalizes them or not.

There are more discussions of our differences later in the book that will either make things clearer, or muddy the waters even more.

Lola Key

Male brain-female brain. Male reasoning,-female reasoning. Male way-female way. Is there a difference? Are we presupposed to think differently or act differently simply due to our sex? Is there anything in our genes, in our chromosomes, that makes or predisposes us to think and act differently?

They have kids as I understood. Kids, plural form, presupposes years of being together. What do I think about that? Whenever a person, male or female, tells me passionately that She and Her Sweety Little Hubby are having wild sex on daily basis with the same flame for 10 years, I can only say: BULLSHIT!

In a long relationship, and I have had two long ones, it is perfectly normal to have periods without sex. I wouldn't like it to be like that, but it is the truth. Admit it to yourselves people, there is nothing to be ashamed of. Once you admit it, you will start your deep introspective in why this is the case? Are you annoyed with some of his bedroom habits? Is it the thing that he is too yours, that there is no magic in it anymore? Is it that you would technically like something wilder? Something kinky? Is it you, after all?

What I honestly think is that Mrs. Perfecta is Mrs. Aperfectlyertoherself. Let me put it this way. When I am truly in love, which I now am, it is like my body, heart and soul are filled with this emotion. Like a cup that is full of liquid. There is simply no space for some new liquid to be poured into. And when the glass is half full (in Mrs. Perfecta's case, half empty, I'd say), there is plenty of room for the new "liquid" to be poured into. Sorry for the insinuation. She just wanted you to push harder, to make her feel more special, to make her feel full. This is something Mr. Perfecto hasn't been doing for a while; guaranteed.

I know a lot of examples of women who emphasize this. I am not some kind of moralist, don't get me wrong. I am not a person who is always faithful to a single man. I have cheated in my life for I'd rather not say how many times. But I am completely against this point of view. And I don't understand it. Ok, there is maybe the possibility that women who constantly cheat on their partners while at the same time claiming that their partners are perfect are in fact lying to their lovers. To make them look like angels in their lovers' eyes. Like, look at me, am I so angel-like, I can love, I do love, I just don't know what got into me and this is temporary! Bullshit! Or, even worse, such girls do believe that their husbands or partners are perfect! This can probably be the case only if they are with some morons who don't treat them the way they are to be treated and women desperately try to pertain in such a relationship.

This is so much related with what we talked about in the previous paragraph, with the truth. I guarantee that such women are not honest to themselves. This also has a lot to do with insecurity I wrote about. These women are so insecure that they don't want to admit to themselves that they are weak, their relationship is not perfect, it is okay to fail, just stand up again. Women these days simply go for the easiest solution. I am not emotionally fulfilled, okay, let me jump into another man's bed. This is not how things are done, ladies. Stay with your man in times of trouble like our grandmas and great-grandmas. Or leave him if you are not meant for each other, you are not going to die, and you will survive. Or cheat on him if you have to. Just be honest to yourselves.

The other point you made in the paragraph of not understanding us has really put a smile on my face. A man doesn't understand how a woman looks differently, talks differently, smiles differently with sexy lingerie. Oooh, Mrs. Perfecta, now we are talking exactly the same language!

My urban friend D whom I met few years ago in the club, says: "When we go out, it is Me who chooses who will be hitting on me." And that is the truth. You men keep forgetting our magical, seducing beauty, our irresistible fragrances that you cannot resist. Are we going to let it come out or not, depends on whether we are satisfied with ourselves. And when we are, for example, when we think we look stunning in the new underwear that fits us perfectly, we simply let it go. And we are the ones who choose, who make it happen. Touché, Mrs. Perfecta.

Claudia

DO I UNDERSTAND MEN? DO I UNDERSTAND THE HUMAN RACE?

There are many popular sayings, jokes, and stories around how difficult it is to understand women. Even Freud wondered: "What do women want?" When we girls get together and talk our hearts out, we wonder what men want, what they think, and admit to ourselves that we don't understand them. Nonetheless, often times I wonder if I understand some of my girlfriends. And it's then when I conclude that human beings are just impossible to understand, and that is, after all, the beauty of being alive and open-minded: learning every day a new aspect of how wonderful (or dreadful) human souls can turn out to be.

AY, AY, AY, PERFECTA!!

Next, you'll know my opinion about the Perfecta story. This girl was totally baffling to you, she enraged you at some point and left you completely perplexed. However, and again this is my humble opinion, I think I know what she was up to.

First of all, as you said very well, nobody with the "perfect" husband would be remotely attracted to another guy. Unless, I figured, life has always been completely perfect for you and you need to experience danger, living on the edge and being close to losing everything. That could be a reason to try to cheat on Mr. Perfect.

Having said that, I believe that the moment she discussed her "perfect" husband to you and got you immersed in all the emotions you describe (jealousy, sadness, fear), which made you utter the defining moment phrase "We are never going to have sex; ever", everything changed for her.

That is NEVER, EVER, what a woman wants to hear. Even if it comes from the ugliest, least undesirable man on the face of the earth. I once heard that coming from a lesbian friend of mine. We've been friends for almost thirty years now and often times we traveled together and shared a hotel room. What she said to me was: "You are the only woman I can share a room or even a bed with and not be slightly aroused." Although I have never had the any interest in other women, and especially not in her, I felt a little offended. It is weird, it is crazy: but not being wanted by someone is not something a woman takes well.

Remember the days when a gentleman would say to a lady "I don't want to hurt you," meaning "We're not going to have sex," and for that purpose they looked for "certain" kinds of girls? Well, I bet that even in those days they were a little offended. Even when they thought that sex before marriage was dirty, and after marriage, an obligation.

Evidence of that appears in the first ten minutes of this Cuban movie, "Fresa y Chocolate" ("Strawberry and Chocolate). If you just watch the first ten minutes, you will see an illustration of what I mean. This guy takes his official, steady girlfriend to a hotel room, to make love for the first time. Apparently, she's still a virgin (and maybe he's too). When she comes back from the bathroom, she seems to have second thoughts: "You asked me out to go to the movies, and you bring me here, to this dirty, sleazy place...Sex is all you're interested in." He puts his clothes back on and says to her: "I'm not just interested in sex. I'm interested in you. And I'll prove it to you: we won't have sex until our wedding night, in a five start hotel." In shock, she turns around and goes: "What?" For what happens next, you need no subtitles...She ends up marrying someone else, who probably "didn't respect her" so much (in the old-fashioned sense of the word).

You say that Perfecta said "Ok" (after you told her you'd never ever have sex), "in a cheery and upbeat way". Good mask, Perfecta, but I'm sure you were hurting like hell inside!!

THE "WHO-PICKS-UP-WHOM" ISSUE

Historically, men have picked up women, but it's always been believed that there is something that a woman does (consciously or not) to cause that to happen. The bottom line is women are always the ones manipulating the situation and in control.

Before I became a teenager, I felt like the ugly duckling. I believed that what made you attractive to men were a very pretty face and an outgoing personality. And I thought I lacked both. Ok, I had a good body, but...would that be enough? I wondered. As I grew up and starting going dancing and meeting boys, I realized that there were other things as well that men found attractive and that, amazingly enough, I seemed to possess. That empowered me. After a while, I noticed that whoever I liked at a party, somehow ended up approaching me. I started feeling more self-assured and even though I didn't understand exactly how things worked, I was confident that I would get the man I wanted...just by wanting him.

In your Perfecta story, you describe the way you discussed with her who caused the two of you to meet. You were sure you were responsible for that; however, she begged to differ...and that made you hit the roof!

Particularly so, when you heard the reason: "I was wearing sexy underwear that day." What follows is several explanations I have for a woman to say such a thing:

a) *She was bluffing. Perfecta thought that excuse sounded sexy enough, which was just what you deserved after telling her that the two of you would never, ever, have sex. She knew it would have that effect on you: it'd make you furious and always wonder what it would have been like to actually see that sexy underwear that you never got the chance to have a peek at, being that you closed all doors to sex with her.*

b) *It was true, and she believed that wearing sexy underwear empowered her just like wearing a suit can transform a man's personality. In my case, I can tell you that wearing red (my favorite color) underwear completely changes my mood. Whenever I go to the bathroom and see that color, I cheer up and feel I can do anything. Crazy? Nah!*

c) *Extremely tight and/or ultra-low rise pants can be very revealing. You can notice or even see people's underwear nowadays and what used to be embarrassing in the past is now trendy. Today you can either guess someone's sexy underwear just because their clothes are too tight. Or, they are almost worn on the outside! And looks like that's a cool thing these days. Maybe Perfecta imagined you could notice her sexy underwear even though she never undressed for you.*

In any case, her little revenge for that "We'll never ever have sex" sentence was making you furious and baffled. She knew the effect she was having on you when she said "I was wearing sexy underwear that day". And, my friend, you fell for it!

It even added to your anger the fact those other women you talked to agree with Perfecta. "You don't understand. It makes a difference", they all said. Sometimes women just want to feel they are part of an exclusive group of human beings that nobody can really understand. It is probably our revenge for having been in a lower position for centuries. Many women enjoy not being understood by men, and they laugh at them when uttering sentences like "It makes a difference."

Some theories say women have a so-called "magical thought-process": they stare at a dress in a shop and their purpose is for the man next to them to understand they want that dress, and probably even buy it for them without her uttering a word. There is also the famous "What's wrong?"-"Nothing" exchange between a man and a woman. She would love it if he understood what is going on with her without answering the question in words or without even the need to ask the question. There is no logical cause-effect: you just have to "get it" and men don't "get it." When this happens, many women get furious or at least frustrated.

Why would women aim at not being understood? It makes sense when they complain with "Men just don't get it" kind of statements. But why would they intentionally try not being understood? Mysteries like the Bermuda triangle, the Pyramids or U.F.O.'s are attractive. Men love solving problems and revealing mysteries. And women want to be attractive for men.

I didn't find it surprising that it was Perfecta who eventually "dumped you" (even though you never had a "real" relationship and the whole thing was mostly emails and phone conversations). You exhausted her with your questions and theories and she needed to stop being your guinea pig. She realized she had "a perfect husband" and it was pointless to continue talking to you (especially when you promised there would be no sex involved!).

HOW TO MAKE A WOMAN FALL IN LOVE WITH YOU

The following is an excerpt from my memoir "Violent Tremors: Journey to Overcome the Legacy of Slavery." This will lay the foundation of an emotional combination that I learned from someone way better with women than I am.

Meeting Future

After my final lesson with Kasaun, I continued to go to Santo Rico and the Pickup Artist meet-up. One day they booked a PUA celebrity; Future! Neil Strauss had talked about Future in his book "The Game". It was a big deal that he was there. There usually is a nice crowd for the meet-up, but this time we were in a larger room and there were no empty seats. When it was time to start you can tell who it was we all came to see. A small crowd of people who recognized him formed a circle around him at the door as he tried to make his way to the front. He shook hands and lightly joked with a few people like a politician. When he finally got to the front he introduced himself and briefly spoke of his history. He talked about his time with Mystery and Neil Strauss. Then he proclaimed "I'm turning over a new leaf. My entire game will be completely honest. No more routines, no more lies, I'm not repeating a single line of game!" He put his hand over his face and pressed his fingers across his eyes. It seems like he was trying to keep himself together and not cry.

I was a little taken aback. Most of these gurus would come peacocked and talk about how great they were. This man just wore a button down shirt and a pair of jeans. More importantly, he was hurting. He was sad over a girl. She had broken his heart. Apparently, she found out that he was a famous pickup artist and she promptly dumped him. "Women don't understand that this isn't me. I just do this for work. This is how I support myself. I'm tired of all the lies. I'm tired of it. I once went from approach to close (had sex) with a girl in a British accent. I went on a number of dates with a girl wearing Rasta hat that had fake dreads coming out of it. I'm done. What's the point of all the lies? When she finds out it's over. From now on, when I meet someone I like I'm just going to tell her what I do for a living and whatever happens, happens." He paused, looked down to the ground while shaking his head.

"You know what? What the hell are some of you guys doing here? I've seen a lot of you guys before. Some of you even were in a boot camp with me. Are you addicted to meetings?" He then pointed directly at one of the guys and called out his name. I don't remember what it was. "You! What the hell are you doing here? How many classes have you taken with me?" The guy mumbled something. Everyone was trying to see who it was, but the room was packed with people. "I don't understand how some of you guys can keep taking the same classes and not figure it out by now! Listen, stop taking classes and get out there and live! How many thousands of dollars do you need to spend before you realize this? You know what? I'm going to do something that I've never done before. I'm going to teach you guys something that I only teach in my advanced classes. Usually, you would have to go through many courses and spend many thousands of dollars in order to learn what I'm going to teach you now."

He went over to the board and wrote "How to Make a Woman Fall in Love with You." Most of the class pulled out something to write with and some people held up recording devices as not to miss a single word this young man was saying. "I honestly hope that the father of my future wife doesn't hear a recording of this on the Internet one day. These steps are what I noticed always happens when a woman truly falls in love with a man. This is just the way things happen. And I know that me telling you all this is like giving a bunch of pyromaniacs a stick of dynamite and saying 'don't light that.' But I want to be clear, do not do what I'm about to tell you on a girl unless you actually do love her! Trust me; you can fuck a girl up completely. Don't do this, do not! I want to tell you guys this because so many of you simply just don't get it."

He talked for a few minutes more then began with all the steps. Step one was "Lead an Interesting Life." "This is what most of you guys don't get. You have to lead an interesting life. There has to be something special about you. You need to get out of the house and do something! I would like nothing more in the world than to play my Xbox and smoke weed all day, but that simply isn't interesting." One of the guys in the middle of the class slowly and timidly raised his hand while holding a pen. Future stopped talking and pointed at him. "Ummm, could you explain what you mean by an interesting life?" The guy said. "What?" Future said in disbelief. He then looked around the room, I did too. The entire room was completely puzzled. "Oh my God! You can't be serious! You have to have something personally interesting about you! You can't possibly do any game unless you have that. I'm looking at your faces, how can you not know what I'm talking about? Do you really think the game is a series of lines that you have to memorize?" The same guy slowly raised his hand again. "Yes?" Future said. "Could you give some examples of what leading an interesting life is?"

Future pressed his hands over his temples in frustration. "Oh my God! You can't be serious! This is a question that you have to answer for yourself! Only you know what makes you happy. It has to be something that you love that has nothing to do with women. A lot of people are talking about Mystery. I can tell you that it's truly amazing to see him in action. I learned directly from him. He tried to teach me the things that worked for him. But you know what? I'm not a 6' 4" magician. I tried learning magic tricks and have had some success with it. But you know what? That isn't me! Mystery now has his own television show and I'm happy for him. The company is no longer called the Mystery Method; it's called Love Systems. You want to know why we changed it? It's because none of us is Mystery. We can't be him and if we tried it wouldn't work."

"Me personally, I'm a comedian. This is what I love to do. Mystery could never be me and I could never be him. You know? There was a time that I was really into mangoes. Do you guys have any idea how many varieties of mangoes there are? Do you know where they're grown? Where in the city you can find them? Did you know that there are mango enthusiasts? If you wanted, you could construct entire routines around mangoes. You could have many mango dates already planned out. Listen! I see a lot of you taking notes. Do not go out and study mangoes! I'm just trying to help some of you who don't get it. The game happens all the time naturally. Guys write down what works for them and try and teach other people. But you will totally miss out on what's really happening. The best thing many of you can do is to stop taking classes and go figure out what will make you happy."

This class went on for well over an hour. Here I'm not going to go any further than step one. Even though he told it to the entire class for free, Love Systems charges an arm and a leg for this information. I think Future was just hurting. If this book becomes remotely popular, I know people are going to incessantly ask me what the remaining steps are. So I'll just say that another step is to find a way to fit the girl into your interesting life. For the rest please ask Future.

Listening to Future speak inspired me. He was the only one who was honest. I appreciated that. His steps fit in line with my own personal understanding that I have described as emotional combinations. In addition, I had the ability to do all of Future's steps. Even though he said not to do it… I did. The seminar was on Sunday. Usually, Sunday nights I would go out Salsa dancing. Monday I went to a bar. There I met Aussie. She was visiting America for a couple of weeks before returning home to Australia. I did all the steps right there at the bar. She told me where she was staying and I offered to give her a ride home. I was excited, I could tell that were going straight to her place for sex. She was staying in the village and I found parking exactly in front of her building. It's tough to find parking in the Village, it was great luck. Then I just needed her to invite me in or find a reason to invite myself in.

She unbuckled the seatbelt, turned to me, and said "Isn't it amazing how we found a parking spot right in front of my door? I would've never thought the day would end like this." She was misty eyed. 'She knows we just fuckin right?' I said to myself. She must've noticed the quizzical look on my face and said "Don't you feel like something special has happened?" "Listen, I got to go." I told her. "What?" She was shaking her head 'no'. "There is someplace that I need to be," I reiterated. She sat back into the seat leaned her head back and tried to hold back the tears. "I don't understand… But… We… we…." Then she threw herself on the dashboard. Her face was in her folded arms. I could hear what sounded like whimpering. She stayed like that for a few minutes. "I really need to go," I told her again. She picked herself up, stared forward, and started to take slow deep breathes in and out of her mouth. Eventually, she exited my car and I never spoke to her again. I'm sorry Aussie; I wasn't ready for that amount of emotion.

Even though usually the 'gurus' would plug their upcoming boot camps, I don't remember Future plugging his. I thought it would be a waste of money going to a boot camp. But I wanted to see Future in action. So I paid the money. It was over three thousand dollars for one weekend.

End Excerpt

In my memoir, I said that I wouldn't share. But I decided to share in this book. But by all means contact LoveSystems.com and sign up for their classes. Those guys are truly masters. I remember Future had six or seven steps. Rather than jumping right into the steps, we need to cover the mind of a woman.

Chan

Future's "method", if you can call it that, is what normal people do when they date. It is the natural progression of a relationship or connection. I wish all those men heard and heeded his warning of, "But I want to be clear, do not do what I'm about to tell you on a girl unless you actually do love her! Trust me; you can fuck a girl up completely." Unfortunately my gut tells me that went in one ear and out the other, especially when there were other comments about getting a woman into bed.

Future's words are true. Women do approach dating, sex and love differently. As much as it pains me to say this, his "method" is not a bunch of bizarre suggestions. They are proactive things you can do to show you care about yourself and the woman you are attempting to have a relationship with (not just a one-night stand). These sorts of things are what makes the PUA routines unnecessary and allows nature to take its course.

Aussie was an opportunity to learn more about women that you did not take. Yes she would have slept with you, but what you gave up was learning why she felt comfortable with you right away and why she believed there was a special connection between the two of you. Trust me; this would have been better than the orgasm. It may have even helped you get a little closer to your own emotional growth. I have a glimmer of hope that you realized you were not ready for those emotions, but your stunted emotional growth can only evolve if you take those chances to push yourself towards emotional cliffs. Do not get me wrong falling off is not at all desirable, but worth every scrape and bruise to find the space in your world where you are a confident man, who can exhibit, understand and accept emotions rather than run from it.

Lola Key

When I talk about Americans, I always say that if there is a word to explain you Americans, it would be: pragmatic. You've managed to organize your lives, to ease them in all possible aspects. A pickup artist. I had to look it up in the dictionary since I had no idea what it referred to. We don't have anything like that.

This can be considered good or bad. On the one hand, it is perfectly fine that not all people can do all things. Why would I know how to pick up a guy? And if I don't know, the best thing is to ask somebody who has contemplated about the issue extensively. On the other hand, though, all the truths I have reached in my life are the ones I have reached myself, through long processes of reflecting, or very commonly, healing my wounds. So, if you ask me, nobody can teach you the answers to the questions of heart. Each heart in the world has its own answers. Each woman in the world is a complexity of her own.

Lead an interesting life. When I read it, it sounded silly to me. Yes, that is something we all strive to. But, what does it have to do with picking up a woman? Ooh, it does, it does indeed.

When it comes to this issue, there are two types of women. There are the ones who are completely devoted to their man, who lose themselves when they get a boyfriend/husband and the ones who always keep their interests, their selves and their lives for themselves.

My very good friend, the cruel one from the beginning of my writing, is the first type. She, my dear friend, tried two faculties, and dropped out of education very soon. In the meantime, she returned to our small birth town and had two tragedies that only the person of her mental strength would survive courageously as she did.

First, her brother died, overdosed in bed. Then, all of a sudden, her father died. These two events made her fragile, which is the word I would never have used for her. One man, her current husband, was there. He stood by her in these awful moments, being there every day, every night. What she did not see at the time, and we started clearly realizing is the fact that he is one light year away from her. He is not a people-person, he doesn't have any particular interests, and he is jealous and possessive. She stood by him, soon they got married, had a son, and after, say, three years from the beginning of the relationship, the problems started arising. More about that later.

Why was I saying this here? She agreed to become his shadow, she agreed to put aside her interests, her friends, her music, her sense of humor, and to devote herself completely to him and to his needs. She <u>had her interesting life</u> but she lost it. Now she goes out with us hiding what kind of clothes she is wearing, they do not have sex, and she is having a passionate phone sex with a guy almost ten years younger than her. I know that this is partly because she lost her interesting life and devoted herself to mere nothingness.

This is for people who lost their interesting life. There are some, though, who unfortunately don't know what the sentence means. When I was fat, for example, I did nothing in my life. Literally nothing. Went to work, I was a teacher back then, came back home, ate loads of food, and slept.

Having experienced a problem when my beloved N wanted to leave me (now I understand how unbearable and empty I was), I faced myself and I figured out that I should get to know myself. Not for the sake of getting him back, but for the sake of living. Ok, to be honest, it started as the only way of surviving the emotional pain he caused, but anyways, I had to survive.

I learned a lot about myself. I learned that I can become attractive, which was a shock to me. With 15 kilos more than I have now, I looked like a walking hippopotamus. I didn't think about that at the time. I simply came to terms with how I look, considering it a permanent phase. Can you imagine my surprise when kilos simply started melting! It was the initial push, the sparkle that lit the fire. After that, I really figured out that my body is my temple. I started nursing it, cherishing it. Physical exercise soon became my basic necessity.

I just figured out that one may wonder why I am saying this under the topic of leading an interesting life. It is probably a cultural issue. People around here have become very lazy, passive, bloodless and monotonous. In this part of the world, there is the highest rate of FB users. People don't do the things I do. They simply go home, connect to Facebook, or lie down and watch some meaningless film or series. I hope it is different in America.

What else? What else? Oh, yes, books. Does it work for you? It gives me real pleasure, not the instant one which a film gives you. Knitting. Classical music. Setting long-term goals on the verge of being silly. Mine are to run a marathon and to write a Dostoyevsky-like or at least Murakami-like book. Rituals with your friends. Philosophic discussion with intelligent people.

These are the things I consider when I say: Lead an interesting life.

But once you find yourself satisfied, you will be surprised how more attractive to girls you are. Something like with the thing with sexy underwear. When you are satisfied underneath, you spray the happiness around. And not just happiness. When you are self-assured you are sexy! Let me highlight the sentence. **When you are self-assured you are sexy!** *Don't you think?*

So, the next thing is to find a way to fit the girl into your interesting life. Piece a cake. If only she leads an interesting life too.

What is the most important thing after that is to keep your life the way it is. Don't give up on your habits, don't give up on your rituals with friends, cherish, and nurture your personal life. The key to successful relationship is when both of us are satisfied with our own interesting lives, only then can we truly devote to enjoying together.

Claudia

FUTURE THROWING OUT HIS SCRIPT

This section you wrote about reminded me of the movie "Intolerable Cruelty", with George Clooney, when he throws out his script at the N.O.M.A.N. convention and starts (what was supposed to be) his keynote speech by saying: "Friends, this morning I stand before you a very different Miles Massey...than the one that addressed you last year... because today... for the first time in my life, I stand before you... naked ... vulnerable... and in love." Just like Miles Massey addresses his audience of cynical lawyers with questions such as "What are we doing here? What are you doing here?" Future wonders what he is doing there, now that he's hurting because a girl has broken his heart. He wonders what this bunch of guys with no interesting lives are doing, coming to him time after time for advice and never making the decision of taking the reins of their own lives. His tip, now, is simple, although it sounds like the hardest thing to accomplish for some of the members of his audience: "Lead interesting lives." By that, he means: find your passion and embrace it. That will make you attractive enough for ladies.

Women need to admire their men. Similarly, women need to admire their friends. That is, at least, what I have found in common in my eclectic group of friends. The friends I've had throughout my life, the men I've been in relationships with, all had something in common: I found them interesting, they had a passion to live for and I admired that in them. They were an incredibly heterogeneous bunch of people. However, they had that in common. And that made all the difference.

Therefore, not lying and finding an interesting life for yourself guarantees, in my opinion, a relationship. At least, a relationship of a certain length...Otherwise, you might trick someone into falling in love with you...temporarily. If short term is your thing, then...no problem!

AUSSIE

I could, somehow, relate to Aussie, although what was really going on in her head will always remain a mystery. Why, then, am I saying that I understand her?

A couple of times I felt that way. I was going through a bad breakup, or what I really wanted to have with a guy had never happened and I was heartbroken and disappointed. In any case, I was grieving. And then, either because I was turning to someone to forget or because I found someone by chance with whom I could try to forget, I found myself in a situation in which sadness completely overcame me. I was, yes, with a guy, but he was not, obviously, the one I was trying to forget. That realization filled me with a sense of despair.

It could also be that Aussie thought something very special was going on between you two (finding such a great parking place that easily was a sign for her)...but you "didn't get it" (because you were experiencing a different kind of emotion).

MEN (ESPECIALLY YOU AMONG THEM) DON'T UNDERSTAND WOMEN. DO WE UNDERSTAND OURSELVES?

"I think women understand themselves but are also confused about how to explain what they understand."

Let's consider this question: do women understand themselves? I'd say it all depends on how old you are. I spent years pondering over the meaning of my life, where it was going (if anywhere at all) and getting depressed over the slightest thing. Back then, I also enjoyed discussing this subject with close friends and with the occasional boyfriend (we Argentinians must do this a lot, as it is said that its capital, Buenos Aires, is the city with the highest number of shrinks per person in the whole world!). However, these discussions lead nowhere. I used to envy people who seemed to have planned their lives so perfectly: they chose a major, graduated, got the ideal job, then got engaged; a little later they were married. They spent time taking trips around the world or doing all kinds of fun stuff with the love of their lives, until they felt like settling down and having kids. The rest is quite predictable: they were happy ever after.

Granted: life looks easier from the outside, and sometimes even those perfect plans have flaws that are impossible to notice until a marriage breaks...or murder happens! But as I was growing older, I feared more and more that I would never have what I considered "a normal, happy life".

In my thirties, I decided to spend more time doing things I enjoyed, and that made a difference. It didn't make so much sense now to meditate for hours about the point of my existence. (I've always liked this John Lenonn song line: "Life is what happens to you / when you're busy making other plans."). Instead, I was doing things that I found interesting, and still others that I had put off for years for different reasons. And I had returned to Argentina, where I found less pressure to be successful in everything I decided to do (that pressure was at times brutal in the States!).

Now in my late forties, I'm trying to simplify. All my life I've studied literature and language, a difficult terrain if you hate to wonder about the meaning of life. Unfortunately, these kind of people (yes, like myself) try to interpret and reinterpret everything ad nauseaum, which can be harmful to your mental and physical health. I am not saying that I believe in not questioning or doubting anything. But nowadays I just do it as a game. What matters most is the life going on at present, and every second you spend with your loved ones or doing the things you are passionate about are what really matters now for me. The rest is pointless.

How a Woman Processes Information

Before I embark on this monumental subject, I need to reiterate that women confuse me. I think women understand themselves but are also confused about how to explain what they understand. I've had many interactions with women and will attempt to express what I've learned about how they process information.

After I stopped using scripted routines, I was able to convey exactly what I wanted with the women that I dated. Being upfront honestly had its perks. Once I was clear with them that we would only be having sex something weird started happening after we sealed the deal. Women began to debrief me on how I did. Not how well I performed in bed, but they would recall a series of moments that we shared and comment on them.

It's hard to pin down the correct combination of things that will make women recount everything up until the moment of sex. But I'll let you know what I was thinking after sex. I was either trembling with fear, furiously angry, or both. I would be thinking, "Why is this girl still here?" I dreaded the time after I had sex with a woman. I wanted desperately to kick her out of my apartment, but I didn't want to send a girl out in the middle of the night. Also I knew in the morning I'd feel better and I wanted to be able to be with the woman again. So when the women would start to debrief me, I sat quietly and listened. Mostly because women say weird things and I would use what they say for my 'Women's Words' collection.

From listening and inquiring with women after I'd been with them and talking to random women on the street, I learned that women bunch things together and assess them as one thing. It's fascinating considering I think of things in a straight line. For a man, it's like if A then B. If B then logically C. For a woman, it's like when she thinks of A, she is reminded of Q, Yellow, and the feeling saucy.

This idea is obvious to a woman, but most men simply never appreciate it. Getting frustrated and upset won't get a woman to think 'logically' like we do. Also, just because they don't think in straight lines doesn't make them illogical; it's just not like a man.

While I do appreciate how a woman thinks, I have to admit that it doesn't make much sense to me. It's as if they have the other half of a functioning human brain. It is incredibly frustrating attempting to reason with a woman at times. In the end, I have to admit that she understands things in a way that I don't and I have to accept that fact. This is why I think there should be more women in politics. I have no idea what difference it would make, but women are totally not men! Something would be different.

Chan

When you asked at the beginning for me to describe a woman my mind immediately went to this section. We are creatures born with the ability to multi-task and react to the big picture. This means that we process information in terms of its relationship with every other thing it affects, has affected in the past or has the possibility of affecting in the future.

This is not to say that our process is logical in terms of linear thinking. Rather it is obviously frustrating and why you addressed it in your book.

I (and every woman I have been privileged to meet) do not focus on just one isolated thing/event/decision at any given time. Everything, including the typing this sentence, is done with the past, present and future in mind. Not all of this is done consciously or out in the open. However each word I chose is influenced by how I have used it before, how I am using it now and how the reader will absorb it later. This process allows me to accomplish complicated projects and difficult situations and decisions. I do not have to re-do things because I have already thought about all the factors that have or will have the ability to influence those particular things.

Women cannot choose to turn this thought process off. God knows we sometimes wish we could and just live in the moment. If it sounds like we have little voices in our heads you are not that far off track. It is not a schizophrenic voice, but a nudge from our real self towards the answers. The best way to illustrate this is for me to type what I am thinking about in a certain moment. I am watching the rain, typing by memory, swinging my feet in the chair, thinking about lunch and wondering if I can afford to get my car fixed. All that in one sentence and 25 seconds. Sometimes it even frightens us.

In some ways the process is amazing and almost magical in nature. In other ways, this process it is what holds women captive to their low self-esteem and why we often allow PUA-type guys into our beds and lives. Have I thoroughly confused you yet? See the past, present and future often lead us to that belief that we can change you or give us false hope that we can go backwards and fix our mistakes later. We start questioning every move we make and if a woman has a self-esteem issue our thought process makes a woman believe that her decisions are wrong and never will be right. Therefore we allow someone else to influence the situation. It makes clear decision-making hard. We still are choosing but the choice is sometimes churned up like a tornado.

Lola Key

There has always been this thing about how men and how women process information. I have to admit that such a distinction is getting at my nerves. I refuse to believe that men think black and white. I refuse to believe that women tend to complicate everything. I refuse to believe in male and female principle when it comes to thinking.

I know what you are getting at. You are getting at the standpoint where when a man says: I just want to have sex with you, and he has sex with me on regular basis, it means that once he had uttered the sentence, he stopped thinking about it. But once the woman hears that sentence, she starts contemplating on what had been said and finding the way to bring it up to the next level.

Is it possible that you men can simply switch to the point when you decide not to think? Or is it that you slept with women that are of no good for anything else but of sex? Or is it the point in your lives that determined the situation to be like that? I am not accusing you of anything, I am just saying. It is like, when I utter some thought, some plan, some idea, I think it over again and again. You men don't do that?

Analysis, analysis, analysis. Changing our mind, weighing our words, reevaluating our standpoints. I admit it all. My point is: aren't you the same?

Claudia

TRYING TO REASON WITH THE OPPOSITE SEX

"It is incredibly frustrating attempting to reason with a woman at times. In the end, I have to admit that she understands things in a way that I don't and I have to accept that fact."

In Spanish, "reason" and "right" (as when you say "You're right") are one word. "To have reason" and "to be right", both are "tener razón." So, in Spanish there's a connection between reason and rightfulness (even though having reason -"the power of the mind to think and understand in a logical way "- doesn't always, necessarily make you right). I don't know if wanting to be right all the time is a trait I have because I am a woman. It's probably a personal weakness I should try to correct, as it can often make me unhappy and at times it seems quite pointless. Also, it doesn't seem to go together with good reasoning!

The completely different way of processing information that you mentioned earlier hadn't been so clear to me as it is now that I have lived with the same man for almost 14 years (wow, I scare myself when I read this number!). In the past, I used to believe that either he was right or I was wrong, or the opposite (as you can imagine, mostly I thought the latter was true...). Through the years, and even though it's really hard to comprehend it and accept it, I have noticed that there are times when we are both right in the sense that what we want to achieve is the same goal, or what we are in favor of is the same thing. However, it is unbelievable *how different our positions can be. This will probably be better understood with some examples: at the moment we are in the middle of trying to sell what used to be my mom's house in order to buy a new one for us. We both want a bigger, more comfortable place, and in the same neighborhood. However, we sometimes get into ridiculous fights about how to go about it; we both think we're defending our own rights and trying to achieve the same objective. Still, there are fights about the different ways (more or less conservative, more or less risky) we want to deal with this situation.*

These two very different ways to process information also become a problem when it comes to how we care for and educate our daughter. I am sure he loves her as much as I do and would do anything to see her grow to her best potential. But, but...how we get there can also be reason for heated arguments...

THE TOP THREE THINGS WOMAN SAID AFTER DEBRIEFING ME

Lying in my bed, staring up at the ceiling, and listening to women one after the other tell me all the places where I went right, I began to notice the same stories. The first group of girls would string together all the moments that led us to being in bed and let me know that I had done a good job. Then they would compare my series of events with other guys. This group of guys was either someone that they were dating or someone that they were considering dating.

For the guys that they were just sort of considering they would angrily complain about a moment that messed things up for them. At first, I thought the woman was trying to coax me into wanting her more because other guys are interested in her. But as more and more woman started saying the same thing, I figured that it must be that they feel comfortable enough around me to think out loud.

As for the guys that they were actually considering, I think the women had similar feelings for me and these guys. But where I completed a chain of pleasant events and feelings, the other guys were good up until they did that one thing. It's like she already decided that she was going to be with you, but that one thing collapsed the chain of events that would've allowed her to have sex with you. But also, for some reason my chain of events is somehow related to your chain of events. I don't understand the connection, but I've listened to many tirades about where another guy messed up.

As for the guys that they were already dating, it's the very same thing. On and on women would complain "Can you believe he did this?" and "Can you believe he said that?" It has always been perplexing to me why this is the moment when the complaining happens. The main reason that I engaged in the conversation is to have stories to say to other women. But since this seems like a silly just after sex topic, I always ask "If he bothers you so much, then why don't you leave him?"

In response, I would usually get a laundry list of appealing attributes about the guy. Then they would conclude with "he's a good man." When pressed harder they would simply say "he just doesn't get it!" Then they would inform me that I do get it. I'll be honest, I have an understanding, but I don't get it.

The second group of girls would start off the same way stringing together all the things that I did well, and then they would bring up their significant other. Their difference from the first set of women is that they would complain that their man used to be amazing. They would string together a series of moments that used to make them happy. They would bemoan the loss of an amazing man. As with the first group of women, when pressed they would say that they love him but "he just doesn't get it."

The follow up question is what really bakes my noodle. I would ask them "What do you think changed him?" In response they would say something like "I'm the one who changed him. I nagged him until he gave in. But nobody told him to listen to me." If I only heard those words one time, I would've written it off as nonsense. But this is apparently a thing. Ladies, what the hell? I can't get upset; all I can do is accept that women and men are different, although I don't understand.

The last group of women would start off similarly to the first two groups. But instead of complaining about the men in their lives they're all glowing about a wonderful man. Either it's a man that they just met or someone that they are engaged to. I don't know why women would feel it's appropriate to be butt naked in bed telling me how amazing another guy is. While I truly am happy that you all have found the person that you might want to spend the rest of your life with, it's kind of insulting hearing you gush about some other dude. What's also weird is that they would all declare "I'm going to make him wait (6-24) months to have sex with me. I don't want him to think I'm a slut." I admit, I don't get it, and I can't just say that it's a fluke considering the number of times it's happened. When I ask them "What are you doing in bed with me when you are clearly in love with that other guy?" The response is just as mindboggling as anything else a woman does. They would say "its two totally different things!"

With that I took to the streets and spoke to women about this line "its two totally different things." As a man who likes women, this singular line is terrifying. One by one, women confirmed in one way or the other that "its two totally different things." This led me to try and define who I am to women.

Chan

My debrief to you:

With guys that I considered dating there was always one thing (sometimes so small it was almost invisible to anyone but me) that turned the switch off. I was trying to come up with a good example to illustrate this when one presented itself and there was no way I was not writing about it.

A friend of mine (newly single) began talking to a guy a couple of weeks ago. They are both Hispanic and this is important because culturally they often have different communication needs. They have seen each other in person twice, they talked on Skype several times, and were either texting or talking on the phone any other available time. They had not kissed or done anything else physical but she was very physically attracted to him.

He was supposed to be coming to visit for the weekend and they were talking on the phone as she was checking out at the local grocery. He said, "Can I come inside?" She was distracted and thought he was talking about coming over to her apartment to visit so she answered, "Yeah sure." He went onto to say, "So it is ok if I come inside of you? Are you on birth control? Or do you mind if the day after I go and buy you the morning after pill? The money is no issue."

As most women would do she hung up on him in complete shock. Later that night after refusing the countless texts and calls from him, she finally answered thinking perhaps she had it all wrong and that is not what he meant. (She was trying to rationalize talking to him even though what he said was offensive.) However he had said exactly what he meant and even though she was attracted to him in other ways this incident was a blatant example of a quality that quickly turns a switch off.

Yes, he was just being honest, but please use some common sense and discretion. Just for the record guys, "the come inside you talk" is appropriate only after you are in a relationship with someone. Use protection people it is the least you can do if you are not going to call again.

Unfortunately it is often a problem in the relationship that men just do not get all pieces of our puzzle (more on that later) and we seek it out in other men in order to feel whole. Regardless of whether you believe it or not, we are choosing to be in your bed or not. You may have lied, used practiced routines and every trick you know, but the truth is we would not be there if we did not want to be. Whether we are trying to make up for a deficiency in our current relationship or just looking for fun, even after five martinis it is still our choice. You were (as many other guys are) fulfilling a need for us. Sounds so clinical when a woman says it huh?

**NOTE: When speaking about women making a choice to sleep with you or not, I am ONLY referring to consensual sex. Do not under any

circumstances mistake anything I say to justify sexual assault or rape to a woman (or man for that matter). If you are making the choice for us you do not get to use my words as a way to rationalize your behavior. This was added during my last editing of the piece. It makes me sad to even feel the need to address this but when I thought about who might be reading this book I thought it would be a mistake not to.

Women need two things from a man, a lover and a husband. Most teenage girls dream of finding those two qualities in one person and marrying their Prince Charming in order to live happily every after. In reality it often takes a lot of horrible dates and even more frogs to hopefully find "the one" and this is not even a guarantee. Of course lots of things cloud this assessment and we often see what we want to at the time. I assume men do this as well and that is why we have such a large number of divorces here in the USA.

Later on in the book you touch on the fact that sometimes women just need sex. That is where our need for a lover comes in. Sometimes women need the physical release of an orgasm, the connection of skin on skin or a sense of being wanted/desired. I know very few committed or married women that are happy without the sex portion of the equation. However, women have definitely learned to compromise, which is why vibrators were invented. It should also be mentioned that the amount, quality and variety of sex each woman needs is extremely different. Men seem to have tunnel vision when it comes to sex. Whenever, wherever and however appears to work for them. Women on the other hand have individual ideas of each of these requirements and to make it even more complicated these ideas change with our relationships, age and life situations.

Lola Key

Is it possible that women talk about other men after having sex? And the number is so vast that you have to make categories? Three categories? This really came as a shock to me. When I close my eyes and think of a situation of such kind, I can think about various chitchats, various ways of spending time, not doing anything, going home, whatever, but talking about other guys? Even in the form of comparing how you are better than they are, come on.

As far as I am concerned I have never ever talked about other guys in bed after sex. It doesn't matter whom I am having sex with, if it is my boyfriend or a one-night stand. I think this is rude. Something like your gentleman's code. Why on earth would I be comparing you to another man? I want to say that the other guy was better? Nonsense. Or if I want to say the other guy is worse? Not even that. Whatever I am thinking at the moment like that, I do not say it. You don't compare men in bed, that's just some unuttered code of honor. Whatever I am thinking, I keep it for myself.

I will thus categorize them into two categories, those who say that you are better than the other guys, and those who say that there is a Mr. Perfect(o) somewhere.

The girls in the first category are a rebus for me. I cannot think of a reason why a one-night stand (or alike) would talk about others. Maybe she wants to impress you by saying that you are the best of the best (I feel like puking at the thought of it). Maybe she doesn't have anyone to talk to and simply needs someone to listen to her (I feel like crying now). Maybe they are just stupid and want to talk about anything (I feel nothing, I am indifferent towards them). Or maybe, just maybe, they don't give a damn about you and talk about whatever they want, simply and randomly lining up their thoughts (ahem, this is good, man!) In all the other cases, apart from the last one, I really have no explanation and no justification for such a behavior.

Now, my second favorite category. "It's two totally different things". No, girls, no, mister, it is simply not two totally different things! It is the same thing! The bottom line, when you find the right one, he is the only one to have sex with! Oh my God. Please don't let me be the only one who thinks that way. This sentence: "its two totally different things" is a synonym for weakness! When you are weak, when you don't have the strength to endure the difficult times with your loved one, than you say that sentence. Not just say it, you start believing in it.

I am not saying that I was faithful all the time. Oh no, I was not. But what I can say about myself is that I always gave things their proper name! An adultery is an adultery, it is not a totally different thing.

That is why I don't like present times. All the human values are upside down. I dream about the times when things used to be simple, straightforward, when women were wearing long dresses, when true values were true values, not totally different things. Women would not be debriefing you back then. And you would not be listening to such nonsense.

Besides, a quieter man is considered to be a more intelligent one. Don't you think the same should be applied to women? So, please, next time when you are in bed smoking your cigarette, tell them to shut up. You won't be seeing them again anyway.

Claudia

AFTER SEX EMOTIONS: WHAT TENDS TO SEPARATE MEN FROM WOMEN

"I'll let you know what I was thinking after sex. I was either trembling with fear, furiously angry, or both. I would be thinking "Why is this girl still here?" I dreaded the time after I had sex with a woman. I wanted desperately to kick her out of my apartment, but I didn't want to send a girl out in the middle of the night."

Women and men experience very different physical and emotional feelings after having sex. Right after intercourse, a man needs at least a few minutes to get interested in sex again. Many of them just fall fast asleep until the next morning. Women in general, on the contrary, can't fall asleep right after sex. They need to talk, or cuddle, or both. That is why men fantasize with something like the mechanical device seen in the Argentine movie "The Dark Side of the Heart."

This reminds me of this guy I met in the States, but who also happened to be from Argentina. I'll call him Luis. I found him physically attractive and extremely charming. So did many, MANY other women. And he was an irredeemable womanizer. During the courtship period, he would be interested in everything you said, laugh with you; show the best side of his charming personality. Once we had sex, he'd stay for the night, but the next morning an amazing transformation took place.

I remember once I prepared some coffee for breakfast, and I sat on the loveseat. While he chose to sit on the floor. Ok, maybe a "loveseat" was too much for him (just the name for that piece of furniture is scary enough!). I wasn't expecting him to sit right next to me and cuddle, but at least he could have chosen some other place. He wanted to be as far away from me as possible (without leaving the house yet), and not get too comfortable because he'd be taking off soon afterward. That behavior was so extreme that I found it funny. Ok, he wanted me to get the hint, but did he need to be THAT clear? I knew he wouldn't call me or want to make plans with me for the next weekend; personally, I didn't really want to get too involved with a guy that every girl liked, and who liked every girl. I guess I just wanted to be the first one (or one of the first ones) to get to be with the new guy on campus.

That time, we had spent the night together at my place. But his behavior reminded me of every man's wish come true: a device in their beds to get rid of the woman fast after sex, as seen in the movie segment I cited above.

I have to say that there have been times when I felt like owning a device like that myself. I remember how I really liked this guy (I'll call him David) who was also a teacher at a school where I taught. He taught music and played the guitar beautifully. And, you know, guys who can play the guitar and sing along always seem to have a clear advantage over guys who don't.

He seemed to like me too. Eventually, we ended up in bed at my place. Somehow this closeness had been a little premature; I guess that was the problem, but I'm not sure. I felt that one thing had been our conversations and my fantasies about him; the real deal disgusted me for some reason. So, when he fell asleep, I moved to the other bedroom. It felt so good to sleep alone. And in the morning, my only urge was to have breakfast and have him leave the apartment. After that day, we saw each other for a couple of weeks. Fortunately, it was the summer and there was a trip I had planned long before, which would create a much-needed buffer zone between us.

To continue with the music teacher story, I'll tell you that after I returned, I didn't call and neither did he. A month later or so, when the beginning of classes was getting closer and we were bound to bump into each other again, he gave me a call. He said it was Yom Kippur and he felt like he had to apologize to me since it was a day of repentance, a very important day for Jews. Anyway, that almost made me feel guilty, because I hadn't been a great person to him either.

After that, we ran into each other at work, but all we said was hi, and that was it. I was glad that whatever we were had ended.

MEN JUST DON'T GET IT...(REALLY? GET WHAT?)

When women just say "He just doesn't get it!" again (once more!), they are being mysterious. It's such a general statement, however, we women all seem to agree on what that "it" refers to.

Again, feeling misunderstood puts us women in the same place where all the mysteries in the history of humanity are. It adds to our natural allure. And it makes us part of a sisterhood. We want men to feel they are outside this circle we share with women all over, no matter what culture they come from. We believe there are certain traits that are womanly here, there and everywhere, and that creates an undeniable bond with the rest of the female world. The minute we become teenagers and get our first period, we realize right then that there is at least one thing men will never understand: the physical discomfort, PMS, being afraid of getting red stains all over your light clothes. As we grow up and move on to having babies and breastfeeding, the idea that there are things men will NEVER get becomes even clearer: how could a man ever remotely understand how it feels to have life growing inside of you? To see that your baby survived the first six months of his/her life because you breastfed? NEVER! He doesn't get it, and he'll NEVER EVER get it!

But at same time, we realize that it is not really the point whether a man "gets it." It can be hard for some women to pin down what exactly keeps them together with their men. I know how it matters to you, Daniel, since you are racking your brains to try to figure out why a woman would be lying in bed with you after sex discussing how wonderful her husband or boyfriend is. It sounds as if they are going to bed with you to see if that helps them appreciate what they have at home more, or to try and understand whether there are actual reasons to go back to that home. In regards the "it's two totally different things" statement. I have to say that many women have believed the "Sex and the City" fallacy: that we can take sex lightly, just like men do. I guess it'd be great to really believe that and put it into practice. That would really liberate us as women! But unfortunately I don't think most of us agree on the fact that we can have sex at one place and love at another. That is a man's thought and we want to make it ours, thinking it might make us free.

DO MEN REALLY CHANGE?

"I would ask them 'What do you think changed him?' In response they would say something like 'I'm the one who changed him. I nagged him until he gave in. But nobody told him to listen to me.'

In my country, we have a saying for this: "Women fall in love with Che Guevara, and then ask him to shave his beard." I haven't personally ever felt like that. Just the opposite: many times I felt that the man pretended to be someone else until I completely fell for him, and after a couple of months he would be himself again. And that was not the guy I had fallen for. But that was the real him.

This American boyfriend I'll call Chris is a good example of that. If he had been his real self from the very beginning, we couldn't have even met. Because when he approached me I was at a booth collecting signatures for a 'Help the People of El Salvador Association'. It was a human rights issue, a leftist cause, and the only reason why he came to this booth was because he had found me attractive and wanted to talk to me. Of course he signed, picked up brochures and got my phone number.

We started a relationship. I thought I had fallen madly in love with this guy. It bothered me a little at the time the fact that he was 14 years older than me and divorced, but I soon got over my prejudice.

A few months later, the first Gulf War began. For me, it was a shock to see so many people embrace the idea of war instead of wanting peace. Those in favor of peace were treated as anti-Americans. And what shocked me the most was that my boyfriend not only sided with whatever Bush senior was doing, but also decided to personally gather signatures and messages of support for the troops. He even took that to Washington DC, where he met Dan Quayle and got a pic of himself with this poor excuse for a Vice President.

Thus, my personal experience hasn't been that a guy changed because I insisted him to do so and then I disliked the final product. In my experience, it was more like the example I just gave: someone was trying to seduce me pretending to be the guy of my dreams, and after a few months, the mask fell off. But I've seen women trying to change men. An extreme case was this girl who had a one year-plan, a five-year plan, and a ten-year plan for her husband, I feel sorry for that guy. I can imagine he could have drawn up similar plans for her. After all, we are women, but far from perfect! (ha-ha). I wonder if those two are still together now.

"Women have a desire to fix things and also have an innate sense that they can transform a man by just being around them."

Deep inside, we women know we'll never meet Mr. Right. That knight in a shining armor exists only in fairy tales. So, what's our built-in mechanism to try and make up for this? Believing that, if there's no Mr.

Right available, we might as well create one. Not from scratch, true: we need some raw material, and then, we can make wonders!

For centuries women have believed that although on the surface men seem to be the boss, females have a subtle way of manipulating things so that what she wants is eventually accomplished. Maybe it's all a fantasy, but it's a fantasy we strongly believe in,

LOVERS VERSUS HUSBANDS

For a time I would approach random women just to talk about the men in their lives. When I ask why they are with the men that they are with now, I got many similar responses. They would tell me all of the things that this man does and is to them. Some guys are smart, have good jobs, are in good shape, have a charming personality, are great with kids, partial to a specific interest, own nice stuff, etc.

On the other hand, when it comes to 'players' women <u>all</u> say that they made "a mistake" with that specific man. Consequently, I know many guys whose goal it is to be a woman's mistake, and I have sat through seminars on how to be a woman's mistake. I took issue with the term "mistake" considering these "mistakes" are incredibly common.

When I would ask women what attracted them to the "mistake" their responses were very interesting. They would all tell me how this man made them feel. They would say: he was charming, he made me feel alive, every moment was fun, I felt like a woman with him, etc. What would make these women visibly upset was when they realized that he fooled their senses. Or in their words they realized "he was full of shit."

It became clear to me that women are attracted to different men in different ways. I understand and I accept that. Yet it baffles me to no end that a woman would marry a man and spend the rest of her life with him knowing that she isn't sexually attracted to him. How can you say you love a man and not want to have sex with him? When I ask women this they would say something like "sex isn't that important."

Again, I don't get it. But I must accept that women are different and move on. Use this time to talk to some women you know about how they process information.

Chan

A husband represents to a woman the man that should fulfill all the emotional, intellectual and potential parenting needs. Even those women, like me, who choose not to have children look for the qualities that would make a man a good father. I could write an entire book on this subject alone but let's just say that women do use some form and function of this to identify her life partner. Husbands often try very hard, unfortunately with limited success to understand us and to seek out what makes us tick. The husband portion of what we seek is often what women place as the most important quality especially as we age. Therefore, when husbands give women enough of what we need, we take on the responsibility to make it work in our lives. It sounds like lots of women are settling doesn't it? It makes me sad to admit but I know many women who have settled in their lives, some without even consciously realizing what they are missing.

Other women however have worked to make their relationships full of honesty and allow for open communication. All with an understanding that each partner will do some things that the other does not and frankly will never understand. Yet they trust each other enough for that to be ok. This is not settling but prioritizing what you value in a relationship and choosing the partner who checks all of your boxes and is open to growing with you.

My marriage will never be perfect. However, we both insist on honesty and talking through our problems. There are things that will always baffle me about his behavior and I know he takes lots of deep breaths when I do something he does not understand.

Well Daniel you are right men just do not get it. They treat women the way they want or expect them to be, not the way they actually are. More on this topic later

Lola Key

Why do women cheat? Everyone has a theory of their own. My opinion is very simple. Women cheat when they are not satisfied with their lives. That is why I am simply certain that the story of Mrs. Perfecta is bullshit. Which is even worse, I'd say, because she is not even aware that she has a problem. Years will go by, I think, before she even acknowledges she has a problem with her husband, and then she has to resolve it.

After some time, something in a relationship goes wrong. The period of love magic is over and the period of facing the facts starts. When we realize that not everything is the way we wanted it to be, the first indicator that there are serious problems in a relationship is the lack of sex.

This happens always and from my experience and the experience of people around me, it always happens in the same manner. The period without sex lasts for months. You might be surprised, but it can last for the whole year. Oh, yes, it happens. At the beginning of the sexless period, both partners simply deny that there is an emotional problem, which has caused this lack of sex. We are tired, we have a lot of work to do, we are under stress or we work in different shifts. What happens then?

In my life, and in the lives of my closest friend, the next thing we know and the next thing we start thinking about is a new man. It's not that we have been looking for him; it's just that it simply happened. Again, there are two subgroups of these situations. The first situation happens in relationships where problems are not possible to be solved. Problems between people are so deep that the end is inevitable but they both deny them. Women are then attracted to people that would engage them spiritually, that would move their soul and would be their inspiration. They usually stay in touch with them by phone, email or even Skype.

This written communication lasts for weeks, months. Women deny that something serious is happening, they say to themselves that they are in control of the situation and that is nonsense. Then, when they forget about controlling the situation, when they forget about the consequences, they have sex with them.

These types of women are usually the ones who are so haunted by guilt and remorse that they don't talk about their husbands. The denial phase then gets focused on their husband. They deny his existence when they are with their lovers. They are at the same time obsessed with the idea that they have to find a reason to justify their adultery. The list of reason varies, like: he must have done the same thing once one he went out without me; everybody does this, so why would I be an exception, etc.

How do these situations end? All the stories ended differently. Sometimes women realize that this is just a fling and that their man is the one worth fighting for. Sometimes they realize that they had been living a meaningless half-life and that should rediscover themselves with or without their new lover. Sometimes, very rarely, this other guy turns out to be the guy for them. But in all such cases, I can't believe I am saying this, in all the situations, the adultery was a good thing because it led to facing the problem and eventually, solving them.

The other group that I mentioned at the beginning stands for a completely different type of girls and completely different type of adulteries. We have girls who cheat. Full stop. I think these girls are led by insecurity. But just think, these girls are in constant search for reassurance, appraisal, and compliments. And I think they will always cheat. They will keep searching for their happiness, they will be pretending it is cool to be Samantha Jones, some of them might be bisexual, because it is cool, but deep down in themselves, they will be miserable. But will never be honest to themselves and admit that.

I had a roommate once and oh my God she was something. She was a true inborn mistress. First of all, her physical appearance was really something. She is of breathtaking beauty. With such an appearance she could be with any guy she wanted. But she was with two of them. Every single day was the same. In the morning, one of them comes to our place, and in the afternoon, the other comes to visit us. What came as a complete shock for me was the way she behaved towards both of them. She used to behave so loving and caring towards BOTH that I simply couldn't believe my eyes. Same nicknames, same words, same everything. I tried to talk to her, to let her explain to me why she is doing such things, I couldn't understand, but she was always just smiling and laughing. And when she got drunk, she used to be crying. Insecurity, trust me.

And of course, sorry to have forgotten this, but there is a miscellaneous group. Women cheat. Men cheat. Full stop.

Claudia

DOES SEX REALLY MATTER TO WOMEN?

"...it baffles me to no end that a woman would marry a man and spend the rest of her life with him knowing that she isn't sexually attracted to him. How can you say you love a man and not want to have sex with him? When I ask women this they would say something like "sex isn't that important."

I only understand that "sex isn't that important" for a woman when she's been with a guy for many years, or when she's had children and exhaustion and stress take over at the end of the day and leave them with no energy at all. Many women who have ALWAYS had a boyfriend who then became their husband take sex for granted. They know it's there, readily available, and that a man will never refuse. Women have the occasional headache, their period days, but they take it for granted that whenever they are ready, their men will never say no. That could make them say "sex isn't that important." But when they don't have a partner, or when they are at the beginning of a relationship...well, I just don't believe that sex doesn't matter to them.

I remember once I was at my girlfriend Vicky's place, and another woman friend was visiting her. The three of us talked for some time and then she left. As it happens many times at women's gatherings, when a woman leaves, the others start talking about her (I know it doesn't speak highly of us ladies, but that's the truth!). Then Vicky told me: "You know what she said to me about why she married her husband? Because with him she had the best orgasms."

Personally, I wouldn't say that sex is the only thing that makes me stay together with Horacio. But one of the things is that I feel every sexual moment is enjoyable. It's never happened that I didn't like spending an intimate moment with him.

SAFETY FIRST

Physical Safety

Physical safety is incredibly important to women. Men are usually bigger than them and they need to be cognizant of their surroundings at all times. If a woman or her friends are lax, even a little, then they could become susceptible to violence.

Some women are attracted to 'bad boys' and others that like being rough. I've played those roles before, but they always knew that they were safe with me. If there weren't any rules on safety I would make some up and let her know.

When I would meet a new girl and was sure that we'd be headed to my place later, I would offer her friends my driver's license. Safety is a major issue, so I was always careful to be cool about it. I'd say something like "I like your friend. I hope that's ok with you guys? If any of have any doubts ask me some questions or maybe take a picture of my driver's license."

They would usually chuckle about that and someone would take a picture of my license. Although I never confirmed it, I think women would text or call their friends as soon as they got to my apartment. Every girl, the first time at my place, would immediately request to use the bathroom. I assume that they are confirming with their friends that they are safe and relaying address information while it's still fresh in their minds. I never confronted a woman on what she was doing in the bathroom, as it's kind of weird and threatening. Offering my driver's license to a woman's friends is a courtesy to her friends. They wouldn't have to stay up to make sure that she's safe.

You need to be able to convey to a woman that you are safe to be around. Ask some women you know and trust. If they tell that you give off threatening or weird vibes then you need to work on that. It may seem obvious, but a woman will have nothing to do with you if she suspects being alone with you could lead to something heinous.

Chan

My friends say I over react and I am too careful. I trust my gut and if something feels off I exit the situation and make sure anyone I care about knows what I am feeling. There has been many times when I have learned some information after an incident that reinforces my gut's strong recommendation. On the other hand, when I sense a friend in physical trouble I have been known to kick my way into a situation, literally.

Several years ago I went on a trip with 30 women to this party island on the Great Lakes. It was an annual trip and one of the highlights was a very interesting scavenger hunt. We had been split into teams and my team was struggling to find one of the very particular items. As we entered a bar my friend spotted a guy wearing the item we needed. This guy was sketchy, sleazy and very drunk. I vetoed the idea and said we would just look elsewhere then stepped outside to take a call. When I came back in my friend was missing and so was the guy. Dead sober and irate, I bullied one of the patrons into telling me that my friend had agreed to flash the guy in the bathroom to get the item. All I knew was she was in no condition to defend herself if he tried to sexually assault her. I tugged on the bathroom door and it was locked. I heard my friend struggling and I kicked the door in, straight off the hinges. The guy was trying to touch her inappropriately and I pulled her out and we left. Physical safety is paramount for my friends and me.

Lola Key

Physical safety is very important to us, women. I think it's a rather biological issue. I read in a female magazine that all men are attracted to women with slim waists and wide hips. That got me thinking into whether there is a biological, primeval predisposition for ALL men to like certain women and for ALL women to like certain men. I reached the conclusion that perhaps these for waist and hips may not be always true, but there are some that are true.

All men like sensual women.
All women like powerful men.
All men like devoted women.
All women like strong men.

Feminism, gender equality, role changes. Omnipresent. But women do need to feel secure. We like to feel that we are safe, that we have our guardians even that we are the weaker sex.

And it's not just that. We all like for a man to be powerful. That is the conclusion of numerous discussions with my female friends. What does that mean? He can be powerful in many respects. He can be powerful and super ordinate in bed. He can be financially powerful. He can have a powerful and responsible job. He can be powerful speaker, humorous and witty, the center of attention in any company. He can be intellectually powerful (my choice). I always say to my friends: I want a guy who is capable of screwing me intellectually, by being smarter, sharper and wittier than me.

One of my friends once started seeing a guy whom I have seen a few times when we went out. When she told me she was seeing him, I was shocked. I remember him as being physically completely unattractive, not witty at all, and completely shy? What on earth are you doing with him, I *asked her. Now, don't take this the wrong way, please, I will try to explain it. He became a very influential politician. And she tried to explain to me, and I am now trying to explain to you, that this fact completely changed her perspective of him. It's not that she had hoped to get any money or something of kind from him, which she didn't, I assure you, its that she started perceiving him differently. She started seeing a powerful man, a man she can rely on.*

I don't know if this is biological, inherited or a novelty. I just know it is a fact.

Claudia

PHYSICAL SAFETY

When you are growing up, being a woman, your mom will always tell you to take care of yourself, usually scaring the hell out of you with horror stories of other girls who were not smart enough to follow their mother's advice. So recommendations such as; "Be careful what you drink!" "Don't get into a stranger's car!" or "Don't go to a stranger's place!" have been well engraved in our minds from an early age.

However, when you are very young, you think you already know everything and try to learn through your own experiences. Most of the time, it works, and disregarding your parents' advice is a natural way to develop your own personality and become an adult. Other times, you realize you put yourself in a very risky position. So, maybe your parents should never hear about those times!

I was 17 and it was my first vacation without my parents. I went to a beach with a friend my age. We shared a room in a hotel, went to the beach during the day and dancing at night. In my country you go dancing at midnight and get back early in the morning. But that beach town seemed to be safe enough for us teenagers to lead that kind of life.

Every night we went to the same bar. One night I met this angel-face guy: he looked completely harmless, was from a small town in the province and couldn't have possibly projected a more naive look.

He said he'd pick me up the next evening. I won't lie to you: it did make me a little scared to think that I would get into a car with a guy I had just met. But he looked like such a good guy!

He was there at the hotel lobby the next evening. We got into his car and he started driving around. We were talking about different things, listening to music, but he wasn't saying a word about where we were going, and apparently at the time I was stupid enough not to even ask that very important question. I guess I felt it'd show distrust, and how couldn't I trust this baby-face?

We drove on and on along the beach. Finally, he parked near some kind of cliff. He looked at me, and without a word he reclined my seat and got on top of me, kissing me and fondling me. Until then we hadn't even kissed goodnight and now angel-face wanted to have sex with me all of a sudden. I was still a virgin, and kept thinking: "Is this how it's going to happen?" Saying "no" and "please don't" repeatedly was not helping. I never knew exactly what made him stop, but I felt so relieved when he finally gave up, although that alone was not the end of it. We were in the middle of nowhere and I couldn't possibly get back to the hotel if he didn't drive me. I asked him to take me back to my place. During the drive I had to hear him say how disappointed he was with me: he thought he was with "a woman", and I was just "a little girl." I had to put up with that just because I needed the ride. When I opened the car door to get out of that hellish car and that was my moment to say something: "Thanks for the ride. I wish you good luck on finding the mature woman you're looking for. Just make sure you don't get involved with an elderly lady." And I slammed the car door behind me.

The next day, I ran into him again at the same bar. He pretended not to see me. I've always wondered what made him stop. Probably it was just that he wasn't a criminal, after all, just a confused and immature young man.

Of course after that I took my precautions before just taking off with a guy like that. But now it was because I had experienced this nasty situation by myself, not because I was following mom's advice. Fortunately I didn't need to be raped to learn the lesson my mom had tried to teach me.

Many, many years later (around twenty, to be more precise), I had a deja-vu situation with the person who is now my partner. After we met at that salsa class, we just said good-bye; maybe both of us knew we would see each other again right there, because we really liked those salsa classes. And he also lived around the corner from that place. So one or two weeks later, we met again. This time we were each other's dancing partner for the whole duration of the class. Afterwards, we sat down, had a drink and a nice talk. Then, I mentioned that my birthday was coming soon. As this salsa place used to organize birthday celebrations, I was considering going there for my birthday with some friends. He said something like "You should invite me", because if you were one of the guests, you could get in for free. I thought that was pretty pathetic, but hey, so was I, as at the time I didn't really have many friends who would willingly attend a party at a salsa place. I said Ok, and, of course, the next thing he said was: "I'll give you my phone number, then." I thought the guy was a little desperate, but didn't think much of it, really. I thought he was kind of cute and a good dancer, he was Ok for talking for a while, and that was that.

Horacio called me on my birthday, which fell on a Friday that year. Oh no, I thought, he will want me to invite him to this birthday party I announced, and then I decided not to have."No problem," he said, "we can go out tomorrow and celebrate it, just the two of us." Mmm... Ok, why not?

He picked me up at around nine the next day. It was Saturday night and he was there, which was a good sign already. We went to the old part of town, where there are many bars that serve beer and peanuts. When we got out of the car and he held my hand, somehow, it felt so right. It was just holding hands for a couple of blocks, but just that simple, romantic gesture gave me goose bumps.

We sat at a table in a beer-and-peanuts bar and started one of those first-date conversations. Until he began throwing peanuts into my beer mug. At first I just thought it had been a little accident. But soon enough I realized he was doing it on purpose, and probably thought that was somehow funny and cute. I didn't think so, but let it pass. I'm not going to sentence this guy to death by lethal injection just because he's being a little silly. The night is young. Let's see how this progresses, if it does.

After a couple of beers, he suggested going somewhere else. Because now I was twenty years older than when I went on that date from hell I described earlier, I asked where we were going. He said: "It's a surprise."

We got into his car and headed to the river drive. This ride along the river brought back disturbing memories for me. I was tense, but I trusted that being older would make a difference here.

Horacio stopped at a convenience store, and made me wait in the car. Was this the right moment to escape? There seemed to be some bus stops nearby. I wasn't (still) in the middle of nowhere. But, was this guy scary enough? He didn't have an angel face, but he did look like a good guy: hardworking, honest and humble. While I was lost in thought, he came back and smiled at me, like he had just gotten part of that "surprise."

I was still feeling uneasy. I desperately wanted him to stop somewhere now. Finally, he did. It was not such a completely deserted area as I thought, though we were by the river, near the boardwalk. After parking, he went to the trunk and got his surprise: a birthday cake, with a candle on it, and two glasses of champagne (actually, our Hispanic version of champagne called "sidra", which is not exactly like cider because it does have some alcohol in it). And the cake wasn't really a birthday cake, but something that we call "pan dulce" (panettone or fruit cake), because my birthday is between Christmas and New Year's, when we usually have this kind of stuff.

I started relaxing a little. It didn't seem now like his plan was raping me.

When we got to know each other a little better, I told him how I had felt that first night, so that he would understand why I seemed to be a little uptight. "But wasn't that an original idea?" he said.

Emotional Safety

A woman's emotional safety may seem like a weird topic coming from a man who's been with a few hundred women. It's only weird to you because you don't know anything about women. In the pick-up artist community, I would be considered above average or maybe an expert. There are many guys who are true masters and even grandmasters in understanding women. I've never once heard a man who's been with over a thousand women ever say slut, ho, or bitch (in a derogatory way.)

This is a tricky topic to attempt to express, since most guys don't get that the person a woman is showing you is usually not the real her. That's usually the case for every man and woman, but it's especially true with women. What makes this matter more complicated is that women often accept the role that men think that they are. It's endlessly perplexing that women do this, but they do.

This idea might be incredibly challenging for you, as you may have preconceived notions about what a woman is and what a woman is supposed to be. If you wish to cling to whatever beliefs you have that's fine. But consider this; most of the women that I've been with weren't single. The same thing is true for many other guys like me.

If the first thing that came to your mind is "you were sleeping with dumb sluts," then you have a long ways to go. A large percentage of women admit to me that they don't have, or never had an orgasm. I think the oldest one, who never had an orgasm, may have been in her thirties. For some reason, they accept the relationship they're in and fake it for years. When I ask what sex feels like to them, they say "it feels numb" or "it feels like nothing."

When I ask them what they think the problem is, they never know. Obviously, if they knew they would change something. What I've noticed is that it's the men in their lives. Those guys have expectations of her to be a certain way. It's like the man needs and expects her to be something she isn't. And that image of a woman she isn't has trapped the real her inside. These poor women spend decades faking it in every way. I want you to understand something; the woman who you know would never ever fall short of your expectations is precisely the woman who would lose her mind around people like me.

If there is a woman that you care about, you need to find out how you can make her feel emotionally safe. Communicate with her or female friends you have. Be open to suggestions. Also, write down what you think a woman is supposed to be. Be thorough and get down all of your thoughts and feelings. Look it over, and consider what happens inside of you if women don't meet those expectations. Then consider whether or not a woman would consider your thoughts or reactions emotionally safe.

Chan

I am not going to lie; I threw up in my mouth a little when I read "…man who's been with over a thousand women…" Seriously not impressed.

As a woman it is essential for me to be needed. When I was younger that translated to becoming whatever the guy I was dating wanted or what he projected onto me to be. When I think back at all the stupid things I did to make guys like me and to conform to their ridiculous expectations I want to kick my own ass. All women have done it and some of us will continue to do it for various reasons. I was lucky and found my inner bitch (self-esteem) and starting being only myself while dating rather than what my date was expecting me to be. This failed miserably sometimes and others (like when I met my husband) it worked out perfectly. Does he want me to have less clutter and give more back rubs? You know it! Yet he is also accepting the real me and personally I have finally comes to terms and accepted myself (most of the time).

So although it is men who project these expectations women are equally to blame for accepting them. When you try to be someone you are not, so much of the real you is lost or pushed down and when it does appear, often it is in the form of seeking out a man that will fulfill those missing needs. The real you becomes a prisoner inside of your outer self and over time you start to forget what was the real you and what was the expectation. It is a scary proposition but true nonetheless.

Lola Key

There is a difference in female perspective of what she is supposed to be to a man. In my case, my perspective was one when I was in my twenties and a different one when I reached my thirties.

I think all of us would be surprised to have a clear insight in how many women fake their true selves just to fit in the idea of what their men would want them to be like. Is that damn thing also biological? Do we so desperately want to be loved, accepted or impregnated that we are willing to take on any role that is given to us? Any idea of what a man would want us to be like just for the sake of not being left alone? I know so many women who are like that. And the devastating fact is that these beliefs actually increase as a woman grows older. When a woman is alone in her thirties, she is even more ready to fake her true self, to suppress her needs, if a man is 'on sight'.

Recently, I have had the opportunity to meet a lot of African women. More precisely, I am with them every day since I work with them. Their situation is really terrible. They are completely subordinate. I am mentioning this now just to point out the differences between them and the rest of the world in that respect. They do not have their own opinions, they do not have needs and they do not have any rights in that kind of a relationship. And this all is achieved because they have very strict religious dogma. Imagine what kind of life they lead in terms of emotional safety and emotional and sexual satisfaction. They do not know what it is. And what is in the core of this? Fear.

On the other hand, it is true indeed that a lot of women do not know what an orgasm is. How devastating! Ok, it is a simple fact that we do not experience orgasm the way you do. I think it is just a question of biology again. But once we discover our bodies, once we reach our satisfaction through years of masturbation and sex, we know what feels good for us. We know how to relax, we know how to be kinky for the sake of our satisfaction and we know how to lead a man verbally or non-verbally in order to achieve our own satisfaction.

This is closely connected with the above faking. Women fake their true selves in order to be loved by a man. Women fake orgasms in order to… Wait a second. Why do women fake orgasms? I don't know. I read somewhere that there are several reasons for doing so, some of which might even make sense. For example, because they think there always has to be some kind of happy ending. Ok, all of us would like always to be having mind-blowing sex, with all our partners, every time. But this is not reality. Not all partners are sexually compatible with us, which is perfectly ok. Also, we are not always in the same mental and physical and emotional state. So, not every story has to have a happy ending. Not all intercourses are mind-blowing. I would like us all to realize one simple fact. We should not be having sex for the sake of orgasm, we should be enjoying in it all the way. If we all did so, each would be followed by an orgasm.

Some other reasons why women fake: they do not know how to reach orgasm. Ok, girls, what about masturbation? I don't understand this. It is a perfect way to get to know your body, also a perfect way to get to know your thoughts and what turns you on. When you go through the investigation of this kind, you would know what feels good for you, and you would know how to lead a man to do what is good for you. That is, of course, if you are for any reason, inhibited of saying that yourselves. But, on the other hand, it is indeed sexier when you lead him non-verbally, than by simply giving him the manual.

There are two types of men when it comes to this issue. There are those whom you have a one-night stand or a sexual affair and the other ones. The first ones are usually those who have had hundreds of women.

From my experience, they are so lame in bed that it is beyond my comprehension. The only thing they have in mind is their own satisfaction, which would actually be okay, if they realized that the more you give, the more you get. These guys would not be listening to you to understand what feels good. When a girl fakes orgasms to these guys, I can only say that she is a fool. No wonder she doesn't know what orgasm is!

The second type of men are those who understand that the more you give, the more you get. Nooo, these are not some kind of pussies, on the contrary. These are artists in bed. When they listen to your breath, which leads the way, when they are aroused by your pleasure, when they listen to your heart beat to know when to speed it up, then you are talking about a genuine lover.

Here is the point, when you meet such a man, you feel emotionally and physically secure and there is no need to fake anything, an emotion, a wish, or an orgasm.

Claudia

DOES SEX REALLY MATTER TO WOMEN? PART II

"A large percentage of women admit to me that they don't have, or never had an orgasm (...) When I ask them what they think the problem is, they never know (...)"

It's been said that there are no frigid women, but just men who don't know enough. I guess the women you've talked to assume that the problem is theirs alone, as if sex involved only one person. I understand it wouldn't matter giving up orgasm in a casual relationship, but it is very hard for me to to understand that they would give up orgasm for the rest of their lives. It surprises me that this can happen in this age and era, when everybody is on TV, the Internet, wherever, giving all kinds of advice on how to enjoy sex more. I guess that for centuries it was believed that only "certain kind of women" enjoyed sex, and if you were a wife or a mother then that was not appropriate. But who would believe that these days? There must be something very wrong with all these women's self-esteem.

I remember how shocked I was during my first months in the States when I noticed how much more religious people were and how prudish. And I come from a Catholic, Latin American country! I wonder if religion is part of the reason why some women close themselves to the pleasures of sex or maybe they think others will consider them sluts if they admit they do enjoy sex. Women's minds are like an impossible labyrinth!

LEAD AN INTERESTING LIFE

STEP ONE

This is Future's first step in making a woman fall in love with you. It seems obvious when said out loud but is a major challenge for most guys. I've been to countless seminars, read articles, attended boot camps, posted in forums, read and watched material on gaming a woman, and much more. Only once did someone let the cat out of the bag and was honest.

Everyone has their own brand or technique that they promote. Some people form clans of those who follow a specific technique. This is a testament of greed, ego, lack of patience, and a misunderstanding about women. Women are confusing in general, but no singular technique will work on all women. Guys want to bridge the gap between men and women instantly, so they are willing to pay.

I'm sure that most of the PUA gurus know that you should attempt to lead an interesting life, but there is no way to bottle and sell such a thing. In fact, if you just read this section, threw this book away, and did everything possible to live out your dreams then you would never have problems getting women.

There are no gimmicks and lines to memorize. Even if you don't want women to fall in love with you and you just want random sex, it can only be done if you lead an interesting life. This can be a terrifying thing to some guys. You don't need to be self-conscious about it, and you don't have to be the absolute best at whatever you dream about. Although being the best helps. Every day of your life should be about you doing something that you love and are passionate about. If you don't have that, then you may have trouble with women. A woman might still marry you, for reasons that I don't understand. But I don't think that's a place where you want to be with a woman. It's unattractive. You need to find out what makes you special and be all about that.

Chan

The only thing worse than a man who tries to dictate 100% of a woman's life is a man who has no life of his own.

Men and women both need to find passion in life. It's wonderful if you and your partner find it together, but in order to grow any relationship and further the understanding of your partner, you have to be stimulated outside of the relationship with your own personal passions.

This is what attracts women to men and vice versa. As mentioned previously, and will continued to be mentioned, honesty with yourself AND your partner is important. Do not try to replace the pearls with plastic (fake passions you make up because you think it is what we want to hear or a generic practiced routine passion) because we WILL call you out. And lie? Good luck. You would be surprised how women find a way to communicate with one another. Even as a woman I am often shocked when I just know something that I had nothing to do with. I have no idea how the information got there but it is there and I will use it against you. It will catch up with you and then it will be passed on to future women, which will significantly limit your pool of potential partners.

If you are like me finding a passion does not come easily. Some people are really into gardening, boating, fishing, etc. However, I could never pin down what was my passion. What gets my motor running? What do I turn to when the chips are down to help me get through a rough patch? I honestly came up completely and utterly blank. The things I knew were; I was comfortable being alone, loved animals, enjoyed the process of cooking and was an avid reader but I had to ask myself if those things were strong enough to be considered passions. After years of trial and error I recently figured out that they were not my passions, maybe sub-passions, but definitely not the neon-light passion that helps make me an interesting individual.

Surprise, it is writing. Writing is my passion and when I write everything is brighter and I look more like the woman I want to be. Rather than continuously looking for my passion, I can concentrate on what realizing that passion has done for me. It made me feel attractive again. I have become a better wife, dog mom, friend, sister and daughter. Writing allows me to show and utilize parts of the real me that are integral to my happiness but buried deep inside. Writing did not even make it onto the original list when I brainstormed passions. Do not give up when it seems that your passion is eluding you. Keep trying because it makes all the difference in the world. The hard work is worth your time because this step in particular is not about getting a woman it is about wooing yourself.

Lola Key

I honestly believe that when a person leads an interesting life or is satisfied with herself/himself, or allows herself or himself to meet new people, visit new places, do new things, or when you are simply open to people, or when you are self-assured, or when you are busy exploring things that put a smile on your face, I believe that this undoubtedly brings balance in all the spheres of your life.

This is not like some voodoo thing. It's more like a physical law, like some new physical law yet to be established and approved. What does this mean? If you really want to pick up a girl, or a guy (this is universal, it goes both for women and men) you try and try and try. And when you really want something and it doesn't go well, you get desperate eventually. And desperate people reach for desperate measures. Then the above situation happens. The situations when we lose ourselves and turn ourselves into what we think other people would like us to be like. And other people, at least those who are worthy to be a part of our lives, would like us to be ourselves.

So, try to forget that you want to pick up a girl, or a guy. I know it's like when you tell yourself that you are not supposed to think about a button. Close your eyes now. A damn button. But there is a way of doing this. Don't take a giant step. Take a small one. Force yourself into doing one activity that you have not done before. Anything that sounds at least a little bit interesting. It will lead to another, and to another, and to another. And, before you know it, you won't be thinking about the object of your lust. And this is when the object of your lust walks into your life. Or, this is the moment when you change the object of your lust and it walks into your life. In any case, he or she walks into your life.

Claudia

ATTRACTION TO AN INTERESTING LIFE

"First, if you follow your own dreams, you will be happy with your own self. If you do the things that you dream about you will transform your life. Second, if a woman finds what makes you happy attractive you won't need any game or spikes."

I believe in this and have found it to be true for myself. Unfortunately, it proved disappointing to me whenever I realized that for men it could work exactly the opposite way. I found that many men felt jealous, inferior, or threatened whenever I spoke of my dreams or the things that I was actually doing. In those cases, it was good for me to realize just in time, as of course, that the relationship would have been destined to fail. I had a boyfriend who put on this happy face mask whenever I told him about a personal achievement. He'd grind his teeth and say something like "I'm so *happy for you!", when he was actually feeling, very envious. Others would talk to me in a condescending manner or make fun of my dreams. Losers!*

Horacio is a perfect example of someone who was not exactly leading a very interesting life when we met, but he did a 180 and completely changed his career. To be honest, I thought it'd be extremely difficult for him to fulfill his professional dreams. His project seemed too far from where he was when we met. But he persisted and worked hard and got where he wanted. And now he's going even further. That makes me proud of him, and the fact that I find his life interesting makes me even more attracted to him. Also, I am positive that he would have done those things on his own, without needing me around him (though I helped!). Which reminds me of your goals list suggestion: regardless of what the final purpose is (making yourself more attractive to women), having goals in mind pushes people to do their best, and that makes an enormous difference. You feel motivated and happy and that works like a magnet. On the other hand, if you're just moping around constantly, and have no objective whatsoever, people will avoid you like the plague.

Jerry Seinfeld has made some interesting remarks about relationships. According to him, EVERYTHING a man does is just to attract women. He believes even astronauts want to get to the moon just to say to her later. "So, did you see me up there?"

WHY BE INTERESTING?

Since women are inherently confusing I can only speculate why women are attracted to interesting men. Before I share my thoughts on that, I want to talk about what the PUA community calls "Attraction." Every guru has his own list of all the things that women are attracted to. For example: wealth, health, physical looks, personal relationships, intelligence, humor, a wide array of personal characteristics, ownership of various things, age, height, and so on.

Once a guru has his list set, you are to riddle your PUA routines with "Attraction Spikes." Attraction spikes do work, I've done it myself many times. What I don't like about the community, is that guys view the attraction spike as a game all to get into a woman's panties. The attraction phase is incredibly important, yet it's approached as a series of things to simply make up. If you were genuinely attractive, you wouldn't need to pay a guru.

From what I understand about women, they automatically connect a series of things past, present, and future to a given thing. To understand it better, they string together a pearl necklace in their minds and associate that necklace to a given thing. Each pearl represents an event, an emotion, a color, a smell, a sound, a need, a desire, or anything at a point in time past to future. In each pearl, she's assigned an assessment and those assessments relate to all of the other pearls. This is why it's important to be honest. If you taint one of the pearls with a lie, then all the rest of the pearls could subsequently be tainted. If you manage to convince the woman that it was a one-time deal, she will make a lying pearl necklace in your name and keep track of that.

This is why an attraction spike works or doesn't work. The point of the spike is to subtly convey what makes you attractive. The problem is that all women aren't attracted to the same things. Before you meet a woman, she already has thousands and maybe millions of pearl necklaces in her mind. When a woman finds you attractive, she has connected you to a series of things automatically.

If you have the skill to manually connect yourself in a woman's mind, and you are happy with that, then more power to you. Attraction spikes are subtle and are intentionally superficial. Actually being attractive takes effort, but is well worth the effort.

First, if you follow your own dreams, you will be happy with your own self. If you do the things that you dream about you will transform your life. Second, if a woman finds what makes you happy and attractive you won't need any game or spikes.

Lola Key

Different women are attracted to different things. Yes, bare truth. Wealth, health, physical looks, personal relationships, intelligence, humor, a wide array of personal characteristics, ownership of various things, age, height, and so on. When I think about my friends and acquaintances and their taste for men, I realize that they are indeed interested in different things. Some of them are completely subordinate in their nature and they want an alpha male figure. This is the type of women whose goal is to sit at home, be financially and emotionally completely dependent on their halves. They seek for wealthy men. I cannot imagine how a woman like that can be happy and satisfied, but it is probably possible.

Other women, for example, look for dominance. They would like to find a man over whom they would be able to dominate. They would like to be leading the conversation and impose their (usually superficial) attitude. These women usually look for weak guys. And again, I cannot imagine such a combination, it gives me creeps.

And the thing about a pearl necklace. Well, it is meaningful indeed. And that is I think because women tend to analyze everything in great detail. We always analyze what a man has said, his thought, what they might have meant, and all. This is what Sex and the City has revealed about us women. We indeed have these female endless talks and we do analyze each and every aspect of what had happened, what might have happened, what should have happened or could have happened, just to reach the conclusion what it will indeed happen in the future. Instead of reaching some definite conclusion about you men, we even get more confused out of all these theories and hoaxes. That is why we keep observing what happens afterwards. Getting rid of the pearls that turn out to be falsely attributed to you. You lie to us once. We dispose the pearl of truth and there is a very slim chance you will win it back again.

Now, a man needs to manually connect himself in woman's mind. Well-said. This would be a perfect scenario of how to win a lady's attention. How would a woman get rid of all the black pearls and only keep the shiny ones? When you are honestly and truly into winning somebody's attention, this is how you do it. You devote your time and energy into this person. Find out what she is like, what she likes, and don't forget to be your true self.

On the other hand, not all the girls are the ones you want to devote your energy and your time to. That is understandable. And if you want it to be a fling, or a one-night stand, you wouldn't devote your time and energy in becoming her shining pearl. The same goes for us girls, too. If we don't want a serious relationship with a guy, there is no need for us to organize girl talks and discuss strategies. Simply go with the flow

I read in a male magazine that if you want something like that with a girl nowadays, it is enough for you just to visit her Facebook profile and you will see what kind of woman she is. Housewives who constantly post the images of cakes, romantics who post black and white photos of couples in love, chicks with lousy sense of humor who laugh when somebody falls into mud in a film, hipsters who posted the song of Zaz before she became popular, etc. All you have to do to get into their bed is simple: buy a fancy cake for the housewife, buy a rose for the romantics, play a film where Benny Hill is being chased by a naked female police officer for the funny one, and talk nonsense for the hipster. Here are the benefits of social networks. Everything is the way it is on Facebook.

But if you really want to be attractive and if you really want to be a big shot than it does take some effort. Look at it this way, little effort, and little pleasure. And if you take some effort, get to know the girl, if you find that the two of you are compatible, you will enjoy in being yourself, undertaking the effort of becoming interesting, you will actually enjoy every step of the way.

CONTRAST

One last thing before you start to tackle you own personal goals. I learned a concept from Vin Dicarlo called Contrast. I like Vin because his style is a pushback on all of the technical jargon in the PUA community. Contrast is simply coloring of who you are in a different light. For example if you are a petite Asian electrical engineer, who moonlights DJ-ing hip-hop, then you have good contrast. Other examples are a nightclub bouncer who takes modern dance or Wall Street banker who volunteers in a soup kitchen.

If those examples are true, and align with those guys' true selves, then it adds complexity to who you are. Contrast can be applied to many things, but I'd like to focus on being an interesting person. The reason why these contrasting personalities are highly attractive to women is the same as before. Except now you have additional information. I wonder if new pearls are attached to the necklace or are the old pearls colored or changed.

Lola Key

There is a point in this contrast thing, I am sure. Let's first take it to the general level. I think there is some kind of contrast in every person. And I think that there is some kind of rule that can be applied to the amount of contrast in a person. The more a person is disciplined, for example, due to the nature of their work, the naughtier they get after work. The smarter the person, the more complicated he or she is. It is a feature of a person who is interested in numerous things and activities to be more complex, fuller of contrast. And what can make a person's life more interesting than being versatile and all-round?

And from the female point of view, when we meet a guy who is a bank clerk, for example, and at the same time volunteers in a hospital, we would usually say that he is sexy. Or a man who works as a mobile company junior advisor, and drives a bike to remote villages at weekends; or a journalist for a daily magazine who trains to run a marathon race. Sexy, sexy.

For example, I once went out with a friend and some guys were hitting on us in a bar. In 99% of such cases, it's always the same thing. Same stories, same boring replies, blah, blah, blah. And me being polite to the extent not to offend him, but not to the extent that I want to hear for real how he plays football with his friends every Saturday. Or, which is even worse, to talk about my job, or why my last relationship fell apart, or something like that. When I go out, I want to have fun. Not to get bored.

Anyways, some guys approached us and it started as it always does, meaning, blah, blah, blah. It was just when I started answering the shortest possible replies, when I discovered that, apart from doing a boring job in a common company, he runs his own nursing home. He does that as a kind of hobby. I have to admit that I wanted to know more about a person who runs a nursing home, something about his motives, what drives him, so I spent a lot of time talking to him that night. And you know what? It was fun. Even though nothing happened, it could have. And he is just one of the very few guys who I remember from the situations when we go out.

So, contrast is very important. And, definitely, I wouldn't say that it is that we color the existing pearls. We do add the new, shiny ones.

Claudia

ARE WOMEN ATTRACTED TO CONTRAST?

Personally, I think certain contrasts, like the ones you mentioned ("a nightclub bouncer who takes modern dance or Wall Street banker who volunteers in a soup kitchen"), make a man not only interesting but they also show that he has dreams or goals that make him stand out from the rest of the men in the universe. When I met Horacio, he was driving a taxi; but his hobby (it was hardly a second job at the time) was building fish tanks and aquariums. I had never met anyone who was into the pet business, let alone fish, and I found that attractive because it was an indication to me that he had ambitions that went far beyond driving a cab all day. And I was right: now he's the owner of a thriving aquarium supplies store.

I remember thinking as a teen that I could never be with a man who worked in an office. A regular 9-5 job was for me synonymous for a prison sentence. I thought that nobody with dreams and high expectations could possibly hold an office job. Even though I didn't really make a point of refusing dates from this group of individuals, I somehow happened to date men with what I considered "interesting" jobs, which for me means art-related.

Set your Goals

Take a blank sheet and write down all the things that you wish for yourself. This list should not be for getting women, it should be for making you personally happy. What are your emotional goals, financial goals, spiritual goals, fun goals, career goals, contribution goals, relationship goals, and so on? Please take your time in doing this and be sure that every part of you is accounted for. There are many goal-setting workshops on the internet and in real life. If you need extra help determining what you really want.

Once you have a list, select one or two to focus on. If you have two things that contrast, then that's nice. But remember, this is for you! It's better to have one thing to be happy about than to have two just to impress women.

Find time every day to involve yourself in the thing that will make you happy. In the beginning, it might be tough to get yourself going. So take baby steps. Once you have something that makes you who you are, then you can focus on 'game.' Then it will be easy. But by then, it may seem unnecessary.

Lola Key

Set your emotional goals, financial goals, spiritual goals, fun goals and career goals. This can be accounted for both men and women. This is the essence of becoming a true self. And only when you become a true fulfilled person, can you seriously devote yourself to a woman. And once you have achieved all of them, or most of them at least, you will already have become irresistible to women. Just like with sexy underwear, believe me.

Now I would like to turn things a little bit. I would like to be writing about these goals from a female perspective and how important this is to us as well as to you-men. Maybe even more important since we still have not achieved full gender equity and we have to try twice as hard to achieve something men are already endowed with.

First, emotional goals. Again, I am sure that age is an important factor here. There is no other way of maturing emotionally than learning from your own mistakes. I assume all girls think that everybody is kind-hearted when they are in their teens. I assume all girls think that we are to be the way men expect us to be when in our twenties. And I assume that we learn how to be honest to ourselves when we reach our thirties and that we set the goal of being true to ourselves, honest to ourselves. And patient. And somehow I think that we should try to believe that there is some kind of balance in the world, which will eventually be established. Just wait, be true to yourself, and all the things will find their places. My emotional goal is to be emotionally stable. My emotional goal is to be true to myself.

Financial goals. The situation in this respect has changed drastically when compared to the last decades. A serious financial goal was something that an average woman wasn't expected to achieve. Just a few days ago I was talking to my boyfriend about that. We agreed that there are two types of women-those who have a financial goal to find a wealthy husband and those who want to become financially independent. We were discussing those women who are financially dependent on a man. What happens to them when a relationship falls apart? Here, they usually stay in a relationship/marriage because otherwise they would not be able to survive. I belong to the other group. I want to achieve financial independence. I have achieved financial independence. And it's not because of fear what I would be doing if I found myself alone one day. It's because it is fulfilling.

It's because it feels good. It's because I feel I am a fulfilled individual and member of a society. I cannot imagine what my life would be like without financial independence.

Spiritual goals. This presupposes again a deep introspective into oneself. What kind of person do you want to be/become? What are the spiritual values that you want to follow? Are you going to be honest to yourself and get to know yourself, learn your limits and face your fears? Be open to yourself, be honest to yourself and you will be honest to other people. I think this is very much connected with emotional goals.

Social goals. These are the healing moments; moments that you spend laughing with your friends. And it's not just that. It is also the feeling of security, the feeling of achievement, the feeling that you have managed to build a long-lasting relationship with another human being. Last year, for example, I broke off a serious relationship. Everything went wrong. I was in a strange city, I was doing a job which I did not like, where I was hit on by the boss, I thought I might lose my job and have to go back living with my parents (this is something I simply cannot imagine). When I was contemplating on all these terrifying aspects of my life with my best friend, she told me: As long as I have a house, you have a house. As long as I have money, you have money. And that got me thinking how secure we feel when we have real friends! And these are the friendships we have to cherish all the time. These are the relationships that define us and the way we are. We use a similar pattern when we are in a relationship with a man.

Career goals. Why is this important for a person? Here in Eastern Europe people tend to perceive their jobs as means of earning money and nothing else. It doesn't matter if they are doing something meaningful. It doesn't matter if they spend eight hours upgrading their own skills, learning new things, being useful to society, or merely sitting and doing nothing, or even doing something you dislike. Imagine a doctor who doesn't like his job, imagine how he treats patients. Or a teacher who resents being a teacher, what kind of values are transferred to children. I think all these things are underestimated in the day-to-day struggle to live a normal life.

A normal life, as far as I am concerned, is a life where you do the job that makes you happy, that makes you feel alive.

Claudia

YOUR OWN PATH

Remember the movie "City Slickers"? There's a scene there in which the character played by Billy Crystal is talking to Curly, a rugged cowboy. He seems to be about to unfold the meaning of life for him. The character played by Billy Crystal waits in awe for the answer. "One thing," Curly says, referring to what you have to look for in life. "What thing?" "That you have to find out for yourself." It's not the same for everyone, and it helps if it doesn't depend on one person, because you can be very disappointed if things don't turn out well in a relationship.

It happens many times, particularly when you are under thirty, that women meet guys that are "confused," don't know what to do with their lives, and they break up by giving you the "it's not you, it's me" routine. It tends to help if you have an idea of where you are going and what you want in life, before you meet someone you want to get involved with. Many women find it attractive that men have a plan for their lives, although some may find it a bit frustrating if they see that plan doesn't include them.

I agree that "if you find your passion, you almost don't have to do anything else." Men with a passion, with clear goals, with a plan for their lives, naturally make themselves attractive, without any need for tips on how to attract women.

DOES SHE FIND YOU ATTRACTIVE?

Before you go any further, please be certain that the woman is attracted to you. She will tell you in her own way. You just have to be paying attention. And yes, being an interesting person is being attractive. Some of you may be wondering if there is a magical way to express your interesting life. Well there are many ways to express many things. You could spend a great deal of time mastering the language of your passions or spend time living as you really want to be.

If you want to spend time getting used to talking to women, then ask them about the 'woman's words' I've placed in this book. But if you really feel like you must find a way to express who you are better, find yourself a PUA guru. Trust me; if you just focus on you then it will all happen naturally.

Also, you don't need a lot of time to share who you are with a woman. She will work it all out in a few minutes. I've been with a few working girls. Most were uneventful. But a few asked me to move in with them, offered to pay me, or asked me out on dates. This didn't happen because I'm amazing in bed or have a porn star penis. I'm a little better than average downstairs and I do nothing special for sex. I usually don't exchange any fluids with a woman. I don't like the odds of catching anything considering the amount of women I've been with; basically light kissing and no foreplay. What made me compelling are the things that make me attractive.

Are you surprised that I paid to be with a woman with all the free sex available? Sometimes the time between being finished with sex and the time she leaves was unbearable for me. What's interesting to me is why I'm totally comfortable with no women now.

The reason that I brought the working girls up is an Asian woman who called herself Coco. We had amazing sex and I was happy to have found her. I planned to add her to the rotation for a few months. I was set to leave when she told me that I had time left and asked me to stay a while. She started pointing out all of her flaws, entered her cell number into my phone, and asked me out for drinks.

I laid in bed next to her trembling in fear. She sat in the bed clasping her shins with her face buried between her legs. "No one wants a girl like me." She told me. I was sad for her. Working girls almost never have orgasms and that sometimes leads to health problems. Coco was attracted to me after talking to me after a few minutes. She probably could see me integrated in her life. I was especially sad for me that night, because I recognized that I simply wasn't emotionally ready for any women. And although I did continue to try after that, I was never with Coco again.

Chan

One of the things that can make men attractive is unavailability. Yes, you read that right, when you are not available (physically or emotionally) that makes you more attractive. We know somewhere in the far reaches of our brains that we should move on, but for some unknown reason we become fixated on the one thing we cannot (or should not) have.

For Daniel he was a player and upfront and honest about that with the women he approached. I would assume women were attracted to the honesty but also the fact that he was not up for grabs. He was not available for any kind of emotional engagement and definitely not a relationship prospect for the woman. This is attractive to us because women like a challenge and again we like to think we can change you. We think, "Sure he's says he is a player but I will get him to just be with me." It is an age-old story where the woman either gets her heart broken or the man tires of his game and some woman looks beyond his past or finds a way to accept him as is. I want Daniel to be able to re-enter the dating scene and find someone special (see more later) and while I know that you can take the player out of the game can you truly take the game out of the player?

Lola Key

I don't think that there is a strategy of expressing that you are having an interesting life. I think it is very simple. If you fulfill all the aspects mentioned above, that would mean that there is no need for you to preplan anything. If you are spiritually fulfilled, you know what you want and there is no need for you to think of a way to get it. In my opinion, I'd say that this entire fulfillment also presupposes that a person is educated and versatile. So, it will show, don't worry. Just don't think about it. And, again, once you become a fulfilled person, you will not be thinking about how to pick up a woman, they will be all around you.

When it comes to Coco, I kind of feel that you must have felt a great compassion and sorrow for that girl. But that is the way it is. And the best thing you could have done is the exact thing you did-never saw her again. You are not the one to save the world, just move on. She has to help herself, and that is precisely what we are both trying to point out.

CREATE YOUR OWN NECKLACE

Again, please be sure that you are found attractive. You will be a weirdo if you continue without knowing for sure.

Step two Involve her in your Dream

It almost seems superfluous to involve a woman in the thing that makes you interesting, given that she will automatically make her own associations. But you can't assume with a woman, even with all that I think that I know, I could be wrong. You could be thinking that she's into you, but she's just thinking that her feet hurt.

Even if she can imagine herself being a part of what makes you great, she might not know much about that thing. You need invite her into your dream. Every person is different, so you need to base the timeline on the woman. You have to know her a bit. Sometimes you might want to invite her for a day in your dream. Other times you can start with point A, then follow with point B, and imply a future C if she's good.

Chan

Although the Pearl Necklace analogy resonates with me on some level, it is ruffling my feathers and making me feel unpleasant for some reason. Something in the symbolism of the pearls just does not sit right with me or perhaps it is the oyster/vagina unspoken societal connection. As you can see I cannot just think directly about the necklace, instead I think about everything related to it. I do not find it offensive but I honestly sat back a little the first time I read this section. I suppose I also got the unfortunate definition of a pearl necklace in some sexual circles. It works for your purposes here, but I thought it was important that you know that it does bother me a bit.

Lola Key

Ok, women and men have different dreams, different ideals. In a relationship between two people, it's not that they should impose their dreams on the other person.

On the other hand, if you are together, that means that there are a lot of things that you share. Some dreams are mutual. Find them and try to make them happen. It is natural and normal that each person has a dream of their own, the one that is to stay only for her, but some dreams can be made to belong to two people, instead of just to one.

It may not be the best example for this, but I think it will work. My boyfriend loves Formula One, and I do not see the point in men racing one after the other over and over and over. Ok, I know that there are races once in two weeks and I respect his time. For example, if we are to go somewhere that day, we don't go until the race finishes.

He wanted to make this interesting for me and I simply refused to admit that it is anything but stupid. So he took me to see a movie. It was a great movie "Rush", about two famous Formula One drivers. Having seen it, I realized that there is more to Formula One than just repeating circles over and over again. I realized that there is their personality that affects how they are going to drive, that there is this immense fear mixed with all the adrenalin rush, both struggling to dominate, that there are relationships between the members of one team, that there are rivalries, vanities, all of which can be seen in a race. So, Formula One Season 2014 is to start on Sunday and we are going to enjoy in it together. His interest has become our mutual interest.

And this is not that is reserved just for you men. We should also try to involve you in our dreams. When I say dreams, I don't mean just dreams. I think it is important to be patient and tactful and to know how to bring closer the things you like to your significant other. I think being tactful is the essence here. For example, one of my dreams is to go to the Amazon forests and spend two weeks in the wilderness. My boyfriend has never thought about this and probably, at first sight, does not find this appealing at all. But I would very much like to involve him in this dream of mine. If I manage to make this a mutual dream, I can only do this with patience, not with imposing it to him. And if I don't it's not the end of the world. I will NOT stop having that dream just because he doesn't like it. He has his own dreams, I have my own dreams and we have some mutual dreams. But I think, in a long-term relationship, people share dreams. Otherwise, they would not be in a serious relationship.

BE THE BOSS OF YOUR DREAM

You can't be equal partners in your dream, I hate to say. At the very least, you can't be equal partners until you share many dreams and accomplishments together. Women have a way of sabotaging things that they care about. I don't know what that's about. They have an innate desire to improve things. The last thing that you want is someone crushing your dreams.

Giving a woman a role in your dreams isn't an actual job. It's more like she's along for an enjoyable ride. For example, if you are a painter then she can be your muse. But if you are a painter, the last thing in the world you would want is a woman over your shoulder telling you "I think you need a little more red."

Also, don't give her a paying job. That's lame. Some people after being together start a successful business as a couple. That's fine. But if you already have a business, don't give the girl you want a job. If your business is what makes you amazing, then share the products of your business with her. Or find another way to express it. Above all, the role that you give the woman should be fun and enjoyable.

Chan

Being the boss of your dream is very important because we are not your mothers (even though some men certainly fail to see the difference) and the reason the dream becomes attractive to us is because you own it.

I admit that women do tend to sabotage the things we care about the most. Although this is not because we want you to fail, rather it is because we want you to succeed and we feel that you can always do more in and with your life. One of the things that hampered all my dating in the past was that I seemed to be drawn to men with no ambition. Some women are drawn to the wounded or the bad boy or some type of a fixer-upper. I always felt in some way shape or form that if I could get them to love me that I could influence them in such a way that they would increase their ambition.

This never worked for me. If you do not take charge of your dream then not only will I not give you the time of day, but even if you do in the end I would not find it to be attractive because it is not your personal dream. The worst parts of these dating failures were that the guys each had a dream but they chose not to share it with me because I was not "the one". For example my high school boyfriend (and to be honest off and on through college as well) had what I deemed as little ambition. He was just a happy go lucky type of guy that I tried to push along repeatedly toward what I thought could be his best. As time went on we fell apart (I moved on in the direction of a career and he was fine staying where he was) and a year or two later I became engaged. For some reason I felt compelled to be the one to tell him because we had shared such a large portion of our life together and I did not want him to hear it from someone else. Guess what? He had graduated college, had a decent job, was also engaged and even owned a house. Hmmm where did that ambition come from and why the hell was I not good enough to be privy to it? My self-esteem took a hit and I filed it away under losses. Needless to say I was happy for him and very glad that he found someone to share his dreams with. I did not hold a grudge and realized even then that I pushed him away. If I would have allowed him the space to grow at his own speed things might have turned out differently.

Even though I was dating guys with no ambition so I could fix them, the guys I was truly attracted to (my husband) were the ones who had their own dreams and took charge of them. He wants to find a job he loves, see the world and countless other important things that I share and support but are his to achieve. This is not only attractive this is downright sexy.

And vice versa. He shares in my dreams and encourages me to go after them, but gives me space to explore them and work on my own which in turn keeps me feeling attractive as well. It is a win-win situation.

This equal respect and support of each other's dreams is what makes a relationship grow and continually evolve. Remember these steps are to make a woman fall in love with you, not just to go to bed with you. So if what I am writing seems a bit uncomfortable and close to the emotional edge of things, good!

Lola Key

Of course, we all have dreams of our own. If I shared my boyfriend's dream, it would have become my dream ages ago. That means that I cannot be as passionate as he is about achieving his own goal. The *important thing is that I am not an obstacle; that I am his support, supporting role in achieving this.*

The relationship should be partnership where there are some things we do together and some things we do on our own. And the base for all this is trust. If there is no trust, then the beast called jealousy appears. When I trust my boyfriend, and I decide to trust him, I enjoy not only in my own dreams, I enjoy in him having his own dreams and fulfilling them. For when he returns from driving his motorcycle everywhere, his face shines when he sees me since he missed me. Or when I am out with some friends or travelling alone, I can't wait to see him and tell him all about everything that had happened to me.

There is no room for jealousy; there is no room for being possessive. Only if the relationship doesn't work. And if it doesn't work, break it off at once.

BE INVOLVED IN WHAT MAKES HER SPECIAL

Every person has dreams and aspirations. Find the thing that makes the woman happy and give yourself a role. This is the same reasoning as giving her a role for your own dream. If you can successfully insert yourself into as many chains of thought at possible, then you will at the very least become an indispensable part of her life.

Don't attempt to take over her dream. It would be nice if you could enjoy what makes her happy. So try! If both of the things you love are the same thing and you are more advanced, you can work together, but be sure she's allowed her own time.

Lola Key

I like knitting, for example. It would be really meaningless if I wanted to involve my boyfriend into knitting. So I can knit for him and make him a part of my dream in a way.

I like tango. I asked him to join me. He agreed and discovered that it is not just a dance; it is a philosophy of life in which both of us can participate.

I like going to the gym. He likes going to the gym. Oops, this is a mutual 'dream'.

Claudia

SHARING INTERESTS (OR NOT)

When I was young, I thought that the man I'd end up with and I would stay together because, of course, we would share many interests and activities. Ha-ha. Well, I guess it can happen, but I'm not in that situation now, even though Horacio and I have been together for many years. It's also surprising to realize it doesn't really matter. There are many of his interests that I don't find attractive or that I plainly hate. And he feels the same way about the things that are interesting to me. I love reading (in English or Spanish), watching movies (except action, sci-fi, horror, war), traveling and having plenty of friends. He almost never reads (and only in Spanish), likes all the kinds of movies hasn't traveled much in his life, and has few friends. What keeps us together? It's still a mystery. Of course there are some activities we do enjoy together, and they seem to be enough.

Maybe because of my age (although I've felt this way for quite some time), I don't care if he is watching one of his action movies while I am reading a book, or whether he's playing chess online while I'm talking to a friend. We both experienced living on our own before and get along well with our own selves. We share not sharing everything, and that works for us.

Example of My Friend Popeye

I met Popeye and Olive Oyl through a mutual friend. The night we all met, Popeye wouldn't shut up about cooking. My friend and I met them at the train station and for almost an hour we walked and talked about what we should do that evening.

Eventually, we all agreed to go to the supermarket and Popeye would cook us dinner. Even at the supermarket he followed me around giving me more information about food and asking me to squeeze various things.

I'm not sure if at that time that I was aware of my panic attacks around cooking and the supermarket. But I do remember being incredibly furious. I hated hearing about cooking and I hated being in the supermarket. I went to the back of the supermarket and got a bunch of beers so I could drink and be calm while he cooked. I lingered in the back of the store until he bought everything that he wanted.

When we got to the apartment and I noticed how beautiful Olive was. I was so incredibly angry before, maybe her looks slipped past my attention. When the four of us sat at the table I examined them both. Although Olive was stunning, Popeye wasn't at all impressive. When we got our beers opened and cheered I smiled. Not because I was happy with the company, but because I planned to sneak my way in with Olive.

The plan was to hook her with some of my patented emotional combinations, all while talking to and staring right at Popeye. Once I had her hooked, I would move onto a different phase. Popeye rushed into the kitchen and got busy. The rest of us just chatted and played with the dog.

Popeye came back and forth to the table from the kitchen. Each time, he was talking about textures of food, flavoring, and the place where it's from and on and on.

Then he came out of the kitchen with four saucers with food on it. "Try this guys." He said as he sat. It was a circle table and Popeye was directly across from me. Olive was on my left. The food was absolutely delicious. But my heart sank when Olive began to moan. "Ooooh this is sooo gooood. MMmMmmMMM" I was staring at Popeye wide eyed because I wanted to get a full view of Olive without staring. Popeye couldn't help himself, he had to talk about how he made the food. I don't remember the ingredients, but it was something like a five-hundred year old root that he purchased from a traveling gypsy. Olive was nodding her head yes to all he said while we all were focused on him. I tried to get my stuff started but he popped back into the kitchen.

He came back out with four more saucers of food, "this one is accented with the tears of an angel. Tell me if you can taste it." He said. Again it was tantalizing. When Olive began rocking side-to-side moaning "Yes! This is so delicious! MmmMM Oh yes! Oh I can taste the tears!" I thought to myself 'this guy is stealing my thunder!'

By the second mini meal, I had given up on my plan and just accepted that Popeye was just being nice and trying to impress a new friend. So I asked him about what motivates him to cook, how he started, and his entire process. Even though he couldn't stop talking about cooking before, when I began to engage him; he really lit up.

We were all looking at Popeye as he exploded with glee talking about his favorite subject. Even though I was staring directly at Popeye, my eyes were trained on Olive. 'Does he see what he's doing to this girl?' I thought. Olive was losing her mind just from him talking about cooking. Part of me was frustrated because he was doing what I planned. But another part of me was intrigued that you could have a similar effect just by cooking.

After the third saucer of mind-blowing food, everything began to repeat again. Popeye was clearly trying to impress a new friend with his cooking, but I was more impressed with what he was doing with Olive. He wasn't even focused on her. I just couldn't figure out how you could display such a skill to attract a woman. So I asked "How did you guys meet?" Olive got flushed and waving her hands to her face begging "Me me me me first then you and then me ok?" Popeye said, "Okay."

Olive: "Okay so we met at college. It was graduation time and my family had a graduation party for me you know? And, you know I didn't even know him at all. My family and friends were there and this guy shows up with some pastries and

	says 'here try one.' I, my mom, and my grandma all took one, and it was so delicious! My mom asked him 'Where'd you get these?' and ok you go."
Popeye:	"I made pastries from heaven. See first you need a dragon lotus blossom that's only grown once a year on the Caucus mountains. Of course you need molasses, cream, and sugar. But the most important ingredient is love. It took me about five hours to make these six pastries. You need that time to absorb all the love." That's not what he said, but that's what it sounded like to me.
Olive:	"Then I said. 'You made this just for me?' He said 'yes.' Then my mom said 'honey you should keep this one.' Then my grandma said, (in a raspy thick Jewish accent) 'definitely you need to keep this one.' And I did!"

'Even Bubala?' I thought. Popeye just kept on impressing me. I asked if they took turns cooking. They both laughed and Olive said, "That's his kitchen. I cook every now and then, but not often at all. My only job is to eat. He loves to cook and I'm happy to taste different things." I had to know more about cooking because I loved the effect it had on Olive, so I asked more questions. Eventually, Popeye began talking about rice.

Olive slammed both her fists on the table and shouted, "I hate when you talk about the rice! You aren't in that place any more. Now you can eat what you like! Don't talk about the rice!" "But he's asking about how I started cooking!" He retorted. "No! I hate it! I hate the rice!" Then she bolted away from the table, ran into the room next to us, and slammed the door.

"What's in that room?" I asked. "That's the bedroom." Popeye said. "Well what's in there?" I asked him. He waved his hand at the door and said "Nothing! She just doesn't like for me to talk about when I was at college and too poor to eat anything but rice. But I think it's important to know what the human body can survive on."

I was in awe of Popeye. It's incredibly rare that a woman experiences the gamut of emotions Olive experienced, and he did nothing but be exactly who he was. I was imagining the various combinations that I could do with just what Popeye showed me when he said "Now let's talk about the rice!" He talked for about fifteen minutes detailing all the basic nutrients the human body needs and how you can vary different rice dishes to stay alive for years on a shoe-string budget. It was all going in one ear and out the other, but I still tried to listen intently.

He popped up again and went into the kitchen to finish up the final mini dish. With Popeye away from the table, Olive snuck out of the bedroom, plopped in the chair, and pouted with her arms folded. Three of us sat quietly waiting for Popeye to come back with the final dish. After delivering the final dish Olive's mood instantly changed and she began moaning again. I immediately asked Popeye "can you teach me to cook?"

Popeye was of course ecstatic to have a cooking student. I could only last one lesson, as cooking and the supermarket repulsed me. Because that one lesson was so hard for me, I hired two different cooking teachers later. I had the same results with them as well. I had panic attacks just being in the kitchen.

Some of you might be thinking, 'Why is he telling me this?' Most guys like to regale you with their sexual exploits in hopes that you will copy their blueprint. That's foolish. You need to find your own path. After years of trying unsuccessfully to learn to cook I finally had to admit that I could never have the same passion and success with cooking as Popeye does. He found what makes him happy and he also found someone who appreciates what makes him an interesting person. Also, his woman lets him have what makes him happy, and she's happy with the role she plays in it. They are married now with a beautiful young daughter.

If you find your passion, you almost have to do nothing else.

Chan

Popeye was an interesting example since I am also very into cooking and food. Daniel, I think you got it right when you said that if you are passionate about something, someone will notice it and appreciate that and if you are lucky, love that about you. Of course you learned the hard lesson that you cannot just absorb someone else's passion as your own and use it like a practiced routine. (Hear that PUAs NO practiced passions!) That is like looking through a plate glass window for women. It just will not work. The passion will not show up in your eyes and trust me; we have noticed that your smile is little tighter than usual. We know every line around your lips.

You have to find your very own passion. Only when you have not only realized your passion but wear it like a badge of courage will you be unstoppable. It is not a walk in the park but in the end it will make your life and definitely your love life much more fulfilling.

Lola Key

While I was reading the text about Popeye and Olive, I kept thinking: Jesus, is it possible that someone can be that boring? Ok, it is ok for every person to have his or her passion, obsession, whatever, but it is not ok to impose it on others. I resent people who can be so undiscerning as to keep talking about their interests all the time.

This is from your point of view. I mean, if I were you, and if this was an acquaintance of mine, I think I would simply be off very soon. Life is too short to be spent with people whom we don't share the same vibe. Trust me.

But, on the other hand, from the point of view of Olive, at first I had one theory, and afterwards I changed my mind. Namely, while reading this, and when I got to the point how she admires his mastery, I started thinking like: she is so shallow. She must not be having her own interests and she forced herself into being interested in the same thing he is. Then, the following thing crossed my mind: she is just praising him hoping that he would eventually shut up after receiving enough credits.

But at the end, having read your final paragraph, I realized. He has found his life path. She is simply being supportive. And it's definitely that she is very much alike. They are indeed a perfect match.

But still. I could never think of myself as being with such a boring guy! Come on!

THE PEARL CATALYST

DON'T BE A DICK!

It's true that I'm telling you Future's formula for making a woman fall in love with you. It's even true that I did exactly what I'm telling you not to do the very next day after meeting Future. By all means have fun with the first two steps, and if you aren't absolutely sure that you want this woman in your life please skip this entire section.

Breaking a woman's heart for no reason will come back to you. Regardless of karma, all women are somehow connected and they will talk about you specifically. There is no need to miss out on the company of great people. This book was meant to be a guide for men to learn to meet a woman's emotional needs. But please don't be a dick. It defeats the spirit of what I'm attempting to share with you.

Chan

There is nothing in the book that can compare to the first title in this section, "Don't Be a Dick!" This was one of the parts of the book where I leaned to the pro-Daniel side of the aisle.

Breaking a woman's heart for no reason other than test out a theory or routine will not only come back to haunt you, it will influence how all women look at you. If you are a dick we will all know about it. I do not know whether it is something we are born with or if it is learned, but women sense things from other women and we can somehow see how a man has treated her heart. Sometimes we heed this advice and sometimes we learn the hard way.

So guys, we know when you are a bad seed. We do not always choose to acknowledge it consciously but in our guts we know. Some of us choose to ignore your behavior for selfish reasons but it does not mean we cannot sense it from other women. It will ruin your chances at happiness. Don't be a dick.

Lola Key

You are trying to explain to men not to be dicks. From the point of view of a woman, I truly appreciate this. However, I don't think there is much point in it. Men are either dicks or they are not dicks. For those that are, it is not that they accidently treat women the way they do, it is that they purposefully do what they do, in order to be dicks. The more women they use and break their hearts, the more satisfied they are. As far as I am concerned, this opinion is so outdated. I mean, sexual revolution occurred in the last century. My point is that there is no purpose in bragging how many women one has slept with. So, there is no point in seducing every woman you run into. At least, don't seduce her mentally. It is perfectly fine in today's world to say that you just want sex. It is fine for you to tell us that, it is fine for us to tell you that. So, please, do listen to Daniel, stop doing anything emotional if all you want is to get her to bed.

We should all just simply say what we want. Nobody would be a dick then.

STEP THREE – SHARE YOUR VULNERABILITIES

As a man, this step may seem silly, but it has the potential to magnify everything that you've done thus far. These are things that you don't want to share with just anyone. At the time that I met Aussie, most of the time I was a blank emotionless shell. I didn't care about sharing vulnerabilities. They meant nothing to me. It is my hope that you are too ashamed to share your personal shortcomings with others. If you do, then it will make the moment you open up to another person a special moment. If you don't care, maybe you should see a therapist. I did, and I can say that a therapist is worth the trip.

What's a vulnerable thing? Well, are you ashamed of your baldness, or your overweight body? Do you have PTSD or panic attacks? Are you afraid of loving someone? There are many things like this that we all have. If this is a person that you wish to share your most sensitive parts with, then do so. Just be sure to do it in a way that is consistent with who you are.

Lola Key

This is the step that really got to me. Sharing vulnerabilities. This step is not important for making the other person fall in love with us; this is the step that is important for us to feel free, to feel normal, and to feel loved.

Fact No1. All people have weaknesses. We are all ashamed of them. This is so wrong. I think not a lot is spoken about this these days. If we got to understand that most people, if not all people, are faulty in a way, it would be much easier for us to deal with our own faults. And the best way and the only way of dealing with our flaws is to share them with somebody, a shrink, a friend, an unknown person or a lover.

Example No1. Eastern Europe is a place where being a homosexual is a taboo. You are not allowed to express it freely. I mean, you are, but you will for sure get beaten if hooligans meet you with a person of the same sex. Also, our family is a traditional one, traditional in a bad way, I'd say. This means that you are to follow the beaten track unquestioningly. Being a homosexual is not on the track. So, my best's friend's vulnerability was that he was gay. Once he started visiting his own therapist, things started changing for the better. Once he started talking to people, things got better. He is not ok now, it is difficult to be ok in such a society, but he is better. His hunger for love, for understanding, is satisfied. The magic pill, or magic potion is the love and understanding by a human being. Period.

Example No2. My boyfriend used to be a boyfriend of my friend, my acquaintance, to be more precise. When the two of them broke up, I started spending more time with each of them separately. I started to I really got to know my boyfriend and he really got to know me. Without any intent, without any plan, or any thought of anything happening to us, we revealed our true selves to each other. He broke up with his girlfriend, I was in a bad situation with my boyfriend, we were both devastated and alone, and found a person to talk to. Up to that moment, I thought he was a flawless guy, a regular person with no weaknesses and a normal life. Once I got to know his vulnerabilities, once I got to know him as a person, I unconsciously fell madly in love with him. So, the weaker you are, the stronger you are in the eyes of a woman. What a contradiction. But don't overdo it. It is not that you are to play Titanic at your first date and sob. You are a pussy then, and that is something we resent! It is that when you recognize a person who will understand you and who is worth it, just let it go, let your emotions, fears, faults out. There is a double gain. You will feel better and she will fall for you.

Why are Vulnerabilities so Powerful?

It's a combination of a few things that we have already discussed. If you've gotten to this point, you've shown the woman and she has taken a role in what makes you an interesting person. So you have successfully connected who you are in her life. She has strung together a series of events and sensations to you and who you are.

If we continue our analogy of a pearl necklace, sharing the most sensitive parts of who you are will color each of the pearls. If she does like you, then there is a strong chance that she'll accept all of who you really are.

Women have a desire to fix things and also have an innate sense that they can transform a man by just being around them. This is another thing that I debated intensely over with women. While I do agree on some level, i.e. pheromones, women can affect a man, but the magic that women attribute to their vagina is nonsensical. I've had women demand to have sex with me to prove that they change me.

Similarly, women have a tendency to claim a man regardless of the circumstances. I've had women say, "I discovered you first" and "It's too late you're mine now." These women had families, husbands, and boyfriends. But what's more perplexing is that they knew that I'd have someone else over the next day.

I don't truly understand why women believe that they can transform a man just with their presence. But if you share your weaknesses with her, you'll activate that secret feminine power that they believe they have. Maybe she will actively attempt to help you overcome those failings. More than likely, her feminine powers will get to work.

You are now creating an emotional experience. This woman knows an interesting man and she is somehow a part of this interesting man's life. Now she's the only one in the world who has the secret inner power to help and support you in your weakest moments. Again, don't be a dick!

Chan

Women want the men in their lives to be all they can be and I do not mean go out and join the Army. We accept a lot of crap and baggage that comes with you because we believe that the good parts are enough to get us started. Yes, get us started to transforming you to be the "perfect man". Of course as previously mentioned, we cannot change men, however we do not allow ourselves to use that important kernel of truth as a factor in our thought process. By sharing your weaknesses with us you are giving us the opportunity to add to our "to-do" list. You are a work in progress and the more customization we are able to add the better we feel our chances are of having long-term potential with you. Re-reading that I realized that it sounded like I was saying men are robots and we set out to change all your parts to align with ours. That was not my intention but more of a nuts and bolts explanation of what is going on, at least in my head.

When we find the one we love and want to spend our lives with we accept those vulnerabilities even though we know we can never change them because those vulnerabilities make you real. Strange isn't it that the one we choose to spend eternity with we do not feel compelled to fix? Now the urge to fix is always present in a woman's mind, but after we decide that you're our life partner it is not going to make or break our relationship. It makes the man attractive because in our eyes by sharing these weaknesses you have discarded the machismo dick attitude and shown your true colors. Even if logically this is not the case, this is still what we choose to believe. This is the cycle of female-male relationships and it is how we continue to make wedding planners and divorce lawyers' millionaires.

Lola Key

Being interesting and sharing your interests with a woman is ok, I mean, I don't want to underestimate the importance of that. But once you show your true vulnerable self, once there is a human aspect, a gentle aspect of you in the game, you got it. You got her. This is, I think, the fact that shows us that you are not perfect, and this imperfection is actually the thing we fall in love with. We are not perfect nor do we don't want perfection beside us. We want imperfection.

Yes, yes, yes, we do have this tendency to try and fix this. We do have this crusaders' instinct to help, to make things better. Don't you men feel the same? Perhaps this is a biological issue. We are the weaker sex, historically being looked after, being saved. Nowadays, in the times when we tend to achieve this gender equality, we want to approach men as much as possible. Maybe that is the reason for us to be so chivalrously helpful. Or, is it just the fact that when something is rare, when we don't do something by nature, we simply want to do that-out of spite or whatever.

I really am for this emotional vulnerability to be mutually shared, but also let us not be soppy now. Women do not change men easily. Vice versa. Don't plan to cry in front of a woman. Just wait and see if you share the vibe, allow yourself to be honest and simply go with the flow.

And again, I am talking about a true bond between people. I am not sure how vulnerability fits into one-night stands or alike. In these short relationships, there is not time and there is no point in being vulnerable. It is only when you meet a person you want to be in a relationship with (not necessarily to marry him or her) that you would want to be vulnerable. Both men and women are equally vulnerable and equally in need to share their weaknesses with somebody.

Claudia

ME VULNERABLE?

There was a time when showing weakness to a woman was seen as a big mistake. In the last thirty years, men have proved that crying or sharing intimate thoughts with a woman not only is not a sign of being a loser: it can improve the image she has of you. Some say that is being in touch with your feminine side. On the contrary, I've found that sharing my masculine side can scare the hell out of guys. Showing certain traits usually associated with men (a free spirit, independence, high self-esteem, ambition) may work well at the beginning, but after a while men feel like we're trying to compete with them.

I remember this friend who had many interests besides his major, which was already a full-time activity (Electrical Engineer). He enjoyed many sports (some a little extreme, like hang gliding), loved traveling, *dancing, film and he also spoke a couple of foreign languages (he was German and spoke English and French fluently). He was also very much involved in religious activities at his parish. You could say that he had a life full of interesting things to do and that they all made him a very complete person. However, whenever his girlfriend tried something new he didn't know anything about, he felt compelled to try it himself. For example, she decided to take Spanish classes and he believed he couldn't be left behind, so he started taking Spanish classes as well. In a way, I admired the guy's energy and strong desire for self-improvement. On the other hand, that same thing made him a pain in the butt sometimes. He couldn't stand it if a woman was trying, in his opinion, to be better than him.*

THE DEATH OF THE NEG

WHAT'S A NEG?

This term was coined and made popular by Mystery. Neg is simply short for negative compliment. I've witnessed many thousands of negs and I don't believe that guys really understand what it is that they are doing. I've heard "Dude I blew the set because I negged too much," so many times I want to shoot myself.

A neg is specifically a mini emotional combination. Let's use Mystery's quintessential neg. "Wow, your eyes are beautiful." Clean two fingers with your mouth then spread them out, as if to jab her in the eyes. "Can I touch them?" Doing this is supposed to break down her defenses and make her a little self-conscious.

The truth is that they work, but not for the reason Mystery gave. Looking at his model neg, he starts by complimenting the woman. Doing this will cause an emotional reaction. The reaction will be different in different settings. But for the most part, a woman can assume that the man is hitting on her and if given a chance will react accordingly. Next he counters the very thing he started with in a funny way.

This thus creates a two-phase mini emotional combination. What makes a neg appealing to women is that most men don't offer multiple emotional moments. Doing a neg will make you an interesting person. But a neg is incredibly similar to what other PUA gurus are teaching.

David Deangelo's main teaching point is to be "Cocky-Funny." What I like about David's description, is that you are attempting to achieve a state of being with emotional outcomes. This is why he's the richest PUA in the world. Mystery's 'neg' is in fact just cocky then funny. David gives boot camps of just practicing being cocky-funny.

Vin Dicarlo's 'natural game' is similar as well. His point about having contrast is nothing more than attempting to create emotional combinations in the woman. All of the 'game' that I've witnessed and studied is the expression of each individual male's perspective ways of creating various emotions in a woman.

Chan

The whole term and description of Neg freaks me out. It makes no sense to me why this was part of a man's routine to pick up women. The fact that any person (woman or man) would purposely attack someone with a negative compliment in order to get into someone's pants bothers me. Call me naïve or stupid but this is not a way to achieve what you want.

I am happy to say that when I think back, I realize that the women I know, myself included, caught on to this offensive tactic. I remember calling out guys who would hit on me or my friends with these negative compliments. The definition and method of how guys were approaching us was ridiculous and we started to question why in the hell we ever let this work on us since in reality it was actually degrading.

Once again it is because we made the choice. I never said these choices were good, logical or smart. We chose to let those negative compliments work for you. Whether we did it consciously or subconsciously is dependent on the woman and the situation. As I read that last sentence I realized that I am making women seem like cocky, arrogant know-it-alls. We do not know-it-all and even when it seems like we do it is often our instincts kicking in or something that we learned from the past that had been lodged in the recesses of our brain.

My point is not to peacock women to all the men of the world, but to let you know that women make the choice each and every time we sleep with you. These routines and negative compliments that men set out to accomplish are not the deciding factors for us. For better or worse we are in control of that decision. Every man that reads this will disagree with me and will have handfuls of examples to dispute my claim. They might even have a woman who verbally says it was the guy's line that really worked. Trust me when I say if I had a few seconds alone with that woman I would know the truth and it would be that she chose you in spite of the routines and negative compliments. She had already decided to say yes.

I choose to disagree with your **Essence of the Neg.** Why must we play this game? Women are not stupid creatures by design (There are certainly those you could argue fit the bill and blonde jokes exist for a reason). Women can process information just fine. If we choose to file it away and process it at a later time you can bet there is a reason. Whether it be emotional, situational, physical, denial, etc. Again this is a choice we make within our process.

Dating, marrying, loving or merely having sex with a woman is not a game. We do not need complicated emotional combinations to make or keep us interested. Maybe just trying to be you would be a better strategy. Any discussion of "your plan" is demeaning to me. Do not sit there and tell me that you just performed or are going to perform your newest routine on me and how did I feel about it. It makes you look arrogant and in my eyes sad.

I envision men viewing a scorecard where they check off their routine steps and emotional combinations. If they get the woman to have sex with them they get an extra gold star. Then they come together and compare their cards bragging about who scored best. Do not play this as game. You will regret it someday and you know all those stories about the "one that got away"? That will be you.

Claudia

TO NEG OR TO NEG: THAT IS THE QUESTION

I have been the object of negs before, but I had never realized the whole plan behind it until I read how you put it in words and extensively explained it. As far as I remember, my responses to that have usually been: "Next!" Personally, I have no patience for those kinds of comments. What I have found, however, is that many times I started out a relationship with someone (be it a romantic relationship or sometimes just a friendship) with a man I had a fight to begin with. It's happened to me a few times: I'm with a group of friends at a bar, for example, and suddenly someone I hadn't met before (or I hardly knew) starts arguing with me about something: the issue could be politics or anything controversial that I feel strongly about. I tend to have this urge to win arguments, so I fall for that and eventually we go from what started as an argument to quite a pleasant conversation.

But "negs" as a way to get a woman's attention...oh well, maybe it's just me, even though I understand how a man may want to try it as an original way to cause an impact on a woman.

RIP NEG...

The neg was exceedingly popular some time ago. Everywhere I'd go, I'd see a guy openly insult a woman he wanted to be with. When I'd go to PUA meetings, people would debate the appropriate amount of negs to give. Most agreed either two or three, but some guys liked to neg every chance they got.

The problem that the neg faced was that too many people were doing it, without knowing the true purpose of it. The fact is that women started to catch on. Since a few women knew about what men were attempting, all of them knew. So when people attempted to neg a woman, what she was actually experiencing was nothing more than a guy hitting on her.

After Mystery left his PUA crew and starred in his own television show, The Mystery Method became Love Systems. All of the guys at Love Systems agreed, and they simply dropped the neg from all of their teaching materials. I recently saw an NCIS: Los Angeles episode where Calen and G gave a mini lecture on what a neg was and the reason for doing it. Once it's on a syndicated show, everyone knows about it.

Lola Key

Negative compliments. Openly insulting a woman you want be with. I don't know what to say. For me, and for the women I am surrounded with, this is completely inappropriate. I would never choose to be with a man who undertakes such a method. That is all I can say about this.

THE ESSENCE OF THE NEG

We know what a neg is and how it became overused. But let's understand what made the neg so powerful. Doing a neg or any other of the techniques I spoke of isn't a thing that you do to a woman. In truth you are doing nothing more than giving her an opportunity to process the information you gave her at a later time.

It's important to understand that if the woman likes the first set of emotions then by all means allow her to have that emotion. If you are cocky, and a woman likes that, then don't switch to be funny. If you tell a woman that she has beautiful eyes and she likes that, then don't ask if you can touch them.

The idea is if she is at all uncomfortable with what you've said or done, then give her a chance to process that information later. She might still think you're a douchebag but will appreciate that you protected her from responding.

Lola Key

Now that you've explained a little more thoroughly that neg is not necessarily related to the word negative, I think I might understand it a little bit.

"It's important to understand that if the woman likes the first set of emotions then by all means allow her to have that emotion. If you are cocky, and a woman likes that, then don't switch to be funny. If you tell a woman that she has beautiful eyes and she likes that, then don't ask if you can touch them."

Ok, this is something I can completely agree with. Actually, this is a great point you have here. This is how I would like a guy who is hitting on me to behave. I would like a guy at least to try to be witty and funny in his own way. To give it a go. This is precisely what you should do. Do your best and try what you think is appropriate. You will have to take a wild guess in the beginning. Once you see that she feels comfortable with being funny, or being sarcastic, or being pushy, just go along.

Don't overdo it. You will not leave a better impression if you shoot from all the weapons you have. Stick to the one that makes her smile. That is what I would like.

A PERSONAL EXAMPLE

I'll give you an example of something that I've done a few times. Please do not copy me. But if you do copy me, please let the woman know that you did copy me. Although, do what you think will make you happy,

I would start by telling her "You know what? I want to see if you're ready." Then I would lean in and sniff her neck, close to her underarm, and right over her breasts. I'd come up and pause, then give a micro wince as if I smelled something horrible. Finally, I'd do a cold read on her saying something like "Huh. You're a pediatric nurse?" The last part isn't meant to be a joke. I do my best to guess something pertinent about her. The closer I get to reality the better.

There are four movements to this mini emotional combination. The first is when I challenge her to see if she's ready. This is after I'd already established a rapport with her. By looking at her face, you can tell that she's wondering what I mean by ready and ready for what. Whatever the conversation was about is now over and now she is a bit puzzled.

Next is the uncomfortable part, where I violate her personal space. I personally have a hard time just leaning in without prepping her with asking if she's ready. If I don't start with asking if she's ready, women are usually withdrawn as I'm coming in. Although this is a personal violation, it's respectful.

Here is the part where you have to judge her reaction. After I come back up I would have to consider if she liked what just happened. If she did, then I'd shrug my shoulders and move on as if nothing happened. But if she has a concerned look on her face, I'd make a micro expression on my face as if I smelt something horrible, but controlled myself because I'm a nice guy.

The wince would have her wondering if she has a foul odor and not about the violation that had just transpired. It is also important not to linger on whether or not she smells bad, that's why I would try to aptly guess something about her. It's my hope to amaze her or at the very least what about her made me think that. Since my cold read is honest and not a joke, I can answer honestly why I said what I did. Otherwise, I'd have to tell her, "I just wanted to sniff your titties."

While there are in fact four distinct movements, all together they create one emotional experience. The experience itself differs from woman to woman, but in general I come off as an interesting and unique person.

While this works fine as it is, I sometimes like to take is a further step since I know the purpose is to create an emotional experience for the woman. What I would do is tell the woman everything that I plan to do and the purpose of all that I plan. So in this case I'd start with the sentence "I would start by telling…" And I'd continue until the end and change all the 'she's' to 'you's.'

After I tell the woman my plans to sniff her neck and breasts, and the reasoning behind all of my steps, I then ask her to tell me what she thinks. I specifically want to know about how she's processing every moment. A woman's response to such things is usually amazing.

Once we've had a thorough discussion of my plan and its viability; we could talk about it for a while. Then I exclaim "You know what? I want to see if you're ready." By this time, she would be frozen. I like to create those types of situations that blow a woman's mind. For a man, he becomes frozen just by looking at a woman. For a woman, it takes a little effort. Once I see that she's frozen, I lean in and sensually bite her on the neck; thus creating an extended combination.

Do not copy me! Please attempt to understand the mechanisms that I put together with a lot of effort and trying. Learn from it and talk about it, but copying will do nothing but lead to the death of another emotional combination!

Lola Key

It is very cute, as far as I'm concerned, that you have made your own scenario for approaching women. I will later on say something about what I think about it and how I would react if you approached me with these lines. But first of all, I would like to say something about these set phrases, set scenarios and what I think about them.

At first, I used to think that such pre-planned actions are bullshit. Like, every woman or man arouses different emotions, different energy in you, so pre-planning is the same as dishonesty.

However, there is something that happened to me that made me think about this more thoroughly and actually change my opinion about this. I usually never respond when an unknown person sends a message to me on Facebook. I used to think there is literally nothing a person could say in a few lines that would arouse me and attract my attention to the extent I want to chat with an unknown person (whom I usually think is a poor guy for not being able to find himself a girlfriend in person). So, all these addresses by unknown men on my Facebook account are usually the same: Hi, you are so beautiful, I would like to get to know you. Or: You look like my friend from high school, is it you or not? Or, the best are romantics; I really want to puke when I receive something like that.

But once, there was one to which I did respond. Ok, I was in a period of life where I was completely emotionally ruined, but, nevertheless, I did respond, and I did spend some time with this guy.

The message said: Knock-knock, is anybody there? And a smiley. Ok, let me be honest, his photo showed a handsome man, but in some other examples before him, it didn't matter. Why was I attracted by this simple message? It was decent, not pushy, respectful, and puzzling at the same time. Many days and weeks and months later, when we got to know each other, I remembered this initial message and asked him about it. "Isn't it perfect?" He said. For me it usually was. For someone else it might not have been. But this is a good thing after all, similar people share sense of humor, if you use a phrase to approach me which you think is funny, I will respond to it if it is funny to me. And we have a starting point.

Now I will analyze your personal example, honestly and from my own perspective. I would imagine that you are hitting on me in a club by using this approach. I think you probably wouldn't just randomly pick a woman and hit on her. I guess there has to be something, some vibe between the two of you that serves like some kind of encouragement for you to make the first move.

The "Are you ready?" phase is the one I really, really approve. Why? What do I see in it? I see surprise, courage, balls, confidence, diversity and originality.

This is great for me. When somebody is different, when he has a unique approach. One of my girlfriends says that the sexiest thing in a man is his self-confidence. I have to say that, after thinking extensively about that, I do agree.

Moving in to violate my space. Hmm, I have never had an opportunity to experience something like that, so I can only try to imagine how I would feel. I guess the first thing that comes to my mind is the fact whether I liked the person hitting on me or not. Physically I mean. Let's face it; physical attraction is the initial sparkle. If I didn't like the man, I think I would slap him! Honestly! I am imagining a situation where a guy I do not like at all approaches my breasts! I would slap him for sure! But, on the other hand, what if I really liked the guy. Liked in a way being sexually attracted to him. Would I then mind my personal space being violated? I have to be honest. I do mind violating my personal space and approaching my breasts! There is time for being physically close, but this is not a good time. I guess what I want to say is that I believe there is some personal space a stranger is not allowed to cross. That is it.

Guessing game is next. I really like this part. It must have been truly challenging for you, though. To guess something about a woman, what she does, what her habits are, how she lives; perfect. I just wonder in how many cases this actually worked. And I bet each and every woman would enjoy being the object of a puzzle. And these puzzles are the ones where she is complimented at the end. For you wouldn't say that she must be a farmer according to her smell or anything similar.

So, to put it in a nutshell, I do like your personal example, everything except your nose in a woman's armpit.

Claudia

YOUR NEG EXAMPLE

Perhaps I'm just being old-fashioned here, because there are several aspects of your neg example that surprise me.

The first one is that you felt you had to warn other guys that you don't want them to copy you. By this, you are assuming that it's such a great tip that many other guys would like to use it.

Secondly, when you describe the reaction that most women have when you violate their personal space and then make a remark that suggests they don't smell well, I'm in shock again. I guess the only part I like about all this is the way you start describing to her what you would do to her and she responds with her own "plans" for you. I know you will think that this moment is a natural consequence of what you started with your neg, but for me it is the only "redeemable" part of this chain of events.

Whatever a man decides to try to do, you advise him to "Recognize that there is nothing you can do or say to make a women process things faster."

In my opinion, no matter what exactly it is you are doing or saying to try and get a woman to go to bed with you she will always be wondering whether she was too easy or whether she should have played hard-to-get a little bit longer. The urge for sex kills men; anxiety from not appearing to be a slut kills women.

Of course it was harder for women to internalize that they enjoyed sex decades ago. Now we feel it's our right as much as anyone else's. Still, there's a part of us that need to be courted. We are still playing certain games that made more sense in the past.

I remember that as I was becoming a woman (but was still a teenager); my biggest fear of sex was the possibility of pregnancy. It was a nightmare, and it haunted me to think that no matter how careful you were, it could still happen and completely ruin your life. I know I was too brainwashed by my mom at the time, but the reality is that as soon as contraception became so accessible and varied, women took more control of their sexuality and were able to leave ghosts behind. Their minds are now free to enjoy sex, so, what is the need now for being so careful and slow in accepting a sex invitation? True, the coming of AIDS was devastating and that made everyone more aware of all the other STD's. But now that AIDS stopped being terminal, most people have relaxed a little and gone back to freer sexual behaviors. Today, not getting pregnant or getting nasty diseases is more of a personal decision than it was years ago. Therefore, making someone wait for sex makes less sense nowadays. However, the game is played once and again,...and it needs to be played well.

Step Four – Throwing Down the Gauntlet

At this point, if all went well, you are free to tell her how you feel about her. Appreciate her for being a part of your dream. Thank her for supporting you with your weaknesses. Be genuine and let her know how special she is and how indispensable she is in your life.

Most people don't need help in this category. Just be honest and it will all come out. You will be in heaven if she reciprocates and tells you how she feels about you. If that's the case, be happy with yourself and always remember to cater to your woman's emotional needs.

Lola Key

This is just fine for me. Honesty is something I cherish. Ok, I do mind that it is placed here as Step Four, because in my opinion it should be part of the entire process, but ok, I get the picture.

Step Five – Neg her Hard!

What most guys don't understand is why she doesn't immediately reciprocate. Remember that you are trying to create a pleasing emotional experience for the woman. If she's hesitant or uncomfortable, the last thing you want is for her to commit to the first thing that comes out of her mouth.

If you told her things like she's why you wake up in the morning and such, then you need to neg her with the same amount of intensity. So if you say "You are my Sun and Moon and starlit sky," and you notice she's uncomfortable then you say "too bad you're an annoying bitch."

You may not want to do or say something so mean to a woman. You may want to be self-deprecating, but that's not equal to all the loving things that you've just said. Plus it's really lame to be self-deprecating. It's like you are begging her to love you back because you suck. Her feelings will only be hurt if she already cares for you and planned to reciprocate. But if she hasn't figured it out yet, she will be grateful to you for changing the subject.

Usually after I neg a woman hard, she'd chuckle then hit me in the arm. Then we'd debate, tongue in check, about whether or not she really is an annoying bitch. Once you give the woman her own time and space to process what you've said, the 'annoying bitch' part won't ever come up again. When she's talking with her friends about whether or not she should go forward with you, she won't tell them that you called her an annoying bitch. She will appreciate you for protecting her and allowing her time to process.

Chan

I am at a loss for words, which as you have probably figured out by now is very hard to achieve. I am trying to think back to a situation where this might have been done to me and I would have appreciated it but I am coming up blank. It is almost like the part of the book on "Don't Be a Dick!" did not happen.

You know what I appreciate? When a man honestly tells me how he feels. If I become uncomfortable or withdrawn by the admission there is a reason and frankly it is not because I need time to process what you have said. Women are relatively instinctual beings and as you have mentioned we rarely look at situations in a vacuum. So if you tell me that the world revolves around me but last week you told me my dream to become a writer was crap then guess what? I will be withdrawn. I do not need an abrupt change of subject or a Neg. What I need is consistency. I am already all over the map emotionally the last thing I need are more abstract ideas and events in my world.

Put yourself in our shoes. Actually I hope to remember to touch on this in entirety in the conclusion but for now think how you would feel if a woman said those things to you? Not so great is it. And get rid of that machismo smile because we all know it is crap and you are hurt by those negative compliments just as much as we are.

Lola Key

So you think that a woman needs more time to process her feeling? To process and to verbalize? Maybe this is the case. I am talking generally about women. This is not the case with me. When I want to say something, I say it, in some cases I cannot even wait to say it.

The situation is the same when it comes to relationships between men and women. Once I feel that somebody is being honest to me, I cannot wait to reciprocate. This is, of course, when I genuinely feel that a man is honest. If I am not sure, if I need more time to decide if he is honest or not, than negging would be a good option, I guess.

It's like a rescue at the last minute. If you read on her face that she is not comfortable with opening, neg, make a joke, initiate a "quarrel" between the two of you and wait for the next moment to start again. If it doesn't work then, you may neg again.

ASSESS THE SITUATION

Step six – Give her space and Just Chill

Recognize that there is nothing you can do or say to make a women process things faster. The most important time with a woman is knowing when she needs to process what has happened. Once you've finished a given emotional combination, you need to just chill, seriously. Men like to keep pressing forward with things, but that's not how women work. She will let you know when she's ready for something new, or if she's ready to go forward.

I'm not sure if this step was a part of Future's list, but I'm making it part of mine. Regardless of how grand or short-termed your combination is, chilling is a must! In fact, you doing nothing is when all the magic happens.

Mastering just chilling takes time, but once you get it you will literally be like a rock star.

Chan

Chill indeed. I hate being pressured to make a decision on the spot. By the same token I do not want someone giving me negative compliments in a lame attempt to protect my thought process and "allow" me sufficient time to understand and make a decision.

See it is true that you cannot speed up our thought process, but your recommendation to chill is sitting in a minefield. Nothing about the male-female relationship is black and white and the gray can be full of unpleasant surprises.

Yes we need time to process and absorb most things, but each woman's idea and need of time is very, very different. Some women need 15 minutes some need a week. If you are to the point in your relationship where you are sharing your true emotional feelings then you should be able to pinpoint how long her process is based on trial and error from earlier relationship situations.

I don't agree with your statement that, "you doing nothing is when all the magic happens." I think some women (including some friends of mine) need time and space to process things. I, however, am a talker and I prefer to hash things out right away. Lay all the cards on the table and move on with our lives. It is sometimes ugly at first but any man that has made a relationship work with me has always allowed me to talk though things immediately. That is my way of processing and I doubt I am the only woman who uses that form of processing. Case in point my parents. My mother is a talker. A very loud talker I might add. My father, after 40 years of marriage has figured her process. Let her yell (talk) until she feels heard then retreat to the garage, grocery store, back yard, etc. If he actually did something wrong he quickly fixes it and if it was her fault she apologizes to him a few hours later. At times it seems strange and wrong but it works for them because he respects her process.

The bottom line is women take time to process things, but the amount of time is very different for each woman and not adhering to her specific time frame can be fatal to your cause.

How is that headache coming along? If you are not sure about your woman's time frame I feel that it is ok to go ahead and ask her. I would not recommend immediately asking her (unless she is a talker like me) but the next time you have a conversation just ask if she has had a chance to think about X and when might be a good time to talk about it again. Even if she gets pissed at you for bringing it up and invading her processing time, this is a better reaction then the "he doesn't care about me" reaction you could receive if you wait too long. It circles back around to honesty. I hope you all are noticing a theme here.

The other important thing here is vulnerability. By asking a woman about her processing time frame you are showing her vulnerability within yourself by exhibiting your insecurity about re-approaching the subject at hand. This is sexy.

Lola Key

I usually tend to perceive women as the ones who want to give themselves completely in the arms of a man. I am not like that at all, but most of my female friends are. Being the weaker sex, they tend to tuck into the arms of a man where they would feel secure. I may be mistaken.

I, on the other hand, do like to keep my space, to keep my independence for several reasons. First of all, I think that once you let a man sleep in your bed uninvited, for example, it would be very difficult, if not impossible, to say: don't come tomorrow, I need my space. So, if there is some kind of a barrier between the two of you, it is easier for you to control your own time and your own space.

Furthermore, there is this magic in waiting. My experience has proven that (for me at least), there is this magic of anticipation that nothing in the world can beat. That feeling in my stomach when I have to wait for him to call me back, when I know that I have to put a lot of effort to find out more about him. People of the twenty-first century are so pragmatic and everything is within our reach. We have forgotten how valuable a thing is when we have to wait for it and fight for it. Or wait for her and fight for her. Or him.

So, yes, I'd give a great plus for chilling and waiting for whichever reason you pick.

And this is equally important when the relationship develops later on. Each person has to have his own or her own space. You need to keep this for as long as possible. This is so valuable, we all need some space and time for ourselves and we mustn't allow anyone to jeopardize our space.

STEP SEVEN – LET HER GO

If she doesn't reciprocate your feelings or takes too long to respond, then you have to consider letting go. Regardless of what happens with the woman, you've learned some valuable lessons. But there is still one more to learn. Once you get to the point of letting go, let her know. But also ask for her opinion of all the things that you've done. Go through everything that you've done specifically to create a strong emotional experience for her and ask her for her opinions on how you did. Just be friends with her and you'll get amazing advice and help from her.

Lola Key

Sometimes it simply doesn't work. It doesn't have to be you. It can be a wrong moment in our life. It can be you, something you've said or done, or something you haven't said or done. The same may happen on the man's side. It has happened to all of us numerous times. The only thing we didn't know back then and I think I know now is that it is beneficial for both parties to talk about it.

Now I am sorry I haven't talked more to men when we were breaking apart. I could have learned much more about men and about myself.

Claudia

SQUEEZE ANSWERS OUT OF HER, AND THEN...LET GO? (OR VICEVERSA...)

This reminds me of the convenience of having a male confidant (ideally not gay). Many women like to rely on a man when there's no sexual tension so that they can have the male perspective on whatever issue they have with another man. In my experience, most of the time these male confidants are just waiting their turn. I think it is different when a man trusts a woman this way. First of all, because men don't seem to believe (or are just more straight-forward than women about it) that there is the possibility of friendship between men and women. Women do, or at least give it a try. Or hide their intentions better. Or eventually accept whatever kind of relationship a man wants with them, only because they want to be nearby in case he changes his mind.

I will never forget Gustavo, because it was the first time I said to myself: "This is love. What I felt before was just a strong physical attraction. This is it!" This time, I was also strongly attracted to this guy's personality and I felt like I could talk to him about anything in the world. When I met Gustavo, I thought: "The search is over I don't care if I don't meet any other guy in my life, because I've already found the guy I want to spend the rest of my life with!"

A daring thought indeed at...17. But I continued thinking that way for several years. Gustavo, on his part, chose to close all doors to having a serious relationship with me, but accepted meeting me from time to time for coffee and long chats. I cherished those moments with him and hoped for something more all the time. The only physical contact that ever materialized was a few good-bye kisses, given just before a long trip he was going to take to the middle of nowhere.

Those weeks without news from him made sense in that context. No phones nearby, cell phones didn't exist at the time. But as time went by and I thought he had to be back in the city. Still there was no news from him. When I finally got a hold of him, he said: "You should have known this was going to happen." I didn't understand much, but having him as a friend was not helping; and he was closing that door too.

Years later, now with the Internet putting information right at hand, I looked for him. I found that he was living in the States too, and not too far from where I was living at the time (just around 5 hours away). I thought that was a sign, and kept looking until I got his number. I even got to call, but his voice completely froze me. I will never know what would have happened if we had talked then, more than ten years after that last conversation in Buenos Aires. I wasn't strong enough, even after so many years, to take a "no" from him. I guess sometimes it's more romantic to keep the mystery of things; to believe how great and magical a love story could have been, but never was (because of circumstances beyond your control or because one of you didn't dare take a step).

There were other cases in which having a man listen to my side of the story or my strategies helped. And other times, I felt like I was a good ear for a man when he wanted to vent his frustrations about a woman's behavior. But there was always "something else" there, I guess: by this, I mean one of the two had hopes that the friendship was going to evolve into something else. When it didn't, in most cases, the relationship faded away.

HOW TO HAVE SEX WITH DIFFERENT WOMEN EVERY DAY

LOGISTICAL PROBLEMS

After reading "The Game" by Neil Strauss, I tried to imitate one of the players in the book. The guy had a different girl for every day of the week. I wouldn't recommend that unless you like having sex during a woman's period. Women are receptive to having a specific day that you get together every week, but they don't have control of their reproductive systems.

By following that player's lead, two to four times per month there will be no sex. I'm just confused that women would say the same exact thing "Sorry, I thought I had an extra day." I don't have the organs women have, so I'll never understand what it means to think that you had an extra day.

Being flexible allows women to schedule dates when she feels the sexiest.

Lola Key

Having sex with a different woman every day? Come on, what is the point? I would really like a person to tell me what a point of this may be-because I don't see it. Ok, maybe if you are doing some kind of project or an experiment for god knows what purpose. Or, if you want to show off in front of a bunch of losers; or if you are writing a book and using this as some kind of experimental method. I don't see why a normal person would like to have thirty different women a month. Maybe I am a loser.

SOMETIMES WOMEN NEED SEX

Some time ago, I witnessed a guy tell a woman that she was on her period. I was just as surprised as the woman was. We both inquired on how he knew such a thing. He said something about her eyes and her skin. I'd like to think myself a perceptive person and I hadn't noticed anything. I pressed him some more when the woman left and he reiterated the same vague things from before. "You just have to notice the small changes," he said.

I've observed many women intensely and I've never been able to replicate what that man had done. Next I went to the library to learn more about women. If I were able to know a woman's cycle just by looking at her that would be an awesome skill to have.

That's when I first learned about a woman's cycle. My entire life, no one has ever explained to me this vitally important information. Considering all of the pickup artist classes I've been to its mind boggling that no one is shouting this information from the rooftops. I had to go to the library to learn that every month a woman is in 'heat!'

Not only do women have monthly cycles, but they have seasonal and lifetime cycles. At any given moment something is happening to a woman's body. According to the literature, women become antagonistic towards the one they want during that time. I'm 36 years old and I still have no real clue if a woman is in heat.

After years of guessing and questioning the women that I had sex with, I tried a new tactic, random women. When I talk to random women, on the street, they gave me a better understanding. Some try to say you can notice by some outward things, but those things aren't necessarily consistent. In the end, I realized that women themselves didn't even know what was happening in their own bodies. The only ones who can accurately determine if a woman is in heat are her closest friends. When I asked the friends how they know they all said the same thing. The woman would be bent out of shape about something and the friend would interject and say, "you need some sex!"

This is when I learned the true value of a close female circle of friends. They are the only ones who can interpret what's going on with their friend's body. They also are secondary processing so that the friend won't be easily tricked emotionally.

Something amazing happened when I began to talk to groups of women about knowing when their friends needed sex; they offered me the friend. I honestly just wanted to know how they knew, but it usually would turn into an instant hookup. The first one showed me a picture on her phone and said, "My friend needs some sex. What do you think?" She was hot and I said yes. But that combination of words seemed offensive. There was no way I could do the same thing in reverse.

I added that sentence to my 'women's words' arsenal and went to bars with it. I was genuinely offended by the combination of words, but it didn't seem to bother women. When I would ask their opinion about that sentence the group erupts with glee and all point to a woman and exclaim, "she needs some sex!" It's like most groups of women go out because one of them is in heat and they all get together to help her out. It's the friend's job to help her out.

Once I became that guy, the friends would usually show up at my door a few days to weeks later. This may sound like it could be a high five moment, but I began to lose interest in sex after this. Being passed around a group of friends made me feel like a piece of meat. I felt like I should be getting paid. I'm sure some of the girls would've paid and might have even advertised to others. I didn't want that mainly because I want to be able to say no whenever I wanted to.

Chan

I have already mentioned it, but sometimes I just need sex. Women in general need sex for many reasons. To feel sexy, to feel wanted and desired, for physical release, for physical connection, for pleasure, for sanity, etc.… Our bodies are on hormonal cycles and as lovely and understanding as Daniel wants to be, each woman sits on that cycle on a completely different point. Not just a better day for sex, but even a better time of day. I for one am most easily turned on in the afternoon. I am not a morning person and by night I am exhausted from the day. This only changes maybe 1-2 days a month and to make it more interesting these days are different every month and my cycle is allegedly "regulated". So not even I could not tell you if tomorrow I would be more or less interested in sex. If I happened to be interested I still could not tell you what time of day would be the best and why I need it (physical, emotional, etc.).

All that being said, we all know that there are some women who do not have nor heed their internal sex clock. They have a strong libido and are not particular about the who, when, why or how. On the opposite side there are woman that have no interest in sex whatsoever. Some of this is probably due to hormones and some of it is past experiences. Remember, women have difficulty separating past, present and future. This means that each time they think about sex they are thinking about all the things sex with you embodies not just the physical act of sleeping with you. Unfortunately too many women have had abusive sexual encounters that influence all of their sexual choices.

It is very interesting that you mentioned going to her closest friends to see if a woman is in "heat." While I have certainly gone out with my mind set on sex as the end game, I do not recall ever going out specifically to help a friend find sex. At least the women I know will go out together to help a friend get through a man problem, but not to hook her up. To be honest many times I have talked a friend out of going home with a guy because I felt she was too vulnerable. She thought she wanted a guy just for sex but knowing her I knew that she would regret that decision. She was being strongly influenced by a surge of emotions, not a physical need. Your position confused me because I have not seen these groups of women. I do not necessarily deny they exist, I just know that they are not found in my circle of friends.

It is interesting to ponder though what it might look like if my group of friends were to gather and collaborate to help a friend find sex. I suppose it would look something like a wingman situation but a lot of red flags are popping into my head. Women have all sorts of friends, not all of which would be ideal as representatives seeking to fulfill your sexual needs. There are the prettier ones, the funnier ones, the smarter ones and the worst of all, the manipulative ones. Why are you friends with those types of women? Try finding a group of women that gets along that does not have those types. You will not find one. As I think more about it, the more I feel that going to her friends is a bad idea. A man is likely to lose sight of the ball either by choice (prettier, funnier, smarter, etc.) or by manipulation from one of these friends. I do not see a way this would end well and I am curious to know what happened in the situations Daniel spoke about and to be a fly on the wall as the women spoke among themselves.

Lola Key

This is an interesting topic to be discussed. First, let's start with purely physical facts. Hormones do play a vital role in our lives. Some time ago, when I started reading about the influence of hormones to our overall state, psychological mainly, I was shocked that we are influenced by some kinds of hormones during the entire month. PMS, then, standing for PRE and POST-menstrual syndrome, and it lasts all the time.

Furthermore, I had a roommate once who told me that our periods after some time would begin to coincide. She had a theory that when two women are close and share a flat, their periods start coinciding after some time. That is how influential hormones are.

So, I guess it is possible; not possible, but probable, that there are some hormones that very strongly influence us. I have never thought that there is some regularity to this, but then again, I never thought of it intensely. I can just say that we need sex the most when we have our periods, but I always kind of thought that this is the case because we don't have it then.

Claudia

Sometimes (Wo)men Need Sex; Sometimes They Don't!

A woman, among her women friends, will joke about this constantly. We talk about "being in heat" just as if we were animals...but we don't really mean it!

It's been a big progress just to be able to say openly and freely that there are times when we women need sex. In the past, it used to be a man's thing. For them, it was supposed to be a basic need, right there together with the need for food and shelter.

Since the women's lib movement, we've been able to express that need ourselves without blushing. But when it is that we really need it changes with every woman. I would dare say that when you have your period it's definitely not the time you feel the sexiest. But I've heard women who do feel like having sex on those days. Pregnancy does not seem to be the hottest time either...but it certainly is for some women. So, I wouldn't generalize here. It is possible that men want sex more often than women. But then again, it depends on the person.

I would have said that men always want sex if it were not for this male friend, Víctor, who seems to be completely asexual. I didn't know it could happen, but after I thought of my own theories, I read about the subject and yes, it seems it's a reality: there are people out there (women and men) who have zero interest in sex...throughout their whole lives. It's not just a phase.

YOU DON'T NEED ANYTHING SPECIAL

Going through a woman's friend to find out if she's in heat, made all the game I had worked on useless. I had spent a considerable amount of time, money, and energy improving my game to an acceptable level. The chase was the best part of dating women, and it was gone. After ridding myself of women that I don't even remember, I hit the streets again. This time I wanted to know why the hell so many women were having sex with me with almost no resistance.

Talking to enough women and hearing similar responses led me to understand how I somehow entered an alternate universe where women will just have sex with you and go home. It's funny, I'd been to many pickup artist meetings and it never occurred to me to simply ask women. To them it's super easy! Hearing women talking about picking women up made all of my studying worthless. There are five things that you will need in order to have sex all the time. These five things are also an emotional combination.

First and foremost you need to have something interesting about you!! I know I've said this before, but you need some redeeming quality. You need to have something for her to be attracted to. This can't be faked and copied, you need to find that thing and be all about it. Without having something interesting about you, you have no real chance. Everyone has something special about them; you just need to able to express that thing in an acceptable way.

Second, know that sex isn't a big deal to women. Women and men think about sex differently. To most guys, getting sex is like winning the lottery. In fact, guys often say that they got 'lucky' after they had sex with a woman. When a guy has sex it is cause for celebration, because it feels like an intense journey. If you or your friends have ever said the words 'lucky' regarding sex, consider this. At any given moment, at least one out of every thirty women is in heat. Quite often, that moment passes and the woman goes unsatisfied. In time, if unsatisfied, a woman will eventually just pick someone. After her moment passes, she wakes up in the morning regretting ever meeting you. I don't call that lucky, I call that insulting! It means that you were the bottom of the barrel and she took what she could get.

On the other hand, women don't think much of sex. They often talk about how easy it is to have sex with men or women. They absolutely don't understand why guys go to seminars or watch videos about picking up women. When I ask them to teach me how they always have a single sentence answer, "All you need to do is (fill in the blank)!"

Knowing this, you need to convey to them that sex isn't a big deal to you either. This is a difficult thing for most guys to accept. If you really believe that sex is a big deal and you tell a girl that it isn't, she will absolutely know! I suggest you go out and talk to random girls and listen to their responses. For now, just consider that sex could possibly not be a big deal.

Third, you aren't emotionally clingy. For me, this is basically the same as the last point. But the women that I've spoken to emphasized how important and different the two phrases are. So you need to convey to the woman that having sex with her won't mean that you are dating. Also, you aren't going to call and text her incessantly. You aren't going to show up at her job with flowers. You don't want to meet her parents. Again, I think it's the same as the last point, but it's different for women somehow.

Fourth, you will keep her safe. This is something that I mentioned before, but it's extra vital now. It's important that she feel emotionally and physically safe around you, but also she needs to know that you will protect her reputation. You need to convey to the women that you will never talk about whatever goes on between the two of you. I almost never, ever, ever talk about being with a woman! You have to fight that urge to brag.

There are many reasons to never talk. The first is obviously you honestly do want the woman to feel safe around you. The second is you want to keep yourself safe as well! If you blab your mouth her man will want your head. Trust me; I've had some bad experiences. A broken heart is the number one cause of murder! The last reason might surprise you. Women are somehow magically connected. If you tell one woman about being with a woman she doesn't know, it will somehow blow up in your face. My rule is to never talk ever. When women press me about who I've been with, I simply let them know I don't kiss and tell. If you brag to a woman about having sex with other women, she may never have sex with you because she will think that you will do the same to her.

Finally, let her know that you find the real her attractive. That might sound weird, but consider that women all around the world go through hell attempting to live up to impossible male standards. Being physically attracted to a woman is easy. You need to find something else to be attracted to. You and I may be coming from a different place when we say that we are attracted to a woman.

In New York City, if I stand on a busy street, every five to ten minutes an amazingly beautiful woman walks by. If you could have sex with even a small percentage of those women, you'd never leave your house! When I talk to a beautiful woman, I'm actively trying to find something that is non-physical and attractive about her. If there isn't anything there, I walk away! If you accept a woman for who she is, she will feel comfortable around you.

Chan

Redeeming Quality

Everyone needs a redeeming quality, especially a man approaching a woman. Each individual woman measures these redeeming qualities very differently. Sometimes women have a set of qualities they carry with them from youth on and some change with wind.

If a woman is in physical need of sex her standards of redeeming qualities can diminish rapidly and become as small and simple as he is the only one not wearing flannel or he has a foreign accent. Qualities like this still have enough of a redeeming nature that women can explain to themselves and their friends why they ended up in your bed last night. This is not because they feel the need to internally justify it, but rather they are filing it away as an experience and making sure to spread the word if necessary to other women (the whole connected thing). Remember once again that our process involves the experiences of the past, present and future.

I was good friends with a guy who acted immature and was a dork most of the time. One summer we were hanging out a lot and really got to know each other. One night after a particular long day I was out with this group and I could not even find a smile to greet people. Then he got there, wearing a Superman t-shirt and acting immature as usual. As the night went on he came over sat down and proceeded to make me laugh hysterically for the next hour. When last call came around I looked up at him and for the first time saw how smart and adorably cute his was. I leaned up and quickly kissed him. We dated for almost a year. His ability to make me laugh when nothing else could was his redeeming quality (one of many) and what made me look at him in a different light.

Sex isn't a Big Deal

Most women can and do recognize sex for what it is. Sometimes it is just a physical event and sometimes it is a show of love and affection. Believe it or not women are quite capable of identifying the difference between the two. Your suggestion that men need to convey to a woman that sex is not a big deal to them is a bit off point and misleading.

Women make the choice to have sex with a man and they decide whether it is a physical event or a show of affection. If a man consistently treats sex like just a physical event they will find themselves taking lots of cold showers (do I need to remind you of Aussie). Basically it is bad news to assume that every woman wants to take your sexual encounter as merely a physical experience. If she at all indicates affection (do you feel something special...) then acting as if it is just sex for you is a huge red mark in your corner and a huge hit to her self-esteem.

Emotionally Clingy

This is similar to the situation above. Sometimes women crave a pure physical encounter where there is no mention of future relationship issues or feelings. Here is a secret, she still thinks about it. We cannot make it stop no matter how much we want to.

In college I took an Irish American History Class and lo and behold a gorgeous man from Dublin sat next to me in class and his brogue dripped with green fields and Guinness. We flirted throughout the 8-weeks and after the final exam we went out to the local pub to celebrate. Did I mention he had a wicked sexy accent? We did not have anything in common except our love of Ireland and the fact that we both liked to drink beer, which we did in excess that evening.

I did not have any romantic feelings for him brewing inside. Then I made the decision that we were going to have sex, so I kissed him at the bar and told him to follow me. We proceeded to have sex in the backseat of a car (not my favorite choice of location) and we both were in it for one thing only, to get off. However there is no way for me to stop my mind and as I was driving home afterwards I thought of all the compromises and ways I could make a relationship work with him.

I did not want a relationship with him. He actually was kind of a dick. The point is I thought about it even though I choose to go into the situation knowing I only wanted sex. I could not help it. Women are definitely capable of having "no strings" sex, but we also cannot deny or suppress our thought process. It is important to note that these thoughts do not constitute strings because in most of these kinds of situations they are quickly disposed of. My thoughts were fleeting and gone by the time I awoke the next morning but I still have to face that they still occurred.

Keep Her Safe

Do NOT kiss and tell. I hope Daniel **BOLDS** *this phrase.*

Women keep their reputations like diamonds in a vault. When we open the vault to wear the diamonds we expect those who take in their brilliance to enjoy them and then forget they existed. In other words enjoy the hell out of the sex and use it in a private moment in your head if necessary, but do not let anyone else know about the quality of the diamonds or where they are being stored. If you are in it for the conquest and the bragging rights go back and read the section on not being a dick because that is unacceptable behavior and NO woman appreciates it.

I assume, perhaps incorrectly, that a man who is using PUA routines or emotional combinations is quite proud of himself when he feels they have worked. Remember that pride is one of the deadly sins and boasting about your ability to get women into bed only makes it worse. Especially if you are using specific examples. I have known women who made the wrong choice on a desperate night only to be labeled a slut and had their names written on bathroom walls. Maybe you were not brought up to be a gentleman but now is your chance. Think before you talk about a woman because it will hurt her and in turn you.

The Real Her

It is an absolute necessity that when you want to have a relationship (not merely a sexual encounter) with a woman that you accept her for all that she is, not who you want or expect her to be. My husband thinks I am beautiful and funny but the way I argue and daydream drives him slightly insane. We are all made up of positive and negative qualities. Being just physically attracted to a woman is not enough for either one of you; she needs to know that you are seeing the book not just the cover.

I was once a day camp counselor during the summer between my freshman and sophomore year in college. The whole staff partied pretty hard and I was no exception. There was this hot guy on staff and I decided I did not want to be alone that summer so I made it happen. His parents were rich and he was a spoiled little brat and looking back on it, a total dick. I cannot even remember if he was good in bed so I have to assume that I was merely with him to have someone around that summer.

Then came the barbeque. He reluctantly invited me to attend a barbeque with some of his fraternity brothers. Everyone else was bringing a date so he thought he needed to. I said I would go but I never liked hanging out with fraternity guys. There was always something dirty and political about them.

Once we arrived at the party he proceeded to immediately get wasted and subsequently ignored me. After a few hours of trying to converse with some stereotypical sorority girls I pulled him aside and asked to leave. Of course a fight ensued and we moved into a bedroom to get out of the earshot of the rest of the party. One thing led to another and we were making out on the bed and my shirt and bra were off. Fighting tends to turn me on what can I say.

The door to the bedroom opens and in walked my guy's big brother (in a frat each new freshman is given a big brother to teach him the lay of the land). It then became rather surreal to me. The big brother said, "Nice rack. John Doe told you about the big brother rule right?" I was trying to cover myself up but John Doe was holding my arms down. "No," I said. "We share everything. And I mean everything." he laughed.

John Doe did not know the real me or how absolutely horrified I would be in a situation so similar to one I had experienced before. John Doe *did not care about me as a person or even as a sexual object. He was not even using me for sex. He was purposely degrading me. When I re-read this example I thought about moving it because at first it did not illustrate the point. Then I realized it highlighted something very important, women choose to show pieces of the real her as she sees fit.*

I did not show my real self to John Doe because I did not want what we had to turn into any sort of relationship because he did not give a crap about me. This is not healthy and it clearly shows that if you are into a woman it is of vital importance to get to know the real her. It is partially her job to release details about herself, but it is your job to convince her it is safe to do so and then cherish those details when she finally does. And for those that need closure, I made it out of the bedroom unshared and sat out in the car until he was ready to leave 4 hours later. We never spoke again.

Lola Key

First of all, I do agree with you that women around the world go through hell to live up to male standards. I think this partially has to do with the standards of beauty that are presented to us. Maybe then we are talking about some self-imposed standards that us, women, strive to achieve. But, nevertheless, when I was younger, I always thought I could be more attractive, smarter and wittier to be more liked by men.

Furthermore, don't think that being physically attractive is something we don't pay close attention to. Oooh, we do make a lot of effort to be physically attractive. We are always hungry, we go to the gym, undertake cosmetic treatments, wax ourselves completely, we do a lot of things even when we don't feel like it.

It's just like some type of precondition. When we are beautiful, chemistry happens, and only then can somebody take a closer look into what is deeper in us that makes us special.

Claudia

BE FRIENDS TO THEIR FRIENDS

I remember once hearing this guy from Spain, who was dating one of my Argentine roommates, say: "If you want to date an Argentine woman, first you have to make sure you get along with their female friends, and that they really like you...!" Of course I found that to be a bit of an exaggeration, but I guess it happens in many cultures: friends can help you get closer to a girl...or, as I've seen it myself, dig your own grave!

So, I don't know how much the friends of a girl can help you get closer to her, or keep you at a safe distance, but I wouldn't personally think too much about the cycles, the heat thing and this monthly need for sex. According to doctors, we humans are the only animals in heat 24/7, all year round! It's not that I disregard the importance of hormones: I think they are a big part of what we women are like. But it's no hard and fast rule.

FIVE THINGS YOU NEED TO KNOW TO HAVE SEX ALL THE TIME?

First of all, I believe that if all what you want is only sex, and you live in a big city, you don't really need much. There are thousands of women out there ready for a one-night stand, no strings attached, period. But hey, maybe you just want to make sure that you can have sex every single night, and for that you need a formula. Alright, let's go over it!

"First and foremost you need to have something interesting about you!!"

To me, this is a must if you want to see this person at least one more time! Otherwise, it could just happen that you're interested in just spending the night with someone, and then, ciao!

"Second, know that sex isn't a big deal to women."

There are many interpretations for this. If by "a big deal" you mean women could live without it, I disagree; particularly, if they don't take it for granted. I admit that for many women in a long-term relationship, a night of sex may not be a priority tonight because they know they could have it tomorrow night, or the day after tomorrow, or whenever they want.

Now, when women are not in a relationship, they learn to appreciate it more. Even when they are not actively looking for it, they'll miss it and want it. At times they'll feel there's a big vacuum in their lives because they are not having sex, or they are having sex very sporadically.

If "sex isn't a big deal to women" means that nowadays both men and women are free to do it whenever they feel like it, I'll disagree too! I think many times we women would like to think that, just like the Sex and the City girls, love can be one thing, sex another, and if the two don't go together, we might as well have sex at least until we find love. But it is usually much more complicated than that for women. Even when they don't show it at all, there are feelings going around. If they suppress them, it's because they would like to show they are as free as men.

"Third, you aren't emotionally clingy."

Do men and women need to establish certain rules before their first sexual encounter? Maybe. It may mean nothing at all, like we've seen in the movie "Fatal Attraction" (that phrase by the character played by Glenn Close, "no strings attached," doesn't work very well). Or, with fewer fatal consequences, in a Seinfeld episode in which Elaine and Jerry that have dated before decide to have occasional sexual encounters without that ruining their friendship. Even though we've seen before that rules like these don't usually work, we think "it won't happen to me," and we decide "yes, let's establish some rules and make everything clear from the beginning, so we have no nasty surprises later on!"

"Fourth, you will keep her safe."

Here, you mention how important it is to never kiss and tell and how much it matters to a woman that you don't try and ruin her reputation. And how that, obviously, keeps you safe too, considering many women you get involved with are already in a relationship with men who will want your head on a platter after they find out about you.

One thing that I found unusual about my present partner is that he never wants to talk about past relationships, nor does he want me to say anything about other men I've been with. In his case, it's probably a question of jealousy. Even after so many years with him, I cannot be too sure. But I've learned what a good idea it actually is. You are who you are as a result of many things: places you've been to, pain and suffering you went though, people you've met…But, is there any need to discuss all this in excruciating detail? I've been hurt by men who did that. It's as if somehow I was entering a competition with women I hadn't even met (and most probably would never meet). And it was all completely useless.

If the point of mentioning a woman by name is to brag, it sounds even more pointless. Yes, it's probably better for your safety and everyone else's to keep that mouth shut!

"Finally, let her know that you find the real her attractive."

In the movie "Six Days, Seven Nights," a pilot called Quin Harries (played by Harrison Ford) is flying a helicopter with the character played by Anne Heche, Robin Monroe. She's the editor of a women's magazine. He's making fun of the articles typically found in those magazines when he says: "You know how a woman gets a man excited? She shows up. That's it. We're guys, we're easy. Of course for that you can't charge six bucks an issue, now can you?" Deep inside, we know that you guys don't need any sophisticated technique or special outfits when, for example, we're going for a run in a worn-out sweat shirt and baggy pants and you still find us attractive. But we want to hear we're special. Many of us have had a hard time working on our self-esteem, so it's great to hear how attractive *you find us. Even after we've been with someone for a very long time (or precisely because of that!), we need to hear that you guys find us attractive.*

Consider Ethiopia

Even though I've done all the hard work in talking to women about this, some guys still won't believe that this is all you need to have sex with as many women as you want. Since I don't like to talk about my own experience, consider Ethiopia. I've never been to Ethiopia and I don't have plans to go there and have sex with as many women as possible. But what if I were able to communicate with the women there? Could these five principles work for me?

I chose Ethiopia for a reason. The women there are force fed from a young age and given hormones to fatten them up. Apparently Ethiopian men like obese women even though there is a famine in the country. Girls are sent to 'fat camps' in order to make them attractive enough to marry. Some women die from the force-feeding and hormones.

I would find a place to meet women that wouldn't arouse the suspicions of anyone else. Once I connect with one, I would demonstrate something that is interesting or attractive about me. She will let me know in some fashion that she finds my interesting thing attractive. All the while, I'll be looking for things to find attractive about her.

At this point, I take all the things in the following steps and turn it around onto her. I tell her that I'm not interested in a long-term relationship and that sex isn't a big deal to me. Then I would challenge her and ask if she gets too clingy after sex or if she won't keep it secret; because those things are super important to me.

Whenever I find myself becoming attracted to her, I'll let her know specifically what I'm attracted to. I'm looking for special things unique to her, and I'm actually attracted to those things. If she doesn't agree to all of those things then I move on. If she does, we just need to find a quiet place.

I have never been to Ethiopia but I'm confident in my assessment of what would happen. What would happen is after I get one or two women to sleep with me, her friends will start showing up at my door. Sometimes they will show up in groups to give themselves an alibi. In time, even the coveted fat women will show up as well.

How am I so confident? Women everywhere have to try and meet impossible standards just to attract a man. They are constantly going through incredible hoops all the while they have emotional and physical needs. When they want to be physically satisfied, to them "there are no men!" The vast majority of men don't bother with a woman's emotional or physical needs.

These circumstances leave women, in general, vulnerable to abusers and players. Both abusers and players give women the emotional experiences that they crave. Abusers take things to another level.

Lola Key

I couldn't agree more with you on this issue. And it's not that I feel some kind of pity for women who completely underestimate themselves and put aside their needs, just to satisfy the physical and emotional needs of a man. I do not pity them. It is their choice. It is this primeval fear, I'd say, that we will be left alone and not wanted. It is fear and panic that let us be as submissive to a man as possible, and just not be left alone. But I don't blame men for this, not at all. Women are to be blamed completely. I would rather be alone for as much as it takes, than in a relationship in which I have to ignore and disregard my own needs for the satisfaction of a man. The older I am, the more certain I am about this.

Next, let me focus a little bit on this example of Ethiopia. Having had the opportunity to talk to a lot of African women and having had a close insight into how submissive they are, how they completely neglect the existence of their own needs, physical, emotional, whatsoever, I am sure that with your approach, you would be able to have sex with the vast majority of African women. And not just to have sex with them, you would be deity to them.

European women and American women are different in that respect. We have managed to achieve gender equality to a certain extent, we have had experiences with many men, not just traditional ones, and our market has a lot more to offer than the African traditional one, so you have to think how to get us to bed.

Claudia

ETHIOPIA? CONSIDER ARGENTINA!

According to research, my country breaks many records when it comes to the number of eating disorder cases (anorexia and bulimia, mainly), cosmetic surgeries...and shrinks! As you can well imagine, most of the people in those records are women. Surprisingly enough, all that effort to look good for men that could be treated at a therapist's office doesn't really work that well, because women still starve themselves or risk their lives at times on the operation table. It's sad to admit it, but self-esteem is still a big issue for women everywhere, and unfortunately Argentina is a poster case for that.

This leaves us in a very fragile situation in our relationship with men. On the other hand, some recent changes have made that biological clock ticking a little irrelevant. Now women are having kids later on in life (I'm a good example: I had my child at 41) without the fears of the past (science can help here too), not getting married is not a big issue anymore (at least in my country many couples live together instead of marrying and that's quite normal and socially accepted) and embracing professions has helped to improve our self-esteem. But still, there's a long way to go, and now that I'm a mother I realize how much responsibility parents have in helping to build a self-assured personality so that we don't replicate the same situation in our own kids' lives.

Men are too Sensitive

Women are emotional. They express themselves and process things emotionally. Men on the other hand are simply sensitive. I'm a man, and I admit that I too am sensitive, although I've matured quite a bit. Men are super sensitive and I can prove it.

In Manhattan there is a cross street Seaman Ave and Cumming Street. Hundreds of women live on that corner, and some do complain. When guys hear about that corner they laugh and demand to visit it to find women. In the Bronx, Hoe Ave and Faile Street run parallel to each other for two blocks. Hundreds of women live between Hoe and Faile, and I'm sure that they aren't particularly happy about it.

If there were a cross street in Brooklyn called Little Street and Johnson Ave men would openly protest. Men would lobby their politicians to change the name. Property values would plummet considering no man would willingly live on the corner of Little and Johnson!

A lot of men get hung up on what a woman is supposed to be and lose it when women don't meet their expectations. It's totally fine to have expectations for the women you allow in your life. I have expectations as well. But unreasonable expectations will do nothing but create opportunities for a person like me.

Often times, within the first few minutes of talking with a woman she would blurt out the nastiest thing she'd ever done. If I create a safe environment for her to be herself, a woman will confess to things that she has never told anyone. It's quite liberating considering everyone else would attack and shame her for not being perfect. It's an unfair double standard. For example, a woman could admit to having sex with three guys at the same time. For some reason, that isn't the same as me having sex with three women at the same time. Even though it is essentially the same thing.

I dated this gorgeous Arab girl once. We could never meet outside. She was always looking over her shoulder and terrified that someone would catch us. The last time we were together I remember her trembling with fear. She was worried that her brothers would find out. I told her that she's in America now and doesn't have to worry about anything. She told me that her family put her brothers in charge of her, and if she offends them in any way they will put her on a plane back to her country since she wasn't a full citizen. She told me they might kill her if she gets sent back to her country. When she asked me if I were willing to convert to Islam it was too much for me. I never was a Knight in Shining Armor kind of guy. By now she's in an arranged marriage and likely has children.

Women are complex and sometimes confusing. You can't train or force them to be the way you want them to be. It's true that she may marry you, but filling a role isn't enough for a woman. You need to fulfill her emotional needs. This is something that you can't be sensitive about! You have every opportunity in the world to create wonderful emotional experiences for your woman. But if you get overly sensitive about what you think a woman should be and lose it when women don't meet your expectations, then let me tell you something. There is a strong possibility that she is finding an emotional outlet somewhere else.

Chan

This section of the book is what I believe to be the most heartfelt and truthful. Often it is forgotten that women have historically not been viewed as equals. All too often they were viewed as less than or sometimes they were not thought of at all. Men made the rules and women followed them.

Then times changed and women started seeking bigger and better things in life and began taking their piece of the pie. Yet still men were making the rules and most women continued to follow them.

Fast-forward to today, there are now women CEOs, heads of state and mothers with 19 children. However, women are still not on an equal pay scale with men and they are still held to a family standard that was created by men long ago. There is now a standard for women to join the workforce, work as hard if not harder than their male peers and get paid less, birth and raise children and still get a home cooked dinner on the table by 6pm.

It is evident that in our society men still make the rules and place expectations upon women, while less and less women are opting to follow them. Most of us follow bits and pieces of these rules because we want to be loved and cared for by a life partner. Yet there is a key piece missing that will truly allow women to live and men to truly appreciate what a woman has to give. That key piece involves the assumed right men seem to have that they can regulate how a woman should be and their negative reactions when she does not live up to the often outrageous expectations. As long as this is still occurring in society women, as a whole will never have their gifts fully realized.

Women want and need the freedom to be themselves. There is no innate physical or genetic pull in a woman to attain this Stepford Wife level of expectation. Sometimes we choose to kill ourselves climbing the impossible walls men put up. I take responsibility for the fact that some women choose to do that very thing for their entire lives. However, we would not be put in a position to have to make those choices if we were given the freedom to be ourselves.

Now some women are naturally perfect homemakers or "a lady in the street but a freak in the bed", but most of us are a mixture of all things in between. Our real selves often include the "base-line expectations" many guys have. Personally I love to cook, shop for my man, do the laundry, entertain his clients, etc.

Bottom line: quit imposing your expectations on us and I think you will be pleasantly surprised at how we react and how much more we want to be with you.

Lola Key

Women are emotional and men are sensitive. Well, I do agree that women are emotional. And when it comes to men and sensitivity, I honestly don't know what to say. I can say that I think men are sensitive when it comes to the length and size of their penis. I think this is an overrated topic. And I really think this is not as crucial as men think it is. The more important thing for me in terms of this size is how men deal with what they have.

When it comes to this Arab girl, the story about her did not surprise me. The story about how you behaved in the situation did not surprise me either. Sometimes I think that the gap between us is so huge, that it is almost impossible to date and marry some who is not of your religion. I don't say we are better than them; it's not something that can be compared.

MY FIRST COMBINATION

The following will be the second and final except from the massive book that I wrote about my life "Violent Tremor: Journey to Overcome the Legacy of Slavery." Honestly, the book isn't really that good. I shut myself off from the world and wrote for two years straight. Whenever I decide to do something I only focus on that. The book itself is everything that I wished to get off my chest. It's far too many topics and ideas. I needed to let it all out for my own sanity.

It's important to note that I was a virgin until the summer before my sophomore year at college. I only had sex once that summer. I didn't have sex again until my senior year. After senior year I didn't have sex again until three years after that. I had made up my mind that I would wait until I got married to have sex, but it was difficult to do and also I wouldn't allow myself to be close to anyone.

LETTER TO ROSE (EXCERPT)

I'm glad that I started writing; it's changed me. With every new section it takes me days or weeks to finally decide to go forward. Even though I already know what I'm going to say. Every page became progressively harder for me. It's difficult for me to say things sometimes, but this part in particular proves that I lie again and again. Rosa Amarilla, I told you time after time that I'd stop contacting you. I told you I wouldn't write or call. Does writing a message to you in a book count? More importantly, why is it so important to me that I communicate with you and at the same time have absolutely nothing to do with you?

I have no regrets regarding you Rose. If I had to do it all over again, knowing what I know now, I think my heart would simply have given in and I would die before I knew a moment of pain. The little miracle you planted in my heart spread like an uncontainable insurrection. For that I'm forever grateful. Although I still have a long ways to go.

I didn't keep many secrets from you. The secrets that I did keep from you, I kept to myself intentionally. When we were together, I knew something was wrong with me but you made me feel like everything was ok. Basically, I know that I was a weirdo and I'd like to share with you what my experience with you was like.

We spent a few months just spending time together. I enjoyed talking with you and sharing my time with you. I felt comfortable around you and I appreciated that you didn't pressure me into being physical with you. Then we spent a few weeks making out in random places. It had been over three years since I had kissed a woman. I had forgotten how enjoyable it was. Eventually, we got a hotel room and were finally able to be alone.

I remember you were on top and said "I could just slide it in you know? We don't have to do anything tonight." You were confused that I shrugged my shoulders and expected me to say no. The truth is I was convinced that sex felt awful and didn't expect anything from the experience. I knew that something was wrong with me. The plan was to let you enjoy yourself and when you were finished I would lie apart from you and see if anything happens to me. I wanted to see if I would have another 'vision' or see if anything mentally, emotionally, or physically changed. I actually didn't want to have sex with you; I hated having sex. You also said that you didn't like having sex either. You said, "It felt like nothing."

I was mystified when it felt amazing when you did put it in. I was frozen in disbelief at how wonderful it felt. All I could remember is seeing your face above mine as the pleasurable feelings steadily increased. I couldn't understand what was happening and tried to analyze the situation. But I kept getting sidetracked by ever increasing orgasmic contractions. When I finally climaxed I was lost in your eyes and I remember exactly what I was thinking 'People should be doing this all the time!' We began having sex every day until you got tired.

Every sexual interaction that we had I began to assess and mentally catalogue. I was still perplexed why sex with you felt good, but also I wanted to learn from the experiences. One day, the first month of us having sex every day, the sex felt magical. Different parts of your insides were moving and doing different things. When we had sex the next day, I asked you why you weren't doing the things you were doing the day before. You had no idea what I was talking about. I tried to be as detailed as possible but you got angry and shouted "I didn't do anything yesterday! I don't know what you are talking about!" Then you stormed off into the bathroom.

I did the only thing I knew how to do; I studied women. I discovered that once per month women are in heat and it's best to have sex with them then. The materials I read said that a woman's body and mood changes along with her cycles. You kept saying that I was a sex fiend because I always wanted to have sex with you. It's true that everything you did turned me on. Unfortunately for you, even your breathing turned me on. But there was more, I wanted to know exactly the day the sex would feel the best.

I could never get the hang of it. The best day would fluctuate by a week every month. It frustrated me. It was like your body knew I was trying to pin the day down. I asked that you start using the birth control pill. I read that it would make your period regular and predictable. But you said that you were allergic. I tried then to predict based on your mood and changes in your body. I expected you to get mad at me or pick a fight and you never did. So I had to ask you why you don't get upset before your period. You simply said, "I don't do that." That was also frustrating. I did my best to examine your body every opportunity I got. You seemed shy and would always stop me. I didn't understand why you would always try and shield your body from the one you have sex with every day.

I then tried smell and taste to find out any changes. You didn't smell or taste like anything. You were OCD about having any smells from your body. Jelly Bean had a strong scent and it drove me wild. Delicious smelled like perfume and I loved it. Chinita's scent was similar to Jelly Bean's except she always covered it with her favorite perfume. I could smell them both. With you there was nothing. I suggested you grow out some hair on your body and you refused and said, "That's disgusting." I just wanted to smell you.

So I had to exam your body without you know I was examining it. It didn't get me any closer to figuring out the day you were in heat, but I noticed that your body was 'talking.' I confronted you initially about what your body was saying and you vehemently denied it. So I decided not to bother talking to you about it. I would respond directly to your body. It was fascinating, I could verbally respond to what I thought your body was saying and you treated it like it was normal part of the conversation. It was like I was talking with two different women: Rose and Secret Rose. Sometimes the two of you would disagree and I would usually side with Secret Rose.

The more I would communicate with Secret Rose the closer I thought I would get to figuring out when the best day for sex would be. I was wrong. The sex got better for every day, not just one. Then to top it off day of magical sex came during the month that the sex was better every day. It was like Secret Rose knew I was on to her and she was trying to throw me off. I had to figure out what happened and I spent all of my mental energy trying to communicate with Secret Rose. I noticed that she responded to emotional stimuli. So I began orchestrating emotional combinations to see what she would like.

By that time, I had to have sex with you every chance that I got. I wanted to know if what I was doing was working. You suggested that we get another girl, because I wanted to have sex too much. I declined, and I want you to know why. With you I already had two women. Another person added would be too distracting and I probably wouldn't have liked it. I had multiple emotional plans working at any given time. Some would last only a few hours, then some would span a few days, and others would go on for months. For a long time, I believed that keeping the emotional combinations to myself was the best way to go; I was wrong. A few years later I learned that it could be even more effective to explain in detail my plans and the purpose of it.

For two years we pretty much just had sex. We went out to eat a few times and went to the movies as well. All of those things were things we did in between having sex. Even though I was obsessed with observing you I was completely naive about what was going on with you. You began dating other guys. There were three in total. I went out with a girl as well. I thought that you and I were just friends. What kind of simpleton could have sex with his best friend every day and think that they were just friends? Me. Technically, I didn't care about you dating other guys. In my mind, I thought it was healthy for you. I didn't feel jealousy specifically.

My memory of the events leading up to our last day together is unclear. I think it may be purposefully hazy. I can tell you the events that were significant to me. The first significant event we were walking somewhere and debating about the things that were changing in our relationship. I don't recall which guy it was or where we were going. But I recall you saying, "If you don't have a problem why are you walking five feet away from me?" I prided myself on being hyperaware of my surroundings and especially being aware of you. I was stunned to not have noticed that we were so far apart. What's more is that I couldn't walk any closer; no matter how hard I tried. I was confused by that moment.

(End Excerpt)

Chan

Newsflash Daniel: the sex felt better because you cared about Rose. You did not acknowledge the emotional feelings you were having, but your interest in finding Secret Rose was about finding a way to satisfy whatever it is your mind and heart were missing. It seems to me that the problem is that you thought you were doing this grand study on women the whole time, and I think you fully believe this, but with Rose it was different. Even the language you chose to use when describing your relationship was softer and more receptive. For Rose you chose to use your research to provide her the attention she obviously craved and needed during that time in her life.

Have a seat for this next one.

All women have a Secret Person. The real us. The nitty gritty stuff that makes up who we are.

Remember how you said men are always imposing their expectations onto women and we choose without any outward reason to adopt them? Well this Secret Person is the un-adopted, unabridged and uncensored us. When we disagree it is because those expectations and what we want/need are conflicting between our two selves. So if Secret Rose was disagreeing with Rose then it is because unconsciously you were projecting your expectations onto her.

What you say? But I was trying to learn her secrets to make her happy? Those are expectations. Even if you did not explicitly explain what you were doing or what you wanted from her you were influencing every move she made based on your actions and reactions. When you tapped into Secret Rose there was a celebration and her body (and real wants/needs) stood up and took center stage. Our Secret Person wants her body to be worshipped and sex is important. Being wanted and desired goes along with that, but our Secret Person also has emotional needs and gets easily frustrated, which will affect our physical pleasure, if those emotional needs are not being met. Ergo why she suggested another girl and was also why she started dating other guys. She needed more then you were giving her.

Secret Rose was flying high in bed but remember sex is not in a vacuum; Rose needed you to care for her emotionally.

In college I worked at a diner. There was a waiter there that was exotic (read foreign), intelligent and sweet. We flirted shamelessly and hung out (not sexually) many times. This man knew how to go straight to the Secret Me without asking any questions or touching me. I would have gone to the ends of the earth for this man. The way he spoke to me not at me, listened to my ideas and not immediately dismissing them and the way he looked at me with captivated eyes was completely overwhelming. I was currently dating my on-again-off-again boyfriend and the sex was great, but I was not getting the emotional needs Secret Me so desperately craved since the relationship portion was pretty much over.

The Secret Me Whisperer moved away but we were able to speak on the phone periodically. One day he invited me to visit. Note that at this time we had not even kissed, but yet I was more turned on by him than anyone I had met at this point in my life. I braved a borrowed car and a blizzard to travel to see him. That night was amazing. We drank red wine and he spoke to Secret Me. He held me and kissed me gently all night. Regular me thought for sure there would be some expectation of sex and I was fully prepared to engage in that scenario.

However, Secret Me needed the comfort and amazing heart fluttering kisses more than the sex. I can close my eyes 19 years later and still feel his lips. My heart still swells at the thought. We fell out of touch as life moved on, but I think of him often and wish I had thanked him. I would have thanked him for introducing Regular Me to Secret Me, and providing memories that were built to last a lifetime.

Before him I had no idea that I was merely following perceived expectations. I actually thought I was kind of a rebel in the relationship department. Although once Secret Me was introduced I was forced to choose whether to listen to her or just adapt to the guy's expectations every time I entered or thought about entering a relationship. Every relationship since then has included a combination of both.

You cannot deny your Secret Me anymore than you can deny decades of imposed expectations. So I guess my point is to go ahead and listen for her Secret Me, introduce the woman to her Secret Me if she does not know it exists, but be gentle because the process is probably going to be more important to her than losing her virginity. Also know that you will always hold a special place in that woman's heart, so don't be a dick.

Lola Key

Letter to Nikola

When I was back in high school, I immaturely concluded that I was in love with my best friend. I was sixteen. We had an argument, one in which he couldn't forgive me and in despair to get our friendship back to what it used to be, I concluded I was in love. I started chasing after him every day and eventually, he gave in.

We were kids, kids who used to be best friends up to that moment. We shared everything together, we knew each other very well, and at the time, we were a great combination. As kids, we used to be a perfect match.

These first few months and years with Nikola brought first sexual experiences for me. We didn't have real sex, we had petting, and we made experiences with our bodies to the extent that we lined up to seven orgasms in a row. This period was perfect!

When we started having "real" sex, though, we kind of grew up at the same time. And, confusingly enough, the way our lives went in two opposite directions, our needs for sex followed the same path. We simply weren't compatible. But that is the case, like, when you are in a serious, long-term relationship, it is not possible for everything else to suck, and your sex to be great. At least for me it isn't. It is possible if you are not having a relationship with someone, if all you are interested in is just sex. But if it is serious between the two of you, it is not possible.

I kept trying and trying, telling myself that something must be wrong with me, I am not good in bed, and I completely neglected my own needs. When I think of these times, I feel so sorry for myself. We were together for years and years and finally broke up.

Now when I think of him or when I talk to him, there is one thing on my mind. If he were the only male person walking on planet Earth, I would never ever be in a relationship with him. And we were together for seven years. Is it my failure then?

A Difficult Journey

Everyone has to create a path for his or herself. It would be cool if I could say that sex with hundreds of women was a wonderful experience. The truth is that I was focused on learning more about women and I was focused on trying to fix myself. I thought that if I slept with enough women, one would stand out.

I dated many amazing women and there was even one, Sunshine, who I wished that I could spend the rest of my life with. Once I admitted to myself that the problem was that I couldn't allow myself to care for anyone I began to phase sex out of my life and focused on healing. After years of therapy, group therapy, and many other things I think I'm free. For good measure I wrote for two years straight and it was liberating.

It's February 2014, and it's exactly two years since I've been with a woman. I've had a few offers, but I declined and only asked for friendship. It took me half of my life to realize how amazing women are. I want to be able to share myself with someone that I care for. I know that if you are emotionally engaging with a woman the sex will get better each and every month, and she will become sexier with every passing day.

One day I may start dating again. I just want to be sure that I won't want to kick the woman out of my bed as soon as we are done. Maybe I'll date a few women or maybe I will never date again. I've had enough random sex. You are free to choose what is right for you. The grass is always greener on the other side of the fence. Some people may hope for a life like I had. But you will miss out on what a woman truly has to offer.

Let me tell what being with a woman is like. It's like you get locked into fancy room. Some guys fantasize about visiting as many fancy rooms as possible. Some guys get comfortable in the room and watch some television. Some guys wreck the room and some guys complain that the room isn't fancy enough for them.

Almost no one notices the panel of red buttons in the back the room. For the few that do notice the panel of red buttons, some cover it up and others bang on the buttons. Some guys went to a pick up artist guru and have a cheat sheet of button combinations. Those guys are appreciated even though they are using someone else's button combinations.

There is a rare breed of man that is so awesome that the woman comes in the room and presses the right button combinations herself. I wish I was that kind of guy, but I'm not. A person like me would sit in front of the large panel of red buttons and press away. I would note what worked and what didn't. In time I would become skilled at appropriate button combinations. Once I've gotten a handle on the red buttons, levers will appear out of nowhere. With time and effort I get the hang of the levers and the red buttons. Then pedals, horns, and a handle on a chain would appear. I start adding the pedals and the horns to the mix and every now and then I pull the chain. Eventually the women would show up and ask me to move aside. Then she would start pulling levers, pressing red buttons, stepping on pedals, honking the horns and finishing everything off by pulling the chain.

Then the woman would congratulate me on a job well done. As a thank you, she offers me a golden key card and asks me to go through the door. When I leave the door, there is a hallway. At the end of the hallway there is an elevator. There is only one button in the elevator and it's accessed with the golden key card. I put the key card in and it doesn't return. The elevator takes me to a deep sublevel. When I leave the elevator I'm in another hallway. At the end of the hallway is a door. Through that door is a fancy room with a giant panel of red buttons in the back. At this point I could be frustrated since I got the hang of the pedals and horns and stuff. I could be angry considering it seems that I just went backwards. But I'm happy, because I know that I like her red buttons.

Chan

Congratulations. You have finally realized that everything is better when you care about the person you are with.

That Daniel, and all men reading this, is the hardest thing to realize and even harder to institute in your lives.

About your choice not to date again Daniel, I call bulls***. This is actually when dating becomes fun and fulfilling. Notice I said dating not sleeping around. If I need to put a definition of the two in this book then we have bigger problems.

First dates are always awkward at first, but they are also the perfect time for the sparks to fly. Not just physical attraction sparks, (which are important) but those butterfly sparks that tell you there is something here worth looking into. It was interesting that you said you might start dating again but were concerned that you would kick a woman out of bed when you were done having sex. I have a rather novel idea: wait to go to bed with a woman until you begin caring for her!

I know radical right. Our Secret Mes have been trying to get guys to understand and act on this for years. We hop into bed too early with potential boyfriend material because of perceived expectations. (Note: we go to bed with other guys to feed the Secret Me physical needs but once again this is different). Try actually going out on a few dates, spend some time with one another outside the bedroom and see if you begin to care for her. I am not saying no kissing or making out, just no sex (and yes Mr. Clinton oral sex is sex). After you have taken time to see if you care for her then invite her into your bed. I promise you will be a hell of lot less likely to kick her out right away if you follow this path.

I always try to play the devil's advocate even against myself so I do have to mention the danger of holding off on initiating sex with a woman. Lots of women (as we have mentioned) have low self-esteem and since they are used to a man's expectation of sex they will be confused and concerned when you do not jump into their bed or push them into yours. They will begin to feel undesirable and assume that you do not want to be with them. Of course what you are doing is the complete opposite. I see two solutions here. One, you actually have a conversation with her about your concerns and explain that you are choosing to wait out of respect for both of you. Or you can amp up the making out. Only choose this option if you truly can stop mid hot and heavy and not end up in bed, which is not an easy feat for a lot of men. By increasing physical contact of any kind the woman will feel more desired and less likely to assume the worst when there no sex is initiated.

Ah the button combinations example. All I have to say is good luck. I think men are so frustrated with the time it takes to learn a woman's combinations that they have given up even trying. It is of course disturbing that PUA uses generic button combinations on women and they work. Frankly I think they work because women are just so dang excited that a man is willing to try to understand her that we take what we can get. This is a serious sad state of affairs. I just want to mention one more time though that it is our choice to settle on a non-winning combination. The Secret Me knows it is not our unique and ideal combination, but allows us to choose to move forward because in our reality it's usually better than nothing. Good men are hard to find is not just a saying, it is what most women live with on a daily basis.

Lola Key

It seems to me that you have really tried to understand how things between men and women work. And I don't think you've done that just on a superficial level. I think you've gone to a philosophical level. And not just psychological, but also empirical by experiencing all of what you are talking about.

The difference between you and me, for instance, is that you consciously went through all the stages, contemplating, trying to figure things out and work for the best, I was not thinking at all.

The perspective of being with a woman, the one you have, is pretty much the same as the one we women have about how to handle you men. It all seems to us as there is always some complicated manual, which we should carefully ponder before even starting to decipher. And, I believe it is the same with you, we are usually driven by instinct. If it works, it works, if it doesn't we move on.

And there is one more thing in which I am certain after some experience. When people get together, when they start a kind of serious relationship, they shape each other to a great extent. And I don't consider this a bad thing. I don't think that being shaped by your significant other is a bad thing. I think, more in accepting your partner's good habits and vice versa.

If there is chemistry between us, then this entire situation with buttons is not unsolvable. If it is something valuable, then there might not be only one correct combination of buttons, there can be more than one, and we would equally enjoy in each of them. And this fact that your partner changes and shapes you, this is not a loss for you. This is huge gain. When you let somebody change you, and you remain with the person, this means that the change feels good for you. This means that it makes you a better person, a more versatile human being. So, what I actually want to say is that we are not completely shaped individuals, we change during our entire life.

And one more thing, I want to say something about the journey you have undertaken-the fact that you've changed countless girls and then decided to stay on your own for a while. I think this is perfectly ok. As you said, everyone has to create a path for themselves. You are not saying this to show off, you are not naming them, actually maybe you are simply trying to confess your weaknesses-the fact that you were not able to find a proper one, or proper ones, and you created such path for yourself. This is completely okay for me.

Now when I think about my love life between the ages of sixteen and twenty-four, when I was with this Nikola, I have to admit I regret something to a certain point. Now I am completely certain that the two of us are in two completely different worlds. I don't regret the years I spent with him, I have learnt a lot, both from him and generally, during that period of time. But what I do regret is the fact that I was faithful to him. All my girlfriends at the time were changing guys all the time. And, to be honest, that was the proper time for that. I did nothing. That is the only thing I regret from dating him for years.

Claudia

DIFFICULT JOURNEYS...

Having sex with hundreds of women you were hoping at least one would stand out. Like in that movie clip I mentioned before ("The Dark Side of the Heart"): this man is intensely looking for a woman "who can fly," and is devastated time after time when he realizes that is so hard to find. Eventually, he does find someone who can fly and also make him fly too.

In my own journey, there were three times when I thought I had to find that person "who could fly": namely, my better half, my soul mate, the man of my life...Whatever you want to call him.

In two of those cases, the relationship was so short that there was not enough time to get disappointed. I only spent a very limited amount of time with that person: the rest took place in my imagination. Through the years, I've had time to idealize those brief periods of time in which I felt I had met the man of my dreams. And, of course, those dreams are brighter every day, and can only get better. This typically happens when you have to say good-bye too soon, and there's no time to get to know the guy's dark side in too much detail!

The remaining case had time to disappoint me. Therefore, I felt the magic the first couple of months or so, and then throughout the rest of the year, I was just struggling to keep a mediocre relationship alive. He had already disappointed me: he was not the kind of person I thought he was. Still, I kept insisting on going back to what it was like at the beginning. Of course, it never happened, and I suffered until the bitter end.

Once I read a piece of public rest room door wisdom: "The man of your life is the one who stays with you forever." I keep thinking that now that I've been with Horacio for so many years. Maybe this was not the kind of love story I fantasized about. Maybe he's not "the man of my life" in the sense I used to idealize when I was young. But he's with me: we're together, and for me now that means there's a lot of love in this relationship.

SOME PERSONAL COMBINATIONS

PLEASE DON'T TRY THIS AT HOME!

I've done my best not to make this a book about exactly what you should say and do to attract a woman. This is the problem with pick up artists who sell routines. If the routines are golden, then the pickup artist will sell lots of material. Once the routines become popular then they are useless.

You've got to understand that women are completely defenseless when it comes to emotionally stimulating things. This is why most of the things that I presented here are generally themed. It's my hope that you can build off of the general things and make your own way. Women know how defenseless they are against emotional stimulation. This is why they have close female friends who help them process things. If a woman, or a woman in her close circle of friends, has already heard your routine then you will be associated with the other guy. Then you have to hope that the guy before you wasn't a douche.

There is only one way to utilize another person's routines, come clean right away. Telling the woman or her friends right away that you borrowed that routine from somewhere else will effectively short-circuit any associations to anyone else. Be sure not to give them a chance to call you out first.

Coming clean could well be a part of your entire routine. When I first started dating Sunshine, she wouldn't let me kiss her. I understood that she wanted to make me wait a little. My game was terrible because I was terrified to be with her, but I wanted with all my heart to go forward. After a date, we were walking home; I stopped her, spun her around and said, "I bet that you'll be the one to kiss me first." "Okay," she said. I leaned in, kissed her, and said, "You win."

After a brief chuckle, we started to walk again. Before she could say anything I told her that I saw that line on a television movie trailer; I forget the name of the movie. She laughed because she had also seen the movie trailer. She busted on me for a few minutes for tricking her into kissing me. I told her, "I just wanted to kiss you and I didn't know what else to do." She then leapt towards me and began kissing me.

I tell you this so that you don't go out trying to repeat another man's words and actions. It is the least attractive thing that you could possibly do. But if you do want to use someone else's routines be upfront about it. I've used other people's routines and was upfront about it. For me it was like a game, I would ask women to grade me on how I used a specific routine. The idea always is to create an emotional experience. If you can't do that yourself, then you need to spend time working on it.

Chan

I strongly and absolutely agree. Do not try this at home, at a bar, club, football game or any other places you go to try and meet someone.

These routines are what I would call emotional stunting. For the men they are limiting their chances at finding someone who would care for them in spite of their vulnerabilities and faults. For the women the routines are playing a dangerous game with perceived expectations and real woman's lives and their self-esteems.

I appreciate your need to explain these routines. They are a prime example of how important it is to try to understand where the women you meet are in their lives, where they are coming from and where they want to go. However, I worry that guys will not see that important message imbedded in between the "how to get a women to love you" and "how to have sex with different women everyday" suggestions.

Rather, they will see that these routines actually work on women. So we must practice and of course if they work and the women want to go bed who are we to argue?

Dangerous interpretation on my part, but one I fear many guys drawn to reading a book on this subject will take from it.

The ugly truth is the routines are effective at getting women into bed. However, honesty and sincerity are just as effective and can have the added bonus of opening up the path to a relationship if you are emotionally ready.

Should we really be training men to set the goal of getting a woman into bed? Or perhaps we need to concentrate more on men improving themselves and learning how to get to know women.

Lola Key

What is undoubtedly true about what you have said here is that women talk. I am sure you men would be surprised to what extent we analyze things together. Sometimes I think it is maybe not because we would so much like to understand what men really think, but it's because we enjoy in the process itself. But, nonetheless, we talk. So what can you do about it? If you don't want something to be widely known in the women's world, don't do it. It is as simple as that.

I was thinking a lot about what you were saying here about these ways of hitting on a woman. At first I thought, yes, if you are doing something you have been told to do, or something you have seen somewhere, just say it, and go straight with it.

And I genuinely believe that there is something, some kind of chemistry or connection that goes before all the hitting lines in the world. I may like somebody's physical appearance, or somebody may like mine, but if there is no chemistry between us, there isn't a chance of us getting together in any combination whatsoever. Some magazines say that there is something related to smell, that we are mutually attracted by some pheromones or whatever. I wouldn't go that far. I don't want to impose that when two persons are attracted to each other, when there is chemistry, nothing else is important. I am not saying that. I just think that when the condition of this initial mutual attraction is fulfilled, only then can we elaborate on a proper hitting on technique.

But then, I was thinking more about it. And I came out with a different conclusion. If I like someone, if there is this initial vibe between me and a guy, I don't care how he is hitting on me. I don't care if these are lines that he learned somewhere, that he was told to use by somebody else, or if it is something he figured out himself. Of course, I like to believe that having the age and experience I have, I would be able to differentiate a guy who just wants to get me to bed and the one who is honestly trying to impress me with some learned phrases. I think I would.

A TRIP TO BARNES & NOBLE

I used this routine as a template for me to improvise from. As far as I can remember, I've never used this routine on anyone. It's possible that I developed it with Perfecta but I can't be sure. I like to call this the perfect date. This can't be done with every woman. Please follow along mentally and attempt to ascertain the objectives. Also, I made this up when there was a Barnes & Noble located near Carnegie Hall in Manhattan. Now there is a chain store of some sort.

The date would be me and someone special sharing a cup of something delicious at a trendy and comfortable place. I like to start in a place like this just so we can feel each other out. Either one of us can eject from the date if things go awry. If things go perfectly, I tell the girl "I like you, and I want to take you on the perfect date." I'll give her a chance to respond in any way she feels comfortable. Then I continue.

I bought us a pair of tickets for a performance at Carnegie Hall. We rushed to the concert hall, but we're told by the usher that we were too late and needed to wait for the intermission. I tease you a little for making us late. I'm not mad but it was your fault. We could've waited in the reception area, but we decide together to go outside for a walk.

Although it is a busy summer's night in Manhattan, on our walk all I can see is you. Your voice is enchanting and your smile is mesmerizing. I'm awakened from that pleasant day-dream by a sudden summer rain. Holding hands we make haste to the closest shelter; a hotdog stand. As not to be rude to the vendor, we buy one hotdog and share it. We take bites to the hotdog together until the last bite the only thing separating our lips is onion sauce. That was our first kiss.

This is when I ask you 'How much time do we have left?' I asked you that because we were standing right in front of Barnes & Noble. I want to share something with you that I've never shared with anyone else, but I don't want us to be late. You see, my entire life up to this point can be summed up by walking through a Barnes & Noble. Each section and each book is a different chapter of my life. I want to share that with you because you're special.

We dashed into the bookstore and you promised to keep track of time. We walk, hand in hand, around the store as I reveal to you different parts of my life. Along the way there was a large advertisement for a romance novel with angelic models on the cover. I suggest that we pose in the same way the models posed, and a passerby takes our picture for us. That pic is going up on Facebook.

We go to the Romance section to mimic other poses, and one book catches your eye. I wonder if you ever did want to go with me to

Carnegie Hall, because we spent the rest of the evening reading that book together, snuggled on the bookstore carpet.

Let me know explain the intention of all that I just said. There is an overall theme of something that we were supposed to do together, a performance at Carnegie Hall. I wanted the girl to have a sense of a proper thing to do and chose to be adventurous instead.

Next there are open threads of conversation that the woman can talk about. Each more intimate than the next. First, a woman can inquire about comfortable and trendy places to have a cup of something delicious. Next is what types of concerts do I like to go to at Carnegie Hall. This location is perfect given that they have every sort of performance there. Next are the books that would show her my path in life. Finally, she could ask me which romance novels I've read. I haven't read any as of yet.

Each of these open threads can spiral into multiple dates over the course of many years. It's important to create that frame around the woman. If she likes the frame, then she has multiple choices to work with; thus stringing a pearl of moments together in her mind. It's important to note that the woman talking about romance novels with me is somewhat of a trap. What I've done there is given her plausible deniability if our conversation becomes too heated. She'll be safe because clearly 'we were talking about a romance novel.' Also, it creates a secret language known only to us. I like to think that I'm good with a woman's signals, but I'm not. If she asks that we read a book together, I'll understand that she wants to move forward with our relationship.

There were a number of specific emotional moments that I could talk about specifically, but I want you to tell me how you felt and what was going on in your mind as you heard those things. I could spend time talking about each emotional moment and even specific language techniques, but I would prefer to get your response. END

If you are confused, I'm sorry. Starting with "The date would be me and..." then ending with "End" is the entire routine. I would say something like this from beginning to end either over the phone or face to face. Then I'd ask the girl to express to me how she felt moment to moment and what went on her mind. I've done something like this a number of times, and women usually lose their minds at this point. They would be wide-eyed and short of breath. It looks like emotional overload.

It's so exciting to watch a woman process a multitude of emotional moments. What I really sometimes want to ask is what she if feeling right at the moment. But I just wait and allow her to figure out what is happening.

Consider for a moment that I gave this girl an interesting fantasy. And yes, this date is an impossible fantasy! Then I gave her some of the purposes behind the fantasy. I even give her the choice to accept the frame around her. If she asks me about any of the open threads that I left before her, then she's accepted the frame. Also, if she ever talks about any romance novels, then she is admitting to falling into my trap.

But the coup de grace is that fact that I'm asking her opinion of the perfect date. I'm asking her to tell me what she thinks and feels about each moment. If I'm telling her this story, then she has to already found me attractive in some way beforehand. In addition, this routine would inform her that I'm intelligent and creative.

Chan

The date sounds quite lovely. What is not as lovely is the fact that so much thinking and what I see as manipulating went into it from your end. You made it into a routine. The definition of routine is something done over and over again. Guess what? That makes me and all the women I know feel like crap no matter how awesome the date is.

It is not special and do not delude yourself that it is.

I will admit that given only the chance to respond immediately after hearing your routine I too may be wide-eyed. However, given even a few minutes I would quickly realize that this was not a fantasy built for me, this was a fantasy built for women in general, to make ALL women fall into your arms. I just happened to be the woman you were trying it out on today. Changing a word or an action here and there is not making it mine.

If you haven't noticed this does not amuse me. You actually said, "Also, if she ever talks about any romance novels, then she is admitting to falling into my trap." Trap? Are you kidding me?

Unsolicited advice: if you have to set a trap then you are not meant to be together for anything. Furthermore if you have to set a trap to get a woman to give you the time of day then you need to work on yourself first. Confidence (not to be confused with arrogance) is extremely sexy on a man.

Lola Key

This is really, really funny for me. I have never thought deeply about what a perfect date would look like but I will now try to analyze each step of your perfect date. Let us assume that the preconditions of me liking you and you liking me are fulfilled. And one more thing I have to say about myself, I am not a typical girl in a way that I really don't like such soppy and romantic dates and combinations, but again, you need to hear various different opinions, don't you?

The idea of sitting in a comfortable place seems perfect, especially because of the fact that each of us can go away if things don't work out. I would like the place to be small and tucked away not to be exposed to looks of other people, to be intimate, let's say.

"I like you, and I want to take you on the perfect date." I have to admit that I would not like to hear this. Let me try to explain this somehow. It would put some pressure on me. When something is announced in advance to have to be perfect, then both of us would have high hopes and this would increase this pressure. I would more like the sentence: Let's get out of here and the rest to be spontaneous. Being spontaneous, that is what I would *like at this stage. Or at least for my point of view, for me to think that the rest of the date is spontaneous.*

Women generally like to create some kind of fuss, to be taken care of or to be dealt with. This would arise some feeling of that kind. And what is more important, you can control the situation. Just don't announce anything. It imposes pressure that everything has to be perfect. And it imposes the obligation the date has to be undertaken all the way to the end of it.

The thing that you are late for Carnegie Hall has its strengths and weaknesses. When you are at the cinema or theatre or something of a kind with somebody you have just met, the good point of that there is some sweet anticipation. What is he thinking about at the moment? Are we going to touch intentionally or accidentally (and it is always unintentionally)? Does he like me? And I somehow think, at least from my own experience, that there is some kind of positive sexual tension in such situations. So, this can be a real hit in some situations. On the other hand, this can be considered as boring, typical, unimaginative, and you don't get the chance to talk, to get to know each other. There will be time for this. So, the idea of being late to Carnegie Hall is a good one!

The story with the hotdog stand and one hotdog and a kiss is really funny. I don't know. This simply isn't my cup of tea. The same goes with the bookstore. It is just too much. The only thing I like about it is reading a book together. I don't know, it seems in a way fake, artificial.

When it comes to your analysis, let me go step by step. Having something pre-planned and choosing to be adventurous instead is something I would give thumbs up. Again, for the same reasons I have already mentioned: being able to run away if things go wrong and enjoying the fact that a guy is putting all his effort to make a girl a center of universe.

Actually, everything that you have elaborated on makes perfect sense from your point of view. But there is one thing that I would say. Some girls are just not that into these romantic dates. But you are interesting, creative and thorough.

Claudia

CARNEGIE HALL, BARNES & NOBLE OR THE ADVENTURE OF A LIFETIME?

Strategies like your "Trip to Barnes & Noble" section remind me of those things men do at the beginning of a relationship, but never repeat and that makes a woman forever wonder why "things aren't like they used to be."

There are moments in a relationship (particularly at the beginning) when everything is pure spontaneity and exciting adventures. Time goes by, though, and with it, all the excitement that made the beginning of that relationship magic. Of course, those are beautiful relationship starters, but hard to keep up. It would be great making a point of never losing that as time passes. But it takes two to tango, and it takes two to keep up the adventure of each day when routine sinks in.

INTRODUCING MY PENIS

While the last routine would've been in an intimate setting this one would likely be in a group setting. Again, this is a template that I used to improvise from, since I don't like to repeat the same things over and over. While the former routine was almost a monologue, this is fun frame that a woman can chose to play with or move on.

I want to again warn you not to do this! Mimicking the previous routine, you may be able to get away with for a while. Saying what I'm about to say to a group of women will be incredibly dangerous. Not because you're talking about your penis to a random group of people, but because it will be highly likely that one of them has heard this before.

It makes me sad to let go of this one. I had actually hoped to use it again one day. It irks me to no end knowing that scores of guys are going to ignore me and flood the scene talking about their penises. The reason why you wouldn't do it is because it isn't you. If it were you, then you would've already done it!

For a long while, after I'm sure the women I'm talking to find me interesting, I would simply start talking about my cock. The origins of why I started doing it aren't important. What is relevant is that not a single woman was offended. They would each play along at different intervals. I had so much success doing it I always interjected my penis into the conversation somehow.

I would give him different roles every time, as not to become boring. Sometimes he'd have superpowers, have a mundane job like a DMV photographer, or an exciting one like an Olympic snowboarder. A simple example would be, my penis is majoring in environmental studies, and takes online courses from the University of Phoenix. Clearly this is a joke, but there are topics of interest within the joke. The women and I can spend the following hour talking about global warming and what can be done about it, the effectiveness of online learning, the practical value of some degrees, or the rising costs of education. Whether she likes it or not, I've just associated all of those things to my penis.

How would I introduce my penis to a group of women? Good question. If there is an opportunity within the flow of the conversation I interject my penis, especially if the women seem fun and playful. If there isn't an opportunity, I go to my default. This is the only thing I usually repeat. I throw both hands in the air and try to get their attention. "You know what? I like you, (I say to one of them) and I think we would be good together. I just want to, well, get something out of the way so that you aren't surprised later…" Then I inform the group of my penis.

In my personal template, I continue with, "My penis is an Islamic Extremist. I just wanted to get that out of the way." While this frame isn't as involved as the first frame, it still takes planning and preparation. I need to be prepared for any type of response. With this type of frame I allow the women to enjoy it as long as they want and they can chose to continue or change the subject. If the subject is changed, then the women can come back to it if they want. The last thing I want to come off as is a guy who actually believes his penis has his own personality; a weirdo.

Allowing the women to express themselves in any way they want could go either way. But if the women have already decided that they like you, then things sometimes become sexual right away. Okay, I have to admit, that there was one iteration of this that I used over and over. I had so much success with it. I would say my default spiel, point to my crotch with both hands and say. "My penis is invisible. I just wanted to get that out of the way so you aren't surprised later." One hundred percent of the time, at least one woman would make grabbing motions toward my penis. In which case I would bust on them for being bad and say, "I said invisible!" For a courageous few, they would simply reach out and grab my cock. If a woman and/or her friends grab my cock, then it's checkmate. I don't know why having an invisible penis worked so well, but now I can't do it anymore.

I use Islamic Extremist as a template for good reason. Obviously, I'm not an Islamic Extremist. Nor am I even Islamic. First, it instantly adds dimension to my personal character. Next, I get to create instant tension between women and my penis. I'm not against Islam or anything; I just wanted to be mindful that creating tension is a good thing. An example would be if I were talking to a group of liberal females in NYC, I would tell them "My penis is a Tea Party Activist, and he's keen to rolling back your voting rights." This would have the same effect as an Islamic Extremist.

If they respond in any way, I make it clear that I'm a Christian and I'm comfortable having friends with different views. Clearly my penis is like a brother to me. If they continue to ask questions, or talk about scenarios then I will shout "Alalalalalah Jihad!" In fact, my penis will declare Jihad to almost anything. They have to be pressing me for more information. I won't just volunteer information; it's kind of weird just talking about your penis without responses.

While its fun declaring Jihad, it's important to recognize the plan is to have the women play along. Although I would never ask them to, I would hope that they would tell me the religion of their privates as well. It would be a fun game that they have to choose to play along. For example, if a woman tells me that she has a Mormon vagina, I could definitely declare Jihad again. Instead, I would inform her about a Facebook post where my penis declared a Fatwa on all Mormons.

Does my penis have a Facebook page you ask? "Of course! Everyone is on Facebook. Look him up his name is Mohammed Browski." I've had this Facebook page for years and never used this routine. I recently used it to play an online role-playing game, but other than that I've never used it. Having a Facebook page ready just for that occasion is bordering on weird, but if the women were playing along it's their fault. I used to have a pic of Anthony Wiener's junk up, but Facebook made me take it down.

If the women again continue down the rabbit hole and friend my penis on Facebook, then it allows me to have a secret relationship with them. Friending my penis online provides an incredible amount of cover, and readymade plausible deniability. Once we are friends, my penis can send her private messages, poke her, and even post on her wall. If she ever has a sexy picture, my penis will definitely comment, "I just shed a tear for this photo." It's all a game that can be played as long as she is still interested in playing.

The real goal of this routine is to start naming other parts of my body. If the women are still engaged I can declare, "Yeah, my ass is a racist. I won't let him on Facebook. Every time I let him near the computer all he leaves is shit on the screen!" This is a little less intimidating then talking about my penis. Sometimes I lead in with my butt. It's just hard to do anything with a group of girls spanking and fondling my butt. The plan is to give personalities to as many body parts as the women are engaged.

Again, this routine was dynamic and edgy. Although there is less verbiage, it takes a little more skill. This is because you will need to go with the ebb and flow of the emotional states of the women you are talking to.

Chan

First, it was interesting from a reader's perspective to find several pages on this topic. Who would have thought that so much explanation would be necessary? Harsh comment: I think your therapist would agree this is telling of why you thought you were a weirdo to begin with.

Second, if a guy ever said any of those things to me in public I would slap him. I do not care how sneaky you think you are being I guarantee it will not work with every woman. If we were already dating or seeing each other I would be embarrassed and shocked, not intrigued or turned on. If we had just met or were acquaintances I would honestly slap you and/or walk away. This might seem a bit much but even in my younger more liberal years I would not have stood for that kind of ridiculous conversation.

Those sorts of comments are meant for private conversations or whispers in the ear. As I was trying to think of an example a thought popped into my head concerning a friend of mine. She is now married and the mother of two. But at one time she was definitely the most liberal of our small group of friends. Many trips to the local bar ended with guys trying to pick one or all of us up. She was quite often a raging bitch, which oddly enough attracted many guys, but if one of them said anything inappropriate or degrading to one of us they received the full wrath, which often included a pretty significant shove. These penis comments would be deemed inappropriate to her and therefore would never have worked in our group.

Dynamic and edgy huh? I think the routine was more about ridiculousness and poor judgment. Basically you did not convince me that I needed to be introduced to your penis before we are actually engaging in a sexual act. Then if you have a name or story about it that would be an appropriate time to talk about the subject. Although personally I find guys that name their penises cowards. That however is a whole other book. This fired me up and I think it would be wise to heed extreme caution before trying to use this sort of routine.

Lola Key

What a contrast we have now. After this soppy and romantic hotdog sharing in the sunset, we have a penis into the story. Ok, let me be honest now. If I was to choose between two guys, the one that would take me to Carnegie Hall, for a walk in the sunset and to a bookstore to read a romantic novel, and the one who would be representing his penis as an Islamic Terrorist at a first date, I would undoubtedly and without any thinking, go for the one with the penis. I guess these pre-planned romantic scenarios seem so dishonest and fake to me. And you being you, taking risks, introducing your funny side, I love this. I really, really love this.

Ok, I admit, if I was with my girlfriends out and if a guy approaches us out of the blue introducing his invisible penis, there is a high possibility that we would consider him a real weirdo. But if some kind of contact has previously been established and we got the picture that you are a normal guy and not a pervert, this would be perfect. We like unexpected things, we like men who are at the verge of being polite and impolite. And again, if this initial precondition is fulfilled, this might be a real turn on, bringing the penis into the picture.

I always tend to care more about those guys who are rebellious, courageous, who are the ones I need to make an effort to get close to them. This, I think, is what you need to achieve. You need to be interesting and puzzling enough in the beginning so that she becomes the hunter. In my world, this cannot be achieved with these romantic chitchats. It can, however, be very much achieved by introducing your penis.

Claudia

INTRODUCING YOUR PENIS

As shocking as this technique may sound initially, I found all your derivations of the topic were fascinating and hilarious! I understand why you don't want other guys to use it (in which case, it should never be published, just like any great grandma's recipe!). However, the same beginning could take you down so many different roads (depending on how fruitful your imagination is) that it doesn't really matter if other men try to imitate you here.

Its funny how we women talking about our vaginas wouldn't sound as good. I guess it's widely accepted that a penis almost has a life of its own (then, all the career possibilities for it are not so unreasonable); but even though women know by now that their clitoris is the master and also has a life (and maybe a career) of its own, such a conversation could be threatening for men, as they in general don't seem to understand very well how our clits can be more important to us than our vaginas, where you believe our world is centered.

I REITERATE. DON'T TRY THESE!!

I know that this is going to fall on deaf ears, but I have to try nonetheless. These routines were developed specifically by me, for the women that I talk to. You aren't me!! For people who know me, they would recognize that those things are something that I could say to people. There is no real power in taking someone else's words and using them as your own. You won't learn anything from it, and if the women you are with find out then it makes you unattractive.

Please understand that I tried and failed for years. Those two routines that I shared with you came from many years of study, practice, and deep thought. I parted with two of my favorites, which I never even tried. Now I can never really use them. Women may even expect me to attempt either of those with them. If I don't, they might ask why I don't try. There were so many penis personalities that I wished to try: running for State Assembly and third degree black belt in Bruce Lee's style Jeet Kune Do. Now they are effectively dead routines.

Do yourself a favor and develop emotional combinations for yourself. When they come from you they are more powerful. Plus, the more you exercise that creative muscle, the easier it will be to make up new ones.

Chan

I have a headache again. I close my eyes and take a deep breath and still cannot believe that you are suggesting to men to make up emotional combinations (or routines) to practice and use on women. The thorough process of putting together the combinations in the privacy of their own homes is not the problem because this may help to encourage greater confidence in some men. Rather, what bothers me is that they will be using it generically for ALL women. We are not a number or notch on a belt. If you learn nothing else from this book remember that women are unique individuals and one size does NOT fit all.

Lola Key

I completely agree on this when it comes to your advice to other men not to reiterate. That is something I wanted to point out from the very beginning of my writing. And I think we share that opinion. If another guy reads this and repeats the same lines, I am sure it would be a complete failure. That is why the very idea of attending this course that you mentioned seemed pointless to me.

Furthermore, I have to admit that I do have a problem with everything that is planned in advance, even if it is 100% original approach, which you have thought of on your own. In my opinion, things don't work like that. We are all different. We like different things, we are in a different mood every day and night and so being spontaneous is a way to go. Always. You should be thinking extensively at home, talking extensively to your friends and a therapist about different women, different approaches, deduce on your own. Just don't go out with a line prepared at home. I guarantee that it would be a failure.

This doesn't mean that men and women aren't to think about how they will hit on each other. This doesn't mean that you should quit your guru classes or whatever they are called. And this doesn't mean that, for example, we girls aren't to spend hours and hours talking to each other about how guys react, what each of their words mean, their verbal and non-verbal communication. We should be thinking about that, we should be talking about that, just don't prepare the lines you are going to say before you see the girl, before you feel her pulse.

CONCLUSION

I know it seems like I was talking to a generic guy this entire book, but the truth is I wrote this book specifically for three random women that I have yet to meet. It would've been simpler to just hire one woman. I honestly wish I could've afforded ten different women but I think three is sufficient enough to get a good response.

I'm excited to hear what they have to say. Maybe it's because it's been so long since I've interacted with women? Or maybe it's just because I always find a woman's response to anything intriguing. I want to know about how you felt throughout the process. I want to know what you thought about. I want to know what you think about me and if your opinion of me changed at all. I'm interested in knowing if you changed or learned at all after reading and writing.

I know that I'm getting more that whatever I'm paying you for this. Even if this book never sells, I will be fascinated at whatever you write. If this book does sell, I'll contact you and offer you bonuses based on sales. I'm honest and I know that you are worth it. I look forward to hearing from you.

Chan

When I applied to review this book I was at the start of my freelance career and thought it would be an excellent piece to begin on. Time in a Pick-up

Artist community and women reacting to the book sounded interesting. And interesting it has been.

Before the book I felt that PUA was disgusting and demeaning to women and provided false hope to men. Teaching someone to "pick-up" a woman (any woman) is a game and one where I believe nobody wins.

While reading the book my emotions ran hot, cold, tepid and raging fire. I have what some call a short fuse for certain things and the treatment of women just happens to be one of these things. I consider myself a strong woman in most aspects but as you can see from some of my examples even I have my weak moments. My concern does not rest with me, but rather the countless other women in my life who have not found their inner strength and who these emotional combinations could seriously damage if used on them. Their fragile self-esteems could not take the manipulation.

I am trying hard to put myself in an unconfident man's place, someone who lacks the instinct and composure to approach women on their own. What I keep seeing in all this is fear and fear is an internal demon that one has to fight and conquer alone. This happens during the process of learning and coming to terms with who you are and what makes you tick.

Confidence, self-esteem, honesty...these three things are what will make the PUA and emotional combinations obsolete. There is always the argument that there is no need to make them obsolete in the first place. However, if being true to yourself and being happy were a possibility why in the world would anyone want to rely on a routine?

Daniel I liked you from our conversations via email. When I read that you had chosen celibacy for yourself I felt proud that you recognized your issues and was striving to become a better person and learn from your mistakes. That better person poked his head out in places all through this book. Sadly though, that better person did not write this book.

I hope you meant it when you said be honest.

It seems to me that you have taken these emotional combinations, creating them as a way to understand women better so they will be superior to PUA routines because they are focused on what the women wants/needs. Yet these emotional combinations are still used in the same manner as the old routines were used just with a shiny new coat of paint. Adding "women's words" and finding a woman's Secret Me does not make these combinations any less like a routine. You still have to practice these emotional combinations and as previously mentioned the emotional combination still lends itself to using a generic combination for ALL women. Women want to feel special and no matter which way I read it I cannot find a place where a woman will feel special if a man used an emotional combination to get her into bed.

It is obvious that you have learned a great deal from and about women and some of the ways we process information and how we react to certain things or events in our life. The parts of the book that encourage men to listen and take in what women are saying are brilliant and this advice needs to be shouted from the mountaintops.

However, a page later you are explaining how to take these things and manipulate them to be used in an emotional combination that can be used for the sole purpose of going to bed with different women. There were times throughout the book where I felt like you got it, all women are different and we are all awesome in our own way. Then there are times when I would have socked you on the arm because you were placing women in a generic group again. While I see that you are trying to essentially soften and emotionally charge the process for men to meet women, I also see that you are leaving out the one important thing that really matters.

Women are independent creatures from one another. We feel, think, react and act differently than each other.

Unlike men there are very few of our characteristics that can be stretched over the entire sex as a whole. We make our choices according to our circumstances, past, present and future. Even if it appears to you and even to us that a decision is made spontaneously, it is not. Even when we do selfish things we are still choosing based on all of the things that lead up to that point and will continue on after that point.

As women we do not follow lines, we follow curves and dips. It might be helpful to think about the mind of a woman like a maze. When a woman makes a decision (trying to get to the end of the maze) we are running along a constant hedge (present circumstances) and getting caught up by dead ends (past or future). By the time we get to the end we have witnessed and felt all of that. And it all happens in a nanosecond.

It is important for me to mention again that as a woman we choose to go to bed with you.

I spoke a lot about women choosing to ignore some of the maze hiccups and go with a less-than stellar guy anyway. There is always a reason a woman disregards the signs saying no exit in the maze and it is always a choice. Women of course do not always think consciously about the choice, especially since romance books spur our fantasies about the fate and the magnetic pull between two people. I suppose that is why teaching men "emotional combinations" or routines to pick-up women is so frustrating and disappointing. We are unpredictable in some things while like clockwork in others but you have to get to know us first as individuals!

Women rarely want to be treated like a number. Of course there are fantasies, which include domination, degradation and the like. As a whole though, women do not want to be #5 in your bet to sleep with 30 girls in 30 days. There is no pleasure or comfort in knowing that the male population is using a set of practiced routines in an attempt seduce us. On the contrary it sends shivers up my spine. Women want a man who recognizes that she is a separate human being from all the other women in world (Secret Me). Now to be fair some women will listen intently to the practiced lines, laugh, call you out and still go home with you. By that time though you are looking at her as an independent being that recognized your faults and chose to be with you in spite of them. Strange how that can change everything isn't it?

There is a large group of women that are vaguely aware that PUA exists in the world and really only have the knowledge from romance novels, TV and movies. If they have had firsthand experience they probably do not even know it happened, which I suppose is the point of the routine.

Just because we are sometimes unaware of the routines this does not in any way, shape or form validate them or the teaching of them to men.

What about the men that are shy and afraid of approaching women? Those men stricken with fear at the thought of being rejected? Both good points but still not good enough to have me switching sides on this one. This is where the false hope comes in. PUA and even the emotional combinations allow guys who would not normally for whatever reason be able to, approach and pick-up women. Yet neither of these is providing them with any insight into what exactly the individual woman wants or needs. Nor does it influence them to find someone to care about and have an emotional relationship with.

No one wins in this situation. I am not saying that no self-esteems have benefited from using these routines because I am sure plenty of men can now stand taller. Yet what are these men really gaining? To me they are just gaining a manipulative way of conversing with women and acting with practiced lines to get them into bed and perhaps an STD.

I admit that Future had some decent advice. The honest truth though is that women do not want a practiced man. Barbie broke up with Ken for a reason and I would venture to say that it was his inflexibility that finally got to her. Women want a real, honest and sincere man who has faults and has made mistakes and who admits them. We are not interested in the guys that have to be told to be interesting. You are told to be interesting in high school by your guidance counselor to get into a good college, not to find love. You either are interesting or you're not.

Perhaps it comes down to getting to know who you really are. Men need to take the time to know themselves and be comfortable alone with that person. Being comfortable in your own skin is what leads to having enough self-confidence to talk to a woman.

Perhaps I am ask too much of men. Flashes of men and women who are socially awkward are crawling across my mind right now. Is it fair to keep from them the tools to overcome those fears and find happiness? I honestly am not sure.

A large part of me thinks that some folks are just meant to be shy and they learn the best way they can to adapt in social situations. Yet the part of me that rescues puppies says do not deny them anything that could lead to love.

Oh no I said it. The most avoided word in the book (besides Future's piece). Do we not all want ultimately to be loved? Whether it is by one or many, the need is deep in our genetic make-up.

Is it possible that PUA routines and emotional combinations could lead to love? Maybe. I admit that they certainly lead to more introductions then would normally occur. Which can be a wonderful start but they are not an effective way to mentor these men so they can truly engage a woman and build a relationship.

I realized as I typed this conclusion that I have been approaching this as a woman and very subjectively. Which is why Daniel wanted my opinion. As a woman I looked at the emotional combinations only in the context of getting to know a woman with the potential for a future relationship.

Shame on me for being such a girlie girl.

For a second though I would like to address the effectiveness and usefulness of the emotional combinations on sex. The PUA routines were created to get men laid. Blunt but correct. The emotional combinations though are not just to get a woman into a man's bed, but also to increase the sexual experience for both parties. There is certainly nothing wrong with making sex better; actually I do not know anyone who would argue that point. Anything that can increase the physical or emotional connection during sex is definitely going in the right direction. If we look at the emotional combinations linearly (like a man might) then the combinations are just a means to an end. It then ceases to become about the experience.

I want to come back to point I mentioned earlier when speaking about the negative compliments. I think within this idea and really all the ideas in this book men need to take a step back and think about where the woman they are approaching happen to be in these situations.

I know this book covers how women process things and ways to learn and understand women but the reality is that none of the things discussed here really addresses men putting themselves in our shoes. All that was really happening was an explanation or a teaching if you will, of how men can use how women are perceived to understand and react to things, to get a woman into bed. I am back to the headache. Men use these emotional combinations or routines for a goal oriented interaction with a woman regardless of how the woman is actually feeling during that time. I want to believe that Daniel has uncovered a secret way for men to begin the long and arduous process of understanding women. But the truth is that until men actually think like a woman they will never know.

When you approach a woman and go through your routine and she calls you out on it, laughs and stills goes home with you, you think awesome it worked I so know women. That woman has decided that you minimally fit her requirements of redeeming qualities and she wants/needs sex. Those are actions not feelings. What put that woman in that desperate position? Where and how did she learn to see through your routines? What is her history? How is she subconsciously viewing the situation? Is she attracted to me? I feel at this point I am beating a dead horse.

Men and women are different. It is what makes life unique, amazing, horrible and downright scary. We think, feel, act and react differently not just between the sexes but also within the sexes. None of the emotional combinations or PUA routines will work with every single woman. It just is not possible to create something that hits all the button combinations for ALL women. Men are going to have to take the time and pay attention and learn about the women they are interested in. It is a fact of life and love.

Daniel-I think your book is important. It may seem the opposite as you read my reactions but I think if it does nothing else it has helped you personally get to a point in your life where you have learned that women are treasures and although it may take a bit of work on your part, finding out how to make them shine is worth it. I did mention earlier that I thought your idea of not dating was in my opinion a bad idea. If you believe all the words you have written in this book then you are ready to begin dating.

However, be cautioned that your emotional combinations need to be spontaneous not planned and rehearsed. Use your knowledge to actually have a conversation with women you are interested in and let the combinations come naturally. And you know what? At a point those natural combinations will lead to sex. By that time you will no longer have the fear that you will kick a woman out of bed after sex because you will already be invested in her. Even if it turns out that she was just going to be a physical connection for you, you will know that you gave her the respect she deserves. That may or may not sound like a load of bull but it is how I feel after reading your thoughts.

Usually at the end of a piece like this it is normal to write a few paragraphs summarizing your findings. Fortunately for the reader I am not a normal writer. I am just going to leave you with this advice:

Look and listen a little harder to the women in your life. They will provide you with the questions and the answers. Treat them with respect even if they do not treat themselves that way. These things will help to make you a great man. I cannot promise it will get you in every woman's bed but I can promise that the beds you get into will be far better than just another conquest. Good luck.

Lola Key

We are different in many respects. As I wrote at the very beginning, I expected this to be the case, primarily because of the part of the world we live in. My society has shaped me a lot and yours has done the same to you. And that is perfectly ok. Why? Because both you and I are people who are satisfied with themselves. When I disagreed with you, I just wanted to say that I think differently, not that you are not right.

I want to say that what I liked the most about all this is the great and imaginative idea you came up with to randomly choose three completely unknown girls from who knows where and to ask them to comment on your writing for the sake of issuing a book. That is a brilliant idea. Congratulations on that. And I do believe that you would like to share your possible future wealth with your co-writers. This I guess means that I believe you to be a good person. And isn't that the most important thing and the most valuable thing you could have acquired from this whole experience?

Everything I wrote is what I honestly think. I believe you understand that and that you agree with that. I decided to read chapter by chapter and to comment on what you have written. Once I have read the particular chapter, I thought for a minute or two, and honestly typed whatever I thought about. I intentionally didn't go back. I wanted this writing to be in accordance with my instinct of male and female relationships, not in accordance with what a proper thing to say is.

So, that's it for now. Who knows, maybe we get the chance to meet each other one day and to discuss this male and female relationships in person.

Claudia

You are right: your book did sound like you were talking to other guys and giving them tips on how to pick up a woman (even though you keep warning them against trying some of your suggestions at home!). And that is probably the best, as I get to eavesdrop on a conversation among men, about how you guys think we women are. We don't get many chances to hear your frank opinions, to tell you the truth. So, in that sense, it's been eye-opening.

On my part, I've tried to do my best at telling you my honest opinion about some of your techniques or stories with women. I've tried to make sense about some of the things that happened to me in the light of your perspective. And I just hope you can use my writing to go one step further in your interpretation of that mysterious (little?) thing called "a woman's brain"!

Part 2

Guys, It's All Your Fault!

The first part was highly informative and entertaining; at least for me it was. Did you notice the things that the women rejected? They weren't calling me a liar, considering how honest I've been. They simply rejected some things. Why do you think that is? Sometimes there were things that they totally skipped over.

What I imagined would happen in Part 1 would be that the women would realize at the end that I had been interacting with their 'Inner Woman' the entire time. This was my first time attempting what I normally do face to face, with a mini book. In person, I'd be able to adjust. Leaving the women to their own devices yielded better results that I'd imagined.

I just assumed that women rely on their 'Inner Woman' to assess certain things. While that is true in general, the reality is quite different. I spent so much time honing my ability to connect with and excite this 'Inner Woman' that I didn't appreciate the inner struggles that women face.

From my observation, Lola has a deep connection with her 'Inner Woman' and probably relies on her too much. Chan is aware of her 'Inner Woman', but there appears to be some conflict there. Finally, Claudia has some sense of her 'Inner Woman', but her 'Inner Woman' seems suppressed. I feel incredibly lucky to have three very different women.

For the women reading this, you may relate to one of these writers and may take offense to what I just said. If that's true, I'd like for you to take out a sheet of paper and write down what it is that offends you. We'll talk about that later.

I want to reiterate why women cheat. They cheat because their 'Inner Woman' simply takes over given the right set of circumstances. Guys like me could have a conversation with a woman's boyfriend and totally ignore the woman. Yet, a few minutes later, she would be making out with us behind her man's back. The woman would say something like "I never do this," or "I don't know what came over me." I lost count to the amount of times women would be in my bed recounting and rationalize the steps that led to that moment.

There is nothing wrong with women, and guys like me don't have any special powers. For some reason, the whole world hates the 'Inner Woman'. Both women and men attempt to suppress and berate her. Men do everything possible to suppress and avoid this 'Inner Woman'. The 'Inner Woman' has an important role in every woman's life. If you have access to your woman 24 hours per day, and you don't engage her 'Inner Woman', then it is absolutely your fault if a guy like me comes along and she gets sidetracked.

Let's find this elusive 'Inner Woman' directly now.

DISCOVERING THE 'INNER WOMAN'

ALL THE PARTS THAT MAKE A HUMAN

NLP (Neuro-Linguistic Programming) is a science, developed by actual scientists. People like Anthony Robbins and Ross Jeffries, took that science and applied it to a specific business model. Anthony Robbins repackaged NLP and turned it into a self-improvement program. I actually like Anthony Robbins' materials. I just wish he would have been honest about not making most of it up all on his own. Ross Jeffries on the other hand, he's just a creepy old guy with extraordinary tools.

Though I'm not a Master NLP Practitioner, nor a PHD in any subject, I have some experience with the parts that are described in NLP. I hope and pray that I do the actual Masters of NLP justice with my following explanation.

The Conscious Selves

In NLP there are many parts that make up the whole self. What we are all aware of is the conscious self. The conscious self has specific duties.

The first of which is an outward expression of the total self. While most people would accept this premise, they may not readily accept that the conscious self is constantly changing. Sometimes it seems the conscious self will represent itself in different ways in different situations. It is in fact different selves in different situations.

Some people rebel against certain conscious selves. For those people, at that time, being their 'real' self is important to them. I hate to break it to those people but that self isn't the 'real' self in any sense. It is nothing more than a part of you that you openly reject. Fighting against conscious selves is futile and barely scratches the surface of who you actually are.

The conscious self again is nothing more than an outward representation of the total self; the duty we all understand. The conscious self has more duties as well. The conscious self has the ability to reason. It understands truth statements. If I say "If it's raining, then I carry an umbrella" the conscious mind will understand that statement and store it in the appropriate place.

The conscious self also has the ability to focus. If the conscious self is usually focused on a singular thing, it has the ability to block all unnecessary stimuli. For example, as you are reading this book, are you aware of what your left foot is feeling? You are aware now that your conscious mind is focusing on in, right?

The conscious self also blocks out stimuli that it deems useless information. For example, here in New York City, there are many apartments that are right next to or above a train line. I've been to people's homes right next to an above ground train line. The entire apartment rumbles every few minutes. The people that live there literally tuned the noise and commotion out. I had an apartment above a train line. When a train would pass by I could feel a slight rumble in the apartment. After a few weeks, I only noticed it when other people pointed it out to me.

Finally, the conscious self has the very important role of protecting the subconscious selves. The subconscious selves don't understand things the way the conscious self understands things. Thus the subconscious selves need protecting from outside attacks or manipulations.

The Inner Selves

The inner subconscious selves are something that most people are vaguely aware of. Understanding what's happening on the inside of each one of us yields greater insight into our daily lives and decisions. While people are aware of 'inner voices,' they incorrectly assume that there is a singular inner self. On the contrary, there are many inner selves and they all have their own purposes.

You are either born with an inner self, or it's created out of necessity. For example, we all have a self who makes sure our heart keeps beating. This is a self that we are born with. Most people take this part of us for granted, but that part is there and will toil away until we die. Later, I'll give you a way to communicate with the part of you in control of keeping your heart beating.

Another inner self would be the part of us that is in control of how we walk. It has a specific purpose and cues when to take over. Only babies consciously think about walking. Once the conscious self sees repetition it either passes it along to an inner self, or it rejects it. Anything that we do repetitively becomes a subconscious self. We have a driving self, a work self, a typing self, a social self, abuse victims have a defensive self, and on and on. The problems arise when these selves have competing desires. That we'll touch on later. First let's consider how the inner selves process information.

If you speak to a hypnotist, he will tell you that the subconscious mind can process information up to thirty thousand times more information than the conscious mind can. This is because the conscious selves are reasoning and filtering out information. The subconscious selves can process all information at once, while the conscious selves weed things out. Unlike the conscious selves, the subconscious selves don't understand logic, negative statements, punctuation, concept of time, and other nuanced things that the conscious selves can differentiate. For example, if I said, "If it rains, then I don't play basketball. If I don't play basketball, I may read a book. I don't like sci-fi so I would read detective novels." While this makes logical sense, if handed over to a subconscious self, as is, the inner self would understand rain=basketball=reading=sci-fi=detective novels.

It's the conscious self's job to understand the world and give that information over to the subconscious selves. Unfortunately, getting past the conscious self is quite easy. Let me share with you some contemporary failures in messaging. With enough repetition, a message can be sent to the subconscious. The subconscious is powerful and accepted messages will usually be acted upon.

If the government had any sense they wouldn't have spent untold billions of dollars teaching people to 'Don't do drugs' or to 'Say no to drugs'. Needless to say, that campaign did not have the desired effect. Telling someone not to do something is a sure fire way of getting them to do it. For example, don't think about a pink elephant. Don't picture a pink elephant with a party hat on its head. You can consciously attempt to fight the image of a pink elephant, but the subconscious is usually far too powerful.

Another big contemporary fail is the Republican opposition to the Affordable Care Act. Almost a half a billion dollars were spent trying to convince people to 'not sign up for Obamacare'. Needless to say, the exact opposite happened. For future reference, if you want to communicate with the subconscious, frame everything you want to happen in the affirmative.

When a subconscious self is created, it usually has a singular purpose. That self will operate behind the scenes without your conscious awareness. This is important because otherwise we'd have to figure how to open a door every time we see one. What's interesting about the subconscious, is that even though the conscious self is actively deleting information it deems unimportant, the subconscious selves are simultaneously aware of the same information and acting on what it believes is in its own best interests.

There was a time in the past when I studied chess for four to ten hours per day. My body understood that studying chess was what we were doing, and it would shut out certain parts of myself. At the time I called it being 'in the zone'. The reality is, a subconscious-self took over. The way you can always tell conscious from subconscious is the time distortion. Subconscious selves don't understand the passage of time.

The reality is, everyone passes in and out of consciousness all the time. People don't notice it when it's partial; like walking. Rest assured, there is a subconscious-self inside of you waiting for the right circumstances to take over. Only that part of you knows what's its trigger is. Later you can ask them directly. For now, I'll prove to you that you have such a self.

Everyone has an 'on my way home' self. However you take yourself home, be it walking, riding the bus or train or driving, you have a self that is in charge of that. Once you've done the same thing enough times, an inner self is created to handle that task. When your body recognizes a certain set of stimuli your 'on my way home' self comes forward and simply takes over from there. People normally don't recognize that inner self until the day they decide to take a detour or decide to not go home. Most people will wake up, at their front door, and realize that they weren't planning on going home at all!

Inner selves take over all the time. The unfortunate fact that people aren't aware of it makes Hypnotists so appealing. Hypnotism exploits the incredible power of the inner selves to take over, by giving subconscious commands. Those commands usually to come from within, but it can come from exterior sources if the conscious self is bypassed. It's important to note, that commands that go against what the person would already do don't really work. Let's consider a PUA using commands.

I first started studying NLP in order to inspire my chess students to excel. I became consumed with NLP once I saw the effects and realized that there were things that I simply couldn't do; no matter how much I tried. I spent thousands on seminars and learning materials. When I couldn't afford more classes, I turned to piracy on the Internet. I opened up my peer-to-peer clients and downloaded anything that had NLP in it. Eventually, I started downloading Ross Jeffries' materials.

Ross Jeffries was the first professional PUA, probably in the world. Quite simply, Ross took the same NLP courses that I took and decided to apply them to approaching women. Although he was the first, he's probably the least unique of the other professionals, since he just strictly utilized NLP.

I read his materials and listened to his seminars, mainly for the NLP. I wasn't that interested in dating women at the time. In fact, I think I wasn't even having sex. To me, it made sense to hear the techniques, that I already knew, applied in a different way. The more mental connections I had with each technique the more I would remember the techniques. But I deleted all of Ross Jeffries' materials after I listened to his "Deep Trance Phenomenon" recording.

Hypnosis is a subject in NLP, in the same way Calculus is a subject in Mathematics. Deep trance phenomenon describes the process of hypnotizing a person with their eyes open. I hadn't taken any hypnosis courses by that point, but I did later. For a time I hypnotized myself almost every day. I have never attempted to hypnotize someone, without their knowing.

In the recording Jeffries describes it like this. "You know what learning is like? Learning is like Christmas. Imagine this. You wake up early Christmas morning, and you're excited. You're excited because there is a big present under the tree and it has your name on it. You don't wait for anyone else to wake up and start tearing open that present. That's what learning is like, and you can have it, if you open up your heart. Now to me, you guys might be confused about what just happened. It's called Deep Trance Phenomenon."

I don't remember the exact words, but I understand deep trance enough to recreate something similar. Potentially, I hypnotized you while you were reading that series of words. The trance could've been stronger if you actually celebrated Christmas. Clearly there's a potential for failure for atheists and non-Christians; they'd reject the premise. First you must realize that both men and women pass in and out of trance all the time. Its just most people don't recognize it as a trance. Let's consider Ross Jeffries' mini statement.

A trance state can be achieved through the senses, but the easiest way is through the imagination. There were two commands that Ross gave, the first I'm ok with. He said, "Imagine this." A common trance state is a daydream. If you imagined yourself, at any age, waking up and going to the big present under the tree, with your name on it, you were just in a trance. I'm personally ok with trance states as they are so common. In fact, the "Trip to Barnes & Nobles" routine I wrote previously is nothing more than an attempt at inducing a trance state. Capturing a person's imagination is fun and usually pleasurable for all involved.

Unfortunately, trance states have many inherent weaknesses. The first of which are subliminal commands. You wouldn't know that there was a command unless you had an understanding about trances. The command given was "Open up your heart now to me." So you can see it better I'll just copy and paste- "open up your heart. Now to me," see it now? Subliminal commands aren't always accepted. If that were the case, then hypnotists would rule the world. You can't give commands that people would object to, as they would subconsciously reject it. In the recording, Ross Jeffries did a long pause within the command. "open up your heart. (Long Pause) Now to me." The conscious mind would hear the pause and understand that it was the end of the statement. In a trance, what is heard is "Open up your heart now to me," because the subconscious doesn't comprehend punctuation. After hearing this routine, I lost all interest in Ross Jeffries.

The Greater Self

When a subconscious command is created, either a new self is born or an old self is given a new purpose. This is a reality for each and every one of us. Problems arise when the selves disagree. The conscious and subconscious selves can be at odds with any other self.

The best book on the market dealing with the conflicts of the selves is "Core Transformation: Reaching the Wellspring Within" by Connirae Andreas. I was fortunate enough to learn from two of the few people who do Core Transformation work Steven Leeds and Rachel Hott at the NLP Center of New York.

I'm a bit hesitant to talk about the greater self. It almost seems like religion. In fact when I first heard Steven and Rachel describe it, I thought "Bullshit!" Even though I did the course, bought the book, and did the exercises for over eight years, the greater self sounded like propaganda to me.

Since I've discovered this greater self within me, I can relay to you what my greater self is like, and how I discovered him. First there are a few NLP presuppositions that you must accept. You have to believe that every part of you has a positive intention for you. For example, in the book, there was a woman who had a part of her that wished she was dead. She had to understand and accept the wishing of her death was a positive intention. Next, you must accept that what each part really wants is to reach the greater self. I'm not sure if they said this or not, but I believe the way to reach the greater self is through one of the inner selves.

There was only one thing that I wanted to work on, when I took that class, the part of me that pushes people away. He was uncooperative during the class and also when I got home. I tried communicating with him for years every day. One day it felt like I found a place inside, and if I touched it, it felt like I was vomiting tears. I stayed with that place inside for a few years. Sometimes I would vomit tears, sometimes I would relive horrible memories, sometimes my body would let go of old beatings, welts would show up on my body, sometimes I'd be in a rage, and sometimes I'd be depressed.

This went on until I thought nothing was left. It turns out that he just stopped talking to me. For a few years I had random debilitating panic attacks. One day, I decided to drop everything and go to the Dominican Republic. I ruined my business, closed out my trading account, and sat at the beach feeling my fear. I told myself that I wouldn't leave until I'm done with my panic attacks. For almost six months, I did nothing be quake in fear. Until it happened.

I reached my greater self. It was like all of my individual selves at the same time, but more. It felt as if I was connected to all things and all times. You could say that it was a spiritual moment. I'm not a Buddhist, but I can appreciate why they meditate so much. I look forward to one day having a peaceful place to connect with my greater self again.

Those are all of the parts. I need to be thorough in case of any future problems. Later we will attempt to communicate with your inner self. Sometimes things will come easily, and sometimes it will take a lot of effort. I want you to know that it's worth it. If you need help, seek out a professional, ask a friend, or at least buy the book by Connirae Andreas.

The Woman's State

With the last section, I attempted to clearly define what the 'Inner Woman' is. She is nothing more than a subconscious self that all women are born with. The 'Inner Woman' is in control of all the parts that make a woman a woman. My stated aim of Part 1 was to communicate with the 'Inner Woman' of three random female writers. I didn't think that I'd be surprised with what they wrote, but women never cease to amaze me.

In the section "How a Woman Processes Information," I successfully attempted to get the three women to accept the idea that women process information the way in which I later said the subconscious selves' process information. My entire thesis was going to be about how women spend too much time allowing the 'Inner Woman' think for her. Chan, it seemed, came back into consciousness a number of times and rejected entire sections of the book. Claudia's 'Inner Woman' seemed almost completely subdued. While I still believe that women utilize this 'Inner Woman' too much, the levels of connectedness is even more intriguing to me.

Men also have an 'Inner Man.' He isn't very complicated and guys don't rely on him much. Women on the other hand, all have a dominant inner self who is always around. When the 'Inner Woman' takes over, I call it the 'Woman's State', as not to confuse it with any other inner part. 'The Woman's State' is a trance state, except with a number of exceptions.

First, it seems that women can access the 'Woman's State' almost at will. Usually, in order to enter a trance state when something has to happen. The 'Going Home' trance needs stuff like street signs and recognizable landscapes. Hypnotists get people into a state with counting and commands. Women can choose to simply be their 'Inner Woman'. Sometimes, a woman can remain in the 'Woman's State' for extended stretches of time.

Being in a subconscious state, you are free to all information at once. It has to feel incredibly powerful to be able to assess things in this manner. Women need to realize the state for what it is, just a state. You don't have super powers, and men have the same ability. Always using your 'Woman's State' to experience the world can be limiting. This is because no inner self understands logic, inner selves' sometimes associate unrelated things, and most importantly the inner selves are susceptible to commands.

In the 'Woman's State' a woman's body will change. Her skin will be flushed, eyes dilated, the hairs on her skin will stand up, her breathing will change, and her breasts and buttocks become firm. Something else amazing happens in the 'Woman's State', women become more attractive. It could be a chemical process that I'm unaware of, but the more connected a woman becomes to her 'Inner Woman', the more attractive she becomes. I suspect this process could potentially continue indefinitely; regardless of age, weight, or gravity. In other words, a woman can be sexier to a man today than she was twenty years ago.

The 'Woman's State' also comes with beliefs that I simply don't agree with. In the 'Woman's State' a woman actually believes that she can manipulate reality with her secret woman's juju. If I were to approach it as pure animal instincts, it makes sense. The 'Inner Woman' takes over and makes the woman feel as if she is the best her. Maybe there are some secret chemicals that tell a man to approach. Apart from that singular instance when a woman is attracted to a man, and she's shooting her secret mind rays over to him, there is no reason to ever attempt this anywhere else. You are an animal, and your 'Inner Woman' doesn't understand a thing about interoffice politics. You need to learn to turn her off at that moment.

One extra, that I understand, is the need to keep the 'Woman's State' secret. It's like Fight Club, you don't talk about it. I think sometimes women genuinely don't know about Fight Club. I kind of wanted to call this book something like "Women's Words: A Glimpse into a Woman's Psyche." The challenge with the 'Woman's State' is that you can't will yourself there with force or logic. A scientist could spend a lifetime attempting to study the 'Woman's State', but you can't look right at it and expect it to respond. The only way to get to the 'Woman's State' is by walking backwards towards it, while pointing at something else, and talking about something unrelated.

Defending the 'Inner Woman'

With a strong understanding about the 'Woman's State', a person could potentially be highly influential in a woman's life. For example, I could myself be a pimp. I could write a step-by-step guide on finding random women and pimp them out. Apart from morally objecting to doing this, it would be a lot of work. As the saying goes "Pimpin ain't easy!" I even said something highly inflammatory, that none of the writers responded to as well. I said "You've got to understand that women are completely defenseless when it comes to emotionally stimulating things... Women know how defenseless they are against emotional stimulation." This statement has truth to it, but isn't entirely true. I'm confused why the writers skipped this.

Men have always known how to get women out of the 'Woman's State'. In the eighties, Iran had an overpopulation problem. Women were having about six children each. Iran made it public policy that women get access to higher education. Now Iran is facing a shrinking population problem and they are struggling to figure out what to do about it.

Men all around the world are terrified of a woman with a purpose, because they are confused about how to be with them. Some guys lash out violently at these women. Let me first clarify about me being a pimp. I could be a pimp, but I would need to seek out women who are lost and have nothing going for them. Then and only then, can I offer the women my 'fun' way of life. There is no need to be afraid of a powerful woman; all that is needed is for you to lead her back to the 'Woman's State'. Or in words more palatable to a woman "reconnect her to her 'Inner Woman.'"

In truth, this isn't really much of a defense. By giving women a greater purpose, the only thing that has happened is that there is a new inner self is competing with the 'Inner Woman'. It's effective as a public policy, but what public policy do you have for frustrated guys? An average man only knows how to interact with the 'Inner Woman'. It takes skill and practice getting passed all of the obstacles, and reaching the 'Inner Woman'. Women, especially in industrialized nations, are usually like Chan and Claudia.

There is really only one way to truly defend the 'Inner Woman' from a man like me. Her man needs to engage her 'Inner Woman' on a regular basis. If a man doesn't do this, it's his fault if she cheats.

Introduction to Your 'Inner Woman'

Men and Women can do the following to communicate with any part of them that they wish. I chose to focus on the 'Inner Woman'. Ladies, what I want you to do is to get a sheet of paper and write "I'd like to communicate with the part of me that is in control of my lady parts." You can chose whatever wording you like, but you need to be specific. Now switch your writing utensil to your non-dominant hand, close your eyes and wait patiently.

I don't know why this works or why it's so powerful, but it does. They don't teach this specific technique in "Core Transformation." I don't do the technique in that book, as would be too involved. That part of you may respond in any way it feels comfortable. It could be a sound, an image, a feeling, or anything. If you get a response and you aren't sure, ask that part a yes or no question. If that part responds in the same way to a yes question, and nothing to a no, then you can move on.

Once you are sure that this part is the 'Inner Woman', you are free to ask her any question you like. Be sure to ask your questions with your dominant hand and let her answer with your non-dominant hand. Whatever answers this part gives you, you are not to object to, get mad at, or attempt to debate. The inner parts don't reason well, they just know what they want. One question that needs to be asked of this 'Inner Woman' is "What do you want?" I repeat, whatever this part replies, you are to be accepting of and thankful for. In fact, you should write "Thank you for sharing that with me" every time, after each response, until you learn not to antagonize any inner part of you.

If you debate and berate this part of you, she might not want to talk anymore. If you seem to overpower her and win the argument, you've got another thing coming! You can't ever defeat yourself. It's impossible! When I was in class learning this stuff, Steven Leeds told us a story about getting warts on his feet. He complained to his wife, who is also an NLP teacher, about repeatedly getting a wart on the same spot on his foot. Rachel suggested, "Why don't you talk to the part of you giving you those warts?" Steven continued the story by saying he debated with his wife about how you can't use NLP for everything, and that he just needed more wart cream. He finally acquiesced when she said he could communicate with his parts for free, and he could still get wart cream if he wanted to. He finished the story after communicating with his inner parts. He didn't give details on the resolution, he simply said, "that part said I wasn't listening to him."

You've got to understand that each and every part of you, is an image of the whole you, with all of your memories and experience except each has its own specific purpose. A few years ago, while talking to the part of me that keeps people away from me, he said this to me, "I know all your tricks, I know all your techniques and I'm not interested, so stop it."

You can ask this 'Inner Woman' how old she is, what makes her happy, how she feels about you, how she feels about the people in your life, what steps do you need to take for her to take over, and so on. Once you've talked to her enough, ask this question to your inner selves, "are there any objections to what my 'Inner Woman' wants?" Of course, phrase it in a way that makes you feel comfortable. If there is an objection, then ask that objecting part what it wants. The odds are high that there are objecting parts. My only goal was to introduce you to your 'Inner Woman'. I'm not qualified to help you resolve any conflicts. I refer you to Connirae Andreas.

When you are done with that, and you had any objections from the first part, then ask yourself "Which part of my objects to (whatever part of my book.)?" Then have a conversation with that part. No one is wrong or right. I just want you to experience something different.

HOW THE PROFESSIONALS ENGAGE THE 'INNER WOMAN'

Thus far, I've engaged the 'Inner Woman' of three female writers, clearly defined what the 'Inner Woman' is, and hopefully introduced the female readers to their 'Inner Woman'. Now I'd like to break down how some people interact with this 'Inner Woman'. The pattern is usually the same, first they find a way past the conscious defenses, and then they engage the 'Inner Woman' emotionally. In the PUA community, they call it hooking, or a hook point. Feel free to do the Google search "hook point PUA." My extensive background in NLP allows me to say specifically, hooking a woman is simply engaging her 'Inner Woman'.

The 'Inner Woman' has primal and biological needs, and most importantly, she's in control of all of the parts that guys like the most! Engaging her is vital and also just the beginning.

Ross Jeffries

Of all of the PUA teachers, after much thought, Ross Jeffries' material is the most flexible and will likely outlast him. This is mainly because <u>all</u> of his material is NLP. You can check out Ross Jeffries at www.seduction.com. That being said, no one in the community likes him. I haven't met Ross Jeffries, but I've never heard a single good thing about him. The PUA community is quite accepting of people, it says a lot when most of the community detests someone.

The fact that Ross Jeffries is such a creep, is what I believe keeps most people in the community away from NLP. Whenever I hear of someone talk about NLP in the community they either visibly grimace or roll their eyes. It's quite a shame that so many people were repulsed from such a great body of knowledge. It's like, Ross got his cooties all over NLP and the community hates it. He's proud that he got a mention in the book "The Game" by Neil Strauss. He has it featured on his site like a badge of honor. Neil Strauss raked him over the coals in his book! Ross Jeffries, in my opinion, is tone deaf and completely misogynistic. Yet, he will likely draw crowds until the day that he dies.

Since he exclusively uses NLP, Ross Jeffries' approach has some difficulty getting past the conscious barriers. It's incredibly difficult to meet someone, or a group, and start doing language patterns. I'm sure that the people who study, practice, and make up NLP techniques could find a way to work on approaches. But that hasn't happened yet. Trying to do language patterns covertly, in a social setting, is a recipe for disaster. But once you get past the initial hurdle of trust, then following Ross Jeffries could be beneficial. Well, by Ross Jeffries, I mean NLP. NLP was specifically designed to verbally interact with the inner parts.

Deep Trance Phenomenon

What Ross would do is create a semi-trance state, then follow it with commands. Sometimes the commands are subliminal, and sometimes they aren't. Ross loves to give commands. This is difficult to do, unless some trust has been established. It's an underhanded way to get people to do things. The problem with doing this, is that if a woman ever finds out that you were giving her commands it's over. If any part of a woman disagrees with a command, she will have an inner sense to avoid you. To me it's far too risky and shady. But it could be fun if done as a couple with full knowledge. Also, I personally enjoy creating trance states without the commands.

Synesthesia

This is the process of relating unrelated things; at least that's how I look at it. Wikipedia says that it's a neurological phenomenon in which stimulation of one sensory or cognitive pathway leads to automatic, involuntary experiences in a second sensory or cognitive pathway. For some people this is a disorder that they live with. But to NLP, it's an intended goal.

The subconscious already has the ability to link unrelated things. The trick is getting the conscious mind to not reject the associations. Of all the things that Ross Jeffries does, this is one of the few routines that other people in the community use. The problem with synesthesia is the same with all the NLP techniques, you need to establish some rapport before you attempt it. Since it's so common I'll just copy and paste a routine I searched on the internet.

Copied from Attractology.com

> *I can't remember where this gambit came from but it has been around in the community for a while and is one of the most field-tested and powerful routines out there. Because it utilizes NLP and Kino, it is recommended to perform this routine as slow and non-sexually as possible.*
>
> *You: Have you ever heard of synesthesia?*
> *Her: No.*
> *You: (acting excited): Are you serious? Omg I need to show this amazing psychology experiment. Here let's go sit down for a second.*
> *Her: Ok.*
> *Her: I'm going to rub your arm real quick and I want you to remember specifically how it feels.*
> *You: Ok (So I rub the insensitive outside 'hair side' of her forearm arm very smoothly for about 3 seconds and then stop) Remember how that felt.*
> *Her: Ok.*
> *You: Alright now I want you to close your eyes and picture a time in your life where time stood still. Where you felt the most fulfilling pleasure you have ever experienced. Where everything in your life was just perfect... See what you saw... Hear what heard. .. Feel what you felt... Now when you feel like you are fully in that moment, wiggle your index finger (She does so and then eventually*

wiggles). Now I want to see these feelings as an energy source running through your body. Give these feelings an energy color. It doesn't matter what the color is. Now I want you to double the intensity and the double the brightness. Now I want you to picture that energy slowly moving towards your right shoulder. Picture it moving down your right arm. Picture it moving all the way into your right hand intensifying as it compacts into the smaller area. Now picture all of that pleasurable energy moving into your right index finger. Picture it all collecting in in tip of your finger. Now as I touch your finger picture all of that energy and feelings transfer from the tip of your index finger to mine. (I touch her index finger with mine and act as if there is real energy passing between us.)

Now you will see that when I touch my index finger on your arm now, it will act as a paintbrush of all that energy and those feelings. (This time I stroke the sensitive, hairless, part of her arm. I then stroke her face and neckline. They are often amazed/turned on).

You see, your mind has incredible control over the physical feeling in your body. I could show you more, but I don't think you could afford me (I say jokingly).

The essence of the routine is to bypass the conscious and create connections that aren't supposed to exist. It's a very effective routine and can be done over and over. What's nice about it is that you are coming clean about it being a routine right away. So there is never any risk of being found out. It doesn't matter that someone else did the same thing. It's a fun and pleasurable experience. Unfortunately, you need relative quiet and few distractions. You also need her to trust you enough to be alone with you and close her eyes.

I've done synesthesia many times. Associating color, sounds, shapes, and feelings to unrelated things simultaneously is something that I may never tire of. I'm just tired of doing the same thing over and over.

I'm not sure if NLP professionals would agree with me, but the "Introducing my Penis" routine was my attempt at synesthesia with the women's eyes open. Having a woman associate a wonderful time in her life, a color, and intense feelings to the tip of my finger is great, but it takes too much effort and staging.

I was a bit edgy by attempting to associate anything to my penis. It's difficult enough to associate unrelated things. But my penis?? I gave him jobs, nationalities, super powers, etc. The only way to do this is with humor. Laughter is the easiest way to get past the conscious mind. If I told you that my right earlobe is a Native American and my left eyebrow is a Bosnian Serb, your conscious mind would instantly reject that premise. But with relevant humor, the association is possible.

Anchoring

In NLP, when learning anchoring they usually refer to Ivan Pavlov's conditioning experiment with a dog. In this experiment, whenever Pavlov fed the dog, he would ring a bell. Eventually, when Pavlov rang the bell, the dog would salivate and get ready for food, even though no food was present. Actually, anchoring is also used by many PUA's as well. How about I let someone else explain.

Copied from Pickupguide.com

> *A more advanced aspect of patterning is anchoring. Anchoring is an application of Pavlov's reflex in NLP (and also in Speed Seduction)* (**Speed Seduction is Ross Jeffries course**)... *The same conditioned reflex can be created in a girl - this is called anchoring. In patterning this means, that every time you see the*

girl light up with delight, smile, laugh or just feel damn good because of the wonderful feelings you are creating in her with your patterns, you touch her in a specific place (the shoulder, elbow, inside of her arm) thus planting an anchor (the ringing of the bell while offering food:), while saying something "it's a great feeling, isn't it?" to mask your touch.

Let's say you've touched her elbow each time you've made her feel especially good three times already. If you now touch that very same spot on her elbow the same way you touched it on three previous occasions (applying the same amount of pressure etc.), she suddenly and unexpectedly has all those wonderful feelings, that were there when you planted the anchor, rush back to her without you having done anything else but touch her elbow (in other words: you just rang the bell without offering food, and she started to salivate:). If you're really good, you can plant different anchors for different feelings all over her body - an anchor of laughter on her shoulder, an anchor of excitement on her elbow, an anchor of feeling romantic on back of her hand and an anchor of feeling horny... on her knee.

It is however important not to overuse the anchors you have planted or she will eventually become insensitive to them. Ring a bell ten times without offering food and the dog will eventually stop salivating when hearing the bell ring.

Anchoring can do done covertly, or it can be done with the woman having full knowledge. The only time I use anchors is during sex. Whenever a girl I'm dating regularly is having an orgasm, I would bite and suck on the same spot on her neck. Then when I want her to remember, like if she has a boyfriend objection or something, I'd bite and suck on that same spot and bring her back to an earlier time.

In all, Ross Jeffries' techniques, or NLP, will have great longevity. More importantly, all of his techniques can and should be shared with the women eventually. NLP is constantly growing and expanding, a man, a woman or a couple can enjoyably study NLP for the rest of their lives.

David Deangelo

David used to be one of Ross Jeffries' top students. Rumor has it that Ross slept with David's girlfriend and caused David to part ways. David Deangelo made his own seduction program and decided to be the total opposite of Jeffries. He created doubleyourdating.com. People in the community say that David Deangelo is the richest PUA in the world. If it's true, it makes sense. He set up a good business model. Guys start off with either the free newsletter or by purchasing his dating manual. Which is an advertisement for his Double your Dating DVDs. Those DVDs have further upsells as well.

David was a great contrast to Ross, in that Ross was a pervy single old man, and David was an attractive, socially adept man with a girlfriend. While Jeffries taught language patterns, David instead focused on improving a man's personality. He's added more programs since I last visited his site, but his main focus was learning to be cocky/funny. After learning things in general about women, being cocky/funny was his selling point. I do think highly of David Deangelo, but I don't wholeheartedly agree with the cocky/funny premise.

Let's consider why it works. Being cocky can be appealing, but in general it's too much for an average girl to accept. But cocky and funny at the same time is unique and interesting. This is because humor is so disarming. Guys who learn this are pleasantly surprised when woman are drawn to them. Yes, being cocky/funny can be very successful. David is the richest PUA after all.

Here's where it fails. I disagree with David's premise because essentially he says that cocky/funny equals sex with a woman. What in reality is happening, is that attitude portrayed is so unique that women are drawn to it. Most guys offer nothing emotionally to a woman. But being cocky/funny, the 'Inner Woman' will be drawn to it… until the conscious minds figures it out. Once you become predictable, you will lose your appeal. But what if she becomes your steady girlfriend despite the predictability of cocky/funny? Unless that guy has found a different way to engage the 'Inner Woman', he is in a terrible place.

That's only the beginning of the potential problems. What if she finds your David Deangelo DVDs, or maybe watches them with a friend? A woman may completely shut you out of her life if she realizes that the first part of your relationship was an act that you learned from a PUA. It's an unavoidable moment.

The way men, who follow this school of thought religiously, handle this is to regularly switch women. The next problem is that women learn together. If one girl has had experience with a cocky/funny guy she will share it with her friends. By continuously being cocky/funny you run the risk of women recognizing it and rejecting you. It's even worse if the guys just copy the cocky/funny routines and do them word for word.

Cocky/funny is great for business, but in the long term does little for the average guy. The premise that cocky/funny equals sex obscures the reality of the situation. The 'Inner Woman' is attracted to unique and interesting things. The fact is, you can choose almost any emotional combination. To start out with, you can keep the funny part. You can do aloof/funny or sexually aggressive/funny. With each one you will have to gauge the effects. For example, sexually aggressive/funny, I picture a man acting exactly like the cartoon character Pepé Le Pew. You can even do the French accent. It has a similar effect as cocky/funny except I wouldn't always do it. I would back off and give the woman space, as there are far too many sexual assaults. I wouldn't want her to associate me to a man who would do such a thing. Thus giving her a chance to pursue me if she'd like.

Also, cocky/funny doesn't need to happen all the time. If the woman trusts you, you can simply drop the funny part. The humor is meant to disarm, why keep trying to disarm? The cockiness can be toned down as well. What I'm saying is, a guy can in fact change at will, given the right circumstances. There are an infinite number of emotional states a man can chose to engage his woman in. Also, the man can and should switch the states when deemed appropriate.

Doing this is incredibly difficult, but exceedingly rewarding. It's difficult because it will take time, effort, and practice to be able to perfect a given emotional state to share with a woman. It could be rewarding if a man can shift and combine emotional state to always keep the 'Inner Woman' engaged. A man could spend a lifetime mastering this.

The Venus Butterfly Technique

In the book "The One Hour Orgasm," Bob and Leah Schwartz shares how they personally connect with each other's primal inner selves. First, you will notice that these people aren't PUAs. I added them here purposefully. Most of the great books, at a bookstore, involving dating and women, all attempt to teach guys a unique way to connect with the 'Inner Woman'. I have to admit, that I've never actually done the Venus Butterfly Technique, as I've never allowed myself to have a committed relationship with a woman. But, if I'm going to study a subject, I study all that I can.

The first part of the book is extremely informative. It is somewhat similar to what I attempted to share here. The trick is the actual technique part. I think the technique part is great, but there are a number of challenges to making it work. The Amazon reviews exemplify the challenges. Some found it amazing, and others hated it. Let's start from the beginning.

The technique requires you to ask your partner almost a hundred questions. The author's actually admit that this part could be logistically challenging. What they failed to clarify, is that you need to ask those questions to the 'Inner Woman'. They suggest you find a quiet place, light some candles, have some soothing music, while caressing your woman, and asking her the questions. Essentially, you are attempting a trance state.

If you look at the reviews, you can feel the anguish people faced with this exercise. The first challenge you must face is whether or not the woman allows her 'Inner Woman' to come forward. Some women are in active conflict with their 'Inner Woman'. The 'Inner Woman' may never decide to communicate. The next issue is, what if some other part is answering the questions? If you are aiming to have a one-hour orgasm, you need to be communicating specifically with the part that is in control of the lady parts.

Another challenge is the sheer amount of questions. The couple also admits this is a challenge. Turning pages and taking notes may break the state. The Schwartz' suggest memorizing the questions and recording her responses. Given that there are so many, it will take a lot of effort. The idea is that once you ask the questions, and get the right responses, the man will take what he's learned and create a 'date' given what he's learned. This is also a great deal of work.

Another challenge that I see for the technique is that you may miss something important. There are so many questions that you may not have the chance to explore them. One of the first questions is "Which way do you prefer to be loved? Do you prefer to be loved by being held, do you prefer being shown that you are loved, or do you prefer being told that you are loved?" This question simply wants to know if the 'Inner Woman' is Kinesthetic, Auditory, or Visual. I say the 'Inner Woman' because different parts operate differently. The conscious self could be visual and the 'Inner Woman' could be auditory.

What's great about this is you will know the best way to interact with the 'Inner Woman', and also the worst way. A person like me can spend weeks to months having fun with just that information. I personally wouldn't stick to only doing the thing that she likes. I would purposefully combine the thing she rejects to create different experiences. Obviously overdoing it is bad, but giving the 'Inner Woman' a variety of experiences leads to the next issue.

People change, and so does the 'Inner Woman'. The problem with asking a long list of questions, and then planning a date with that, assumes that the 'Inner Woman' is static. The book doesn't suggest repeating the questions in any interval. In essence, the questions are a process of discovery. With every action done with the 'Inner Woman', she will learn and change, just like the rest of us.

Apart from those issues, I think the Venus Butterfly Technique is amazing. You take information you gather from the 'Inner Woman' and take a few weeks creating a special date for her. The weeks of anticipation will drive her crazy. Finally, the technique involves the anchoring of orgasmic contractions to various parts of the skin, and an extended tension and release rhythm. You may be wondering why I think so highly of something I've never actually done. Because I've done the technique in a revised form with only words, with similar effect. This is something that I look forward to doing once I'm in a committed relationship.

Mystery

Mystery is the most famous and most influential PUA in the world. He coined most of the lingo that is used and men often quote his manual "The Mystery Method." He had a television series for a while called "The Pickup Artist." Let's understand what about the Mystery Method is so appealing.

I hate to dispel such a compelling work. But there isn't much to the Mystery Method when you take a deeper look. It is just a series of emotional outcomes over a seven to ten hour period. In other words, an emotional combination lasting seven to ten hours. What makes the Mystery Method so compelling, is that he expressed it in a way that men can comprehend. The Mystery Method is quite strict and dogmatic.

To start with, there is the seven to ten hour rule. Feel free to search "Mystery seven hour rule" for Mystery's reasoning behind it. The rule itself is silly, but for a beginner it will shape his actions. Firstly, he has to figure out what to do for at least seven hours. Next, once the seven hours has transpired he can make his move. Some guys often miss their window of opportunity with a woman, making your move at seven hours gives a good target to shoot for. By the tenth hour, if nothing happens, you just eject.

The Mystery Method is divided into nine phases. Each phase has its own emotional outcome. You can use the routines Mystery provides for each stage, but it's recommended that you make your own routines. Since every routine is geared towards a specific emotional outcome, the guy should have a good idea of what to expect. The Mystery Method provides tests to make sure that you are on track. Once you are certain you've succeeded in one phase, you are allowed to go to the next phase.

For example, phase one is nothing more than the introduction. The goal is basically not to raise any red flags, and "disarm the obstacles." Same as all the other PUA's, you need to get passed conscious objections. Phase two is where you 'hook' the target woman. In other words, connect with the 'Inner Woman'.

The first two phases should last five to twenty minutes. Most guys are excited to get this far, but now they have at least six hours and forty minutes to go. The method is so straight forward. You keep doing one phase until you've mastered it. After six months to a year, you will have a solid seven to ten hours prepared.

The problem with The Mystery Method is that it claims that doing the nine phases equals sex. That's just not true. What is true is this, most guys offer women nothing emotionally! The fact that anyone is offering them a series of emotional outcomes over a seven to ten hour period is exciting. I myself have broken most of the rules that Mystery said not to break. I broke the seven to ten hour rule, both ways. I skipped phases, added phases, mixed the phases around, and I've even added my own emotional outcomes. A hundred years from now, no one is going to look at The Mystery Method and say "this is how you get a woman to have sex with you."

The failure in The Mystery Method is in its popularity. Searching Meetup.com, in various cities around the world, if I search for "Pickup Artist" groups, I will invariably find groups that meet regularly and each meeting is a different Mystery Method phase. It's like they are 12-step program with only nine steps. The television show made The Mystery Method even more popular. The fact is that there are too many guys out there doing the exact same thing.

The seven-hour time horizon is what keeps girls from noticing right away what's happening. Even still, women are noticing the emotional outcomes and are rejecting it. It's simple math. There can't be millions of guys doing the very same thing to the same women. Girls will notice the pattern and start warning each other. But did I mention how popular The Mystery Method is? Women are buying The Mystery Method, studying it, and blogging about it. There are far too many women on the lookout for the nine phases for The Mystery Method to be at all effective.

What if it worked and you found a girl that you want to keep? The problem with The Mystery Method, is that after the seven to ten hour time frame, you're left to your own devices. From the woman's perspective, you were initially amazing, but then you all of a sudden became boring. What's even worst, is if she finds your manual somewhere and realized that you gamed her.

The Mystery Method is quite instructive, in seeing what is possible. Its better if a man instead creates his own seven to ten hour periods; or five to six week periods. If a man creates it himself, he can customize his dates for a specific woman. He can do it in a clandestine fashion, or he can tell his woman step by step everything has planned or had done.

The Mystery Method ultimately became Love Systems; lovesystems.com. When Mystery left the group to start his television show, they dropped the Mystery Method and all the rigid rules. Now they focus of personal development and general targets to reach. I've never seen Mystery in action, but the teachers at Love Systems are amazing.

Why did I write this book?

I don't have any aspirations of being a dating guru. I'm not interested in having a following. The truth is, I'm more interested in social issues than anything else. In fact the next book that I'm going to write may seem like a one hundred eighty degree turn from this one. If there weren't a social component, I wouldn't have allowed myself to write this. I've never been keen to advertise what I've done at night.

When I go out, it feels like there is an epidemic of women at war with their 'Inner Woman'. The future of the entire planet will be like Japan is now, with women as equals in the workforce. The birth pangs of this are happening all around us. The problem that the planet faces is the countless frustrated men who have no idea what to do with a self-sufficient, goal-oriented woman. Frustrated men are lashing out all around the world. Many times, these outbursts are violent.

I started this book demonstrating how I could connect with the 'Inner Woman' of three random women. It was in fact more than a demonstration. I need and want women to read this book, and I know that I can be long-winded and technical sometimes. Women, I reasoned, enjoy hearing what other women have to say. I could be wrong, but I don't think this book could be effective without women being involved with it.

Next I described the inner workings of all us humans. Then attempted to introduce the women to their 'Inner Woman'. I did this because I suspect that most women aren't in complete agreement with their 'Inner Woman'. Then I explained how the most popular PUA's connect with this 'Inner Woman'.

In part, I think women want to know these things to defend themselves in the future, but also to have a better relationship with their inner parts. While it may seem at times that I'm talking to guys, I'm aiming for women. I've come to this point to ask you a favor.

I want you to encourage the men in your life to learn more information about how to connect with the 'Inner Woman'. I want you to not be defensive about the entire topic. Most women I know are repulsed by it. It is unfortunate that they call it 'Pickup Artist.' In time, with more attached men going to meetings, the names will change. It's in your best interest. Why? Because none of the men in the community has ever said that they feel emasculated because their woman makes more than them. None!

Before you make up your minds, I'd like to share with you what a man is. In the very beginning of this book, I asked the writers to explain what a woman is. It's fascinating that two of the writers skipped that. I wonder if it's something that can actually be explained. Thus far, I've attempted to demonstrate what a woman is. Now let me tell you about what a man is.

WHAT IS A MAN?

I HATE STUPID LISTS!

I did my best to allow the women to be free and write whatever they wanted. Apparently women love lists and giving advice and it could potentially be good for other women to read. Except I would have to read it first and my head would likely explode out of anger. Let me share with you the first time I rejected the female lists.

I purchased DVD's, went to seminars, and talked to other guys in the community and at various points over a long period they all said, in one form or the other, "you need to buy women's magazines and read the top ten list section." The day I finally took the plunge and bought one, I was sitting next to a group of guys, at a meeting, and they were having a discussion about women's magazines. I asked what was going on, and one of them said, "Dude, you've got to read the top ten lists. They are perfect openers! Guaranteed at least one girl in the set read the article. Plus you can build a connection by talking about the other articles as well."

I listened to the guys talk about various articles and lists and decided to give it a shot. After the meeting, I went to a newsstand and purchase a magazine with sexy woman posing in a seductively classy way. I turned right to the top ten list and was repulsed by it. I recognized right away what that list was- a recipe for an emotional state. I didn't bother with the articles and I didn't talk about the list with any women. I tossed that magazine.

If there is a thing that frustrates me the most about women, is their propensity to suggest an emotional state as the cause of a problem or the solution to a problem. Sometimes they list seemingly random things and suggest that if you accept that list you will achieve the magical state. More commonly for me, since I'm honest about the seduction community, women tell me to quit going to meetings and say to me "it's all so easy. All you need is confidence and to be yourself."

While those words sound reasonable, it makes no sense to a man. How is any guy supposed to use that advice? Women believe that they have some secret knowledge that guys are too clueless to get. It irks me to no end to hear a woman say how easy it is to get a woman. It bothers me when women are perplexed that guys would be confused about women. People like to say, "it ain't rocket science," when they are talking about something easy. For a man, women are more difficult than rocket science. At least rocket science is predictable. Dating a woman will likely be one of the most challenging things in any man's life. Ladies, if you tell a guy that "being himself and confident is all he needs" and they agree with you; he wants to have sex with you.

If women are such masters of relationships, then there should be a woman that all guys listen to for advice. Guess what? There are none! The only women I've gotten good advice from were lesbians who were into picking up women, female recruiters of women, and female managers of women. Everyone else gave me terrible advice!

The first woman that I listened to was Laura Schlessinger. I bought her books and reread them constantly. I did my best to live my life as Dr. Laura said that I should. One day I saw nude photos of her online. The pictures were taken by a man that wasn't her husband. The man said that he had a moral obligation because Dr. Laura was a hypocrite. I was in my early twenties and that news broke my heart. It felt like Dr. Laura had cheated on me. I tried rereading "Ten Stupid Things Men do to Mess up their Lives." To me it felt like a step-by-step plan to fall in love with a woman and have her cheat on me. I've since deleted all that I learned from her from my memory and would never recommend a guy to read anything she's written; unless he really wants his woman to cheat on him.

There was a meeting that a lot of the guys were recommending that I go to. It was run by a couple who worked together to help guys pick up women. These meetings are usually meant to tease you so you can buy their course or go to a boot camp. The woman started first and she was definitely hot. It was annoying and incredibly frustrating, as she spent fifteen minutes talking down to a room full of guys, saying in various ways "it's easy just be confident." The truth is, I had an idea what she was saying, but I was incredibly upset that she had the audacity to believe that she was qualified to teach a man. What made her so special? Just because she was born sexy?

I was tempted to walk out while she was talking, but I had already spent money to listen to that nonsense. It wasn't just me who was frustrated; I could sense the tension from all the other guys in the room. A guy in his fifties or sixties, sitting close to the front, holding a pen, with a blank notepad raised his hand and asked, "How exactly can I be confident?" This woman's tone went from condescending to anger and contempt. She went on and on about how you should just "Be." I know this sounds similar to the Future experience. The difference is one is finding out your life's purpose, the other is achieving an emotional state.

As someone who's studied NLP extensively, I have a number of tools to help me achieve various states. I would not have known how to do this unless I actively sought out the knowledge. Most guys simply can't choose how they wish to feel. Instead of this woman being in front of a bunch of PUA's, how about she tried the same line of nonsense to professional athletes? Essentially, what she's offering is the same thing. Professional athletes are paid millions of dollars to perform. Most of these athletes have no idea how to consistently have peak performance.

They are all constantly trying to find the path to getting to that state. Most athletes have rituals that they do, in hopes that the rituals will take them back to the place of their peak performance. The rituals these guys go through are totally ridiculous, but the reality is that they have no idea how to get to their peak states. The ones who can consistently get their peak states are called All-Stars.

Let's say the Knicks hired this woman to inspire the team before a game. She could potentially give the same lecture she gave to the PUA's. Telling any group of guys "just be confident," will be equally meaningless. If one of the basketball players raises his hand and asks, "How exactly can I be confident?" What do you say? It is a valid question. There should be a process that the guys can do that should lead to confidence. If the woman does as she did in our meeting, and goes off on the basketball players, what would happen? If they lose that game, she would be fired. If they win the game, then they would hire her to yell at team before every game until they start losing! Then they'll fire her. If they win every game, then she would become a staple for the team. But to be clear, the things she said would totally have no meaning to the guys.

Sensing the frustration in the room, this woman's boyfriend stood up, put his arm around her shoulder to signal her to stop talking, then he began talking. Quite honestly, the class would've been much better if the girl never opened her mouth. I think the guy said some cool things, but I was so upset by the woman's lecturing that I don't remember a thing he said. I don't remember their names and I don't care.

Even after all of this, some women may still not understand. Then I'll tell you something that 100% of guys have to deal with. In the community, we call it 'Approach Anxiety.' All guys feel this anxiety before attempting to approach a woman, and it doesn't go away with time. The situation gets hairier with guys like me who also experience severe panic attacks. Although most of the time my panic attacks were unrelated to women, I still regularly experienced them. Tell me ladies, how does telling men in general "be yourself and be confident" help him overcome this anxiety? More importantly, how would that help me in the midst of a panic attack?

When I'm having a panic attack and I see a woman that I'd like to talk to, I allow myself to be terrified and start heading over to her direction. As my muscles tense up and my breath shortens I tell myself over and over "it's ok to be afraid." After I make my labored approach to the woman and her friends I simply state the obvious while being completely afraid. I would point to where I was and tell her "I was over there and I saw you here and I had to come over here to talk to you to find out what makes you so special." I don't say exactly that, as it's different in every situation. But what is the same is that I allow myself to tremble, stutter, break eye contact, bite my lip, be flustered, and anything else my body feels most comfortable doing, as I am genuinely terrified.

I'm pleased to report that 100% of the time that I did this the woman invited me into her circle to talk. It didn't matter if the circle was her bridal shower or her husband was sitting right next to her. It's vitally important to understand the intentions of a routine before it's attempted. With this routine the goal is to have the woman believe her feminine powers were so strong that it made me a nervous wreck, and yet I was still compelled to meet her. After I make my introduction, the woman that I was interested in basically received an adrenalin shot to her feminine ego. Even if her husband is sitting right next to her, she will want to bask in the adoration some random guy is giving her. If I didn't wind up with the woman, she would introduce me to similarly attractive and single women.

By no means is this disingenuous, as I'm always afraid to meet a new woman. Sometimes the panic attacks are about her, but mostly not. Even still, it would take extraordinary effort to approach a woman while having a panic attack.

So what do you think a man would feel most comfortable hearing? Be confident and be yourself or if you are scared allow yourself to be as afraid as you want and go with it? I personally wouldn't do this routine unless I'm really spazzing out. On the one hand a man can chose to accentuate the state he's already in, on the other he has to navigate his way to a state from fear.

Another thing that vexes me is a woman's propensity to state the obvious. If I tell female friends, who dance Salsa with me, that I'm involved in the seduction community, invariably they say, "You don't need that. All you need is to keep dancing Salsa. You're good!" Firstly, I purposely don't date Salsa dancers. They all know each other and I love dancing too much. It would cause me too much trouble. Secondly, what the hell kind of dumb advice is that? You mean all I have to do is spend thousands upon thousands of hours practicing dancing Salsa and that's all that I need to do? Really, is that it? Hey Tiger Woods, you don't need to learn anything about women, all you need to do is keep playing golf! Hey Mr. Obama, if Michelle ever left you, all you need to do is keep being President. You know cuz duh.

I swear, if I get married and have a son, when my son grows up and asks his parents about a girl, and my wife tells him some nonsense about confidence I solemnly swear that mommy will be getting a spanking from daddy! This is a forewarning! So if you dare fill my son's head that women's mantra of letting your inner self shine, then you and I both know that you are asking me to spank you; and I will gladly spank you!

The last time I was exposed to a woman trying to break into teaching guys about women, it was in an email. The email blast showed a picture of a stunning woman, with big and long blonde hair. She was wearing a suit jacket with her arms crossed just below her chest. She posed on a diagonal profile so that you clearly see her heaving breasts. She was selling a course and gave bullet points of what a man will learn from buying her course. I swear to you the first two bullet points were "Learn to have abundant confidence" and "Unlock your true inner self."

I don't remember the other bullet points and I don't remember this woman's name. I was offended and incredibly furious at the audacity of this woman. The only thing I could do is immediately delete the email. Part of me wishes that I went to the seminar and purchased her course. Only to break every cd right in her face and clasp the manual with both hands and rip it in half with my teeth. I would've finished off by piling it up on the ground, leaping in the air, and stomping on her course with all my might shouting "You aren't an expert because you're sexy!" I never heard that woman's name after that one email.

Men are Mission Focused

Part of me wants to say men are 'goal oriented' instead of mission focused. But goal oriented is used so much for job postings, so it loses its pizazz. In essence, job recruiters are asking for men, or women who are 'goal oriented' like men, to apply. Goal oriented describes a thing that men do naturally, but it's used so much that I need to divorce the process from the words.

Women can of course be mission focused as well. Yet, I don't believe it is a natural state for a woman to be in. Mission focused isn't good or bad and doesn't imply one sex is better than the other. Also, I'm no expert on all men.

From my experience, men are intensely focused on something in their lives. Each man is striving to achieve some goal. What's the difference between a man's focus and a woman's goal? Outwardly nothing, but for a man, that mission is all that he is. The mission is all consuming, be it a video game or running a business. Some women can be like this, but men in general live mission to mission.

There are of course some men who become stuck for some reason or another. Sometimes it's a mental issue, and sometimes the men are too stuck in the past to move on. For the vast majority of men, you can find out their personal missions within the first ten minutes of meeting them. Men are so consumed by their missions that they need to talk about them, in order to recruit more guys into the mission. The more like-minded men that are focused on a mission, the more the men become even more deeply connected to the mission.

The place where the focus of a man is most on display is in the military. Recently, there was a fight to allow women fight in the military. Proponents for keeping women out of the military usually said something like "Women won't have that 'split second' decision making." While I think the military is better with women, I actually do agree with the 'split second' thinking thing. It's a hard thing to explain to women.

First, I'll say, in respect to 'split second thinking,' men are better soldiers. When a man is intensely mission focused, all other matters fade away. Pain doesn't register- only the mission. Fear doesn't register- only the mission. All thoughts that aren't mission focused don't exist. A man can achieve this state by playing a fun video game. Imagine that the mission is a life or death struggle to defend the nation. A man would rush into certain death, dive onto a live grenade, or run into a combat zone to save a comrade. He would do all of these things, usually, without any thought; it would just happen. A woman is definitely capable of all of those same feats. The only difference would be that a woman would actually show courage doing those things, while a man would do it automatically.

It's important to understand what makes a man. I would say that a man's mission focus is his greatest strength and his greatest weakness. The best way to illustrate the weakness of a man's mission focus is again the military. In fact, the very thing that makes men better soldiers in the short term is what makes women better soldiers in the long term.

The problem with being mission focused is that a man will neglect or repress everything other than what's mission relevant. The problem with missions is that they eventually end. The success or failure of the mission usually produces the same results in all men; a crash. There is a moment when the body realizes that the mission is over, and then turns everything else back on all at once. Some men gravitate to a new mission to maintain their sanity. Some men try to focus on a new mission, but the reality forced upon him overwhelms the attempt at a new mission. Men aren't equipped to handle those intense emotions all at once. On the other hand, women have tools to deal with emotional trauma and usually don't bottle them all up to begin with.

Even though I've never served in the military, I understand what the veterans are suffering through right now. I didn't understand much about this process until it happened to me. My personal missions usually involved mastering a body of knowledge, or solving impossible problems. I had one particular problem that I had been considering for almost fifteen years. I was in Manhattan on E 23rd street, when I had an epiphany about that problem. When my body realized that the problem was over, my entire body was hit with intense pain. I stood on the street, squeezing my head, and shrieking in agony. I had a complete mental breakdown. It was as if the only thing keeping me sane was that one problem. That day, the only thing that allowed me to function again was a new and more powerful purpose. What was unique about that day was I recognized a pattern that I see in all men.

Once I recognized the problem, I noticed mini mental breakdowns after achieving my goals. It wasn't until years after my major mental breakdown, that I sought help. I went to group meetings and private therapy. Even after all that I'd been through; I kept telling myself that I didn't need it. After a few years of talking I got frustrated and made my new mission healing. This leads me to the point where I am now.

I don't think it was smart to drop everything and only focus on healing, but that's what I know how to do. I'm a man. I don't personally recommend the same thing for other guys. But for the veterans who are struggling, homeless, and thinking of committing suicide, healing is truly worthy mission. You really can go all in with it. There are plenty of outlets and similar people to help achieve that mission. I'm the poorest that I've ever been in my adult life, and I'm living with my mother. Yet, it was all worth it.

Another example of the dreaded end of a mission, that most guys I know face, is the moment they've finished having sex with a woman. It ruined the entire game for me when I realized that it was nothing more than the ending of a mission. Being consumed by the process of picking a girl up, I neglected the truth; I never wanted her in my bed in the first place. "How do you know you want a woman in your bed?" You may ask. I honestly don't know.

Men aren't born Sexy

This is a concept that both women and men, mostly women, don't seem to understand. Reading Chan's last section and observing her attempt to reconcile the "be yourself" theme with the possibility that a man could potentially learn something. It was incredibly entertaining and I was literally thinking "man I'd pay money for this!" And I did! But before I address the women, I'd like to clarify this statement with guys who don't get it.

I've had a number of pointless debates with men about what women are attracted to. These men are convinced that women are attracted to men in the same way men are attracted to women. Some guys point to attractive male models and say, "this is what they want." Other guys who were born very attractive, or have a giant penis, are incredibly cocky and think they are a gift to women. Then there are some guys who are stuck, always looking to the glory days of their youth "I was sexy back then." These different groups of guys to me are all the same, as they don't understand women, and they never even bothered to ask. I bothered to ask.

I previously attempted to goad the three female writers into explaining why a woman would have sex with a man that isn't physically attractive. For the most part I didn't get any response. So I'll just share my experience. There was a time when I would just randomly stop women and asked about what they were attracted to. It was an eclectic collection of answers. Here is something that I want guys to understand. When I shifted the topic and began listing famous models or showing the women pictures, they all agreed that the men were attractive but at the same time admitted that they didn't want to date the men. One woman said, "I can appreciate attractive people, but that doesn't mean that I'm attracted to them." As a man, that kind of doesn't make any sense, but how can I get similar answers from a wide variety of women?

I didn't give up there; I continued to press these random women. I would say something like "if this sexy guy approached you on the street, and asked you out, you are telling me that you wouldn't want to be with him?" I got a number of different responses, but the best was "No! I don't want a guy like that cuz I'm sexy enough for the both of us!"

Women are definitely capable of appreciating beauty, but that isn't necessarily attraction. Our sexual impulses guide each and everyone one of us. Most people don't plan on children, but children seem to always happen. When a man sees an attractive woman, he could be turned on by what she looks like. But he's not thinking, "Nice hips to waist ratio, this women is fertile for making a baby." The same this is true for a woman. While she might not be thinking "baby" that is what the 'Inner Woman' is aiming for.

Basically, a man and a woman are making baby stew and she already brought all the sexy. The question is what ingredients do you have to offer? Being attractive or having a giant penis, is a bonus but not really needed for the baby stew. It's almost better to be born unattractive just to not fall for the male sexiness trap. I've never been behind the scenes at a runway gig. You'd think that all those super models would go for their sexy male counterparts, right? Wrong! The truth is sexy women wind up with the short, old, fat, bald, wrinkly, small penis having, shortsighted guy, and they love him to death! "Why is that?" you ask, because she is sexy enough for the both of them.

For those guys who are caught up in what they used to be, I feel sorry for you. These men are usually caught up in the male beauty trap. There was a time in high school or college when all the girls loved you for some reason. You thought it was your body or your looks. Now you are stuck and always looking back. That isn't what a man is. A man is constantly growing, learning, triumphing, and challenging himself. I hope these words set you free. You were never sexy, the women were attracted to something else.

The vast majority of men become sexy over time. For some reason women don't get this. Women are like truth detectors of the here and now. But they don't really account for the future. The truth is most guys wish they could go back in time with their current knowledge about life and especially women. When I was thirty-one years old, my twenty one year old self would out be of his league compared to the older me. If women were given the choice between those two men, I doubt any would choose the younger me. My forty one year old self would equally shame my thirty one year old self, and humiliate my twenty one year old self. Most guys are a continuous work in progress; which makes the statement "be yourself" extra silly. A great response to that statement would be "I'm not finished yet!"

Ladies, a weird thing happened to me close to the end of my PUA adventures. One Friday evening, I went to a club alone, and picked up two women from a group of guys. Shorty walked over to me and Friend, and the three of us began walking down the street. I was in the middle, and the two women were holding different arms. Shorty turned back and shouted "Fuckin Fagot!" "Oh my God what happened?" said Friend. "He's standing there cryin like a little bitch." Friend looked back and started laughing "Are you serious? He's really crying?" "Yeah" she said, and then she leaned back again and shouted "Cryin like a little bitch!!" Friend started laughing hysterically, Shorty started laughing with her, but it was maniacal shout laughing "HA HA HA HA HA!!"

Part of me felt sad for the crying Arab. I wanted to turn around and hand him my card. I wanted to share with him what went wrong. I was about ten years older than him, and he reminded me of my younger self. But I didn't have the courage to turn my head. Almost all of the scuffles that I'd be in, during the last ten years, were usually because some guy got his feelings hurt.

The truth is I was terrified. There was a group of five twenty-one year old guys, about twenty-five feet behind me, and one of them was crying because I took his girl. If that was it, maybe I could've gone back and said something. But the girls were basically daring him to whip my ass. I was afraid that I was about to be jumped by five guys, and was concerned that I'd be dropkicked in the back; I've had some bad experiences. I usually walk slowly, but when I found out he was crying I walked double time. I acted like I was talking to the girls, while I turned my head as far to the left or right as I could. I don't remember what they were saying; I was focused on making sure no one was coming up from behind me. In the winter, I usually wait at least five minutes while my car warms up. I didn't that night; I just drove off. Also, I drove extra slow, driving down side roads, and constantly checking every mirror.

Here's what I'd like to know ladies. What advice would you give Mr. Crying Arab? They went to the club as a group and everyone was about twenty-one years old. I know what I would tell him, but what would a woman tell him? Some women would tell him to "Man up!" and "Stop being a pussy!" Some others may say, "She's not the right one for you" or "You can do better." I could speculate to my heart's content about what a woman would say, but it doesn't really matter. Women don't understand men, and the especially don't understand how hard it is to relate to women.

At the very least, I wanted invite Mr. Crying Arab to a meeting. I went to meetings because I was addicted to learning. Some guys go because they have a successful career and are confused why they are alone. A few guys show up in order to get a specific girl; I don't think those guys fare well in the group. But the vast majority of guys to go to meetings are guys like Mr. Crying Arab. These guys suffer some inexplicable heartbreak, and they are lost and confused. These guys openly share their past shame in the meetings like an AA group session. Ladies, you have no idea how often you all totally destroy a guy for not "being" what you wanted him to be at that one moment.

The guys who had their hearts smashed and were confused about it are usually highly motivated. I've heard countless stories of triumph from these guys. After a few years in the community, they 'bump' into the woman that broke their hearts. Those women invariably like the new man and want to get back with him. I need to reiterate that men aren't born sexy, but they can get there over time.

The Origin of "Women's Words" or Ending my PUA Mission

Two days after I met Mr. Crying Arab, I met a gorgeous woman and her two friends. We went to a restaurant and shared a meal. It was my custom to share the last weird interaction that I had with a woman. Having a guy cry after I took his girl qualified as weird. A funny thing happen after sharing what just recently happened, the women rejected the story. All three leaned back in their seats and made a disgusted face. They all instantly agreed that I was full of myself.

I was perplexed at the response, given that I've relayed crazier stories to other women in the past. I was so used to women discussing the situation that I was taken aback when the women uniformly rejected the story. They sensed my confusion and began interpreting my expressions. After a few exchanges with each other, they concluded that I made the entire story up in order to impress them.

No one knows when they will have an epiphany that will change the direction of their lives. There I was in the midst of a date, and it all just came together for me. The first thing that I understood was what made all my other stories effective; women's words. That story was devoid of them because there was very little verbal communication in the club. I knew if one of the girls were there to tell these women what happened, they would believe and accept her words. I sat and puzzled and what the girls could've possibly said differently. Women's words, I concluded, are rationalizations of thoughts and actions women make while in the 'Woman's State.'

As not to get to far ahead of myself, I realized at that moment that my 'mission' was over. I will talk more about that later. But I knew because I've experienced the ending of a number of missions. The endings of missions are dramatic and often overwhelming. After that moment, I still attempted to date women, but I could never follow through. I would give up at some point and/or suffer a severe panic attack.

Although I told the women that I was seeing that I didn't want any more sex, Dulce continued to show up. She would meet up with me once per month for years after that. We would have dinner or get a drink, and hang out for the day. In the evening, she would just get in my bed naked and wait. It was good that she didn't touch me, as usually I was having a panic attack because she was too close to me. Most of the time, I would wake up in the middle of the night and realize I had a sexy woman in my bed and we'd have sex. Sometimes I remained terrified. Dulce is a psychologist, and I figured she had some secret she knew about me, so I asked her about it. She said "Danny you're like a normal guy but just extreme. I want to be with you, but I think you just need space sometimes." I thought she would say something technical; I was wrong.

After the date with the three women, I finally recognized that I needed help rather than a new mission. I started going to group therapy and personal therapy. They were helpful for a few years until I took healing to the next level and made that my mission. I guess I am extreme sometimes, but I have no regrets.

I DON'T UNDERSTAND WOMEN!

By now, you may be thinking that I have a good understanding about women. Or at least, I should think I have a good understanding of women. My previous statement about not understanding women still stands. I had a full expectation of the female writers to ignore the very thing that I don't understand, and declare me clueless. Women, all of them, completely minimalize men to the point where they believe that men have no effect on them.

The first time I wrote, in this book, that I didn't understand women, I mentioned Perfecta. The underwear thing didn't bother me, what bothered me was that she really believed that I had absolutely nothing to do with us meeting. David Deangelo says that, "seduction is mutual." I believe this. In fact, I lose interest in a woman if it's just me trying to make the relationship work. But how could I have nothing to do with us meeting? At least she could say I had a nice smile or maybe she liked my shoes. But nothing? I understand that underwear makes you feel sexy, but that had more power than anything else that I did? I admitted being a player; I admitted to doing routines on her, did that really have no effect?

It wasn't a surprise to me that all the female writers also accepted the premise that I had nothing to do with it. They all believed that Perfecta was secretly in control, and that I just didn't get it. I've experienced women 'coming to their senses' quite often. It's just them leaving the 'Woman's State'. When she was confused about what was happening, I think she was genuinely confused about why she was trying so hard to set up a date with me. In the end, she said, "it was too much" for her, I believe that too. I took her to emotional levels that she wasn't used to, and asked her to talk about it with me. How can these writers knowingly write for a guy, who admits to being a player, and declare that I had nothing to do with that situation?

How can those three women I shared a meal with, talk themselves into believing that I made up making a guy cry? The girl I was interested in was an 8 on a really bad day. I was sitting there with women that I just met, was it really that impossible? I don't understand how that could be useful to the species that women universally discount so many things about a man.

While looking for the old seduction forum, which I found at archives.fastseduction.com/, I noticed that PUA's are now coming out of the shadows. They are openly promoting their faces and real names. I guess they're keeping the monikers for marketing purposes. I think the guys in the community are finally realizing that woman go much further than not caring, they rub it out of their consciousness. All three writers think the community is a waste and futile.

It's a weird dynamic, being completely honest with a woman. If you tell her everything, somehow that magically makes it all right. I've told women, in the past, that I'm going to use routines on them to seduce them. I would go step by step of what I planned and say what will happen; and it did!

I don't understand how women can complain about a double standard, when there actually is no standard for women. For example, I have no idea how many children my father has. Last I heard it was thirteen. He may have more on the way. Some of my brothers and sister were born only a few days apart. What has to go through a woman's mind to find such a guy acceptable? It's like, you know he's got other women, and you know he has kids and doesn't take care of them, but somehow it's ok because you know. I've admitted some ridiculous things to women, but it's ok because I told them.

Is it because women secretly want men like my father? Is this why women universally diminish and delete things about men from their consciousness? If that's true, then you can't complain about guys like my father, me, or any guy for that matter. Also, you can't complain that a guy won't instantly do the same for a woman. Its mind boggling to think this is a universal thing.

How is it that women can date and marry rappers that make misogynistic songs? "Those songs aren't about me," you say. They are precisely about you!! What magic goes through your mind to make it all just evaporate? I would have a hard time dating or marrying a woman who made similar songs about men. It doesn't make sense!

About nine months after I met Mr. Crying Arab, I was in Manhattan, walking to a Salsa party. I was completely done with 'the game' and just focused and dancing and healing. I heard someone shout "Hey! Mr. Salsa man!" I looked around, and I saw Shorty in the backseat of a car. She was on a double date with a different girl this time. We forgot each other's names, but it was nice to see her. We exchanged numbers and became good friends.

My time with Shorty was always random. We went out almost every evening and partied for almost a year and a half. It was nice to just have a female friend. We never had sex. One evening, I decided to ask her about her description of the night we met. I asked only for posterity. I wanted to know what words I could've used to get those three women to accept the story. Basically, all she said was that she did everything. We argued back and forth for a while. I informed her that she knew how honest I was, that I've been involved with the seduction community, she went to the club with someone, and I went alone and left with her. She interrupted my reasoning and said something I wasn't surprised at, but will never forget.

"Listen mister! I saw you! I wanted to dance with you! I went over to you! It doesn't matter who I was with. That guy was lame! He thought he could take me to a club, grind on me, and get some. I put a quash on that! And you are supposed to be some big time pickup artist! You were just standing there like a loser! Where was all the game you were supposed to have? You spent all that money learning nuffin! You were just as lame as the other guy. I left with you that night because I wanted to! (She was jamming her index finger into my chest at this point.) I made that loser cry when I left his lame ass at the club! I did that! If you want to learn how to get a woman, you should just pay me and I'll learn you all you need to know!! End of discussion!"

I bet these words are the most palatable to women reading this regarding Mr. Crying Arab. The obvious thing in her statement is a clear understanding that I was just a passenger along for the ride in her reality. I tried to tell her my side of what happened, but she actively fought against hearing it. I don't understand why it's so vitally important that I be a nonfactor in this situation. How can that be at all helpful?

The next most obvious thing about her statement is the time distortion. We were together at that club for about three and a half hours. Most of that time, she was clearly in a 'Woman's State', and time was distorted. Pointing out the three and a half hours to her was what actually set her off. No. I really don't understand. It doesn't make any sense. How could I have nothing to do with it? At least she could say I was wearing nice shoes that day. Nothing? How is it useful to believe this?

Ladies, do you know what a man would ask? They would ask, "How did it all happen? And please go step by step." I feel inclined to oblige them.

THE EDUCATION OF MR. CRYING ARAB

Hello Mr. Crying Arab. Apart from inviting you to some meetings, there were a few things I wish I had the courage to share with you that night many years ago. I'm certain, by now, a good guy like you has been scooped up by a woman. You're probably married with a child by now. Whether or not that is the case, what I intend to share with you will likely be particularly instructive. Unlike any other part of this book, this is just for you- not women. Women will likely be offended, because they don't think the way we do. Also, considering most of that night happened using non-verbal communication, most of what I will say can immediately become applicable to your own life.

I remember that night. It was Friday, and on Friday's I would go to the You Should Be Dancing Studio for Salsa lessons with Frankie Martinez. That Friday, they had a dance party after class. Salsa parties are always fully of gorgeous women, they were mostly off limits for me. I danced to remind myself that I was alive. If I didn't dance, I could go the entire day without feeling a single emotion. In the Salsa community, all the girls literally knew each other. Unless I was sure of a discreet relationship, the women were off limits. Some people in the community still wonder if I'm gay considering I never responded to overt flirting.

I left the Salsa party at around 12 am. I was pretty wound up, since there were some sexy women flirting with me hard that night. I drove around a bit looking for a place to go for the night. Since it was a few days before New Year's Eve, the places that I wanted to go were closed for private parties. I drove past the club, Latin Quarters, and noticed a small line outside. The line told me that there was no private party and also that it might be ok to go in that night.

Honestly, I hate going to clubs unless there is no other choice. Tuesday and Wednesday nights are usually club nights for me. I would never step foot in any club, let alone Latin Quarters on a Friday night. The obvious problem with a club for me is that it's too loud. Not being able to verbally communicate takes away my best asset. Second, clubs on the weekends are always crowded. You're a little bit taller than me. But being 5'7", I can barely see above the crowds.

The biggest problem I have with a club on the weekend is that guys often fight on the weekends. These poor guys worked hard for weeks, bought a new expensive outfit, spent hundreds of dollars on drinks, came with their ten friends, and become incredibly frustrated when girls don't give them the time of day. If one fight breaks out, then it spreads. It's like a contagion. Since I'm usually alone, and there is no way to verbally diffuse a fight, I don't like the situation.

It wasn't a normal Friday night. The weekend crowd, I surmised, are all at private parties. Usually, the line to get into Latin Quarters would wrap around the block. If it weren't a few days before New Year's Day, I would have never gone to that club that night. It was even more encouraging that I found a parking space after a short drive.

It's also important to note that I tried to keep myself to a budget. Usually, I try to limit my spending in a club or a bar to $50. This is another reason why I'd usually avoid clubs on the weekend. After I paid to get in and checked my coat, I only had $25 left to spend. Although I was making about $8k per month, at the time, if I didn't budget myself I'd go broke going out every night.

Being short, alone, unwilling to spend money, having difficulty communicating, and concerned about fights are just the beginning of my problems with night clubs. The issue of the approach at a night club poses a specific challenge, considering you can't just ask the questions that you need to ask. Women set up a circle of defense and it seems easy enough to break through that circle. There is an axiom, that the guys in the community all agree, "Approach the group with the same or greater energy that they have." If there is a rule, I usually break it, just to see what would happen. Although, it is optimal to approach the group with the same amount of energy, I could also have the group follow my lead. I personally get bored by always doing the same thing.

The real issue with the circle of defense is that far too often the one I want isn't available. I feel like such a tool when that happens. It's like a trap they set. The hottest one isn't single, but when you talk to her she'll point to all the ones that are available. If I wanted to pick the other women, I would've approached them! There is always one woman, who is completely shameless and will take her shot at me knowing that the hot one is shutting me down. She'd break the circle and dare me to dance with her.

That scenario frustrates me to no end. The reason it's so frustrating is because women always claim that they are out "just having fun." But it's so obvious that they are coordinating for maximum effect. Mystery says, "Avoid the dance floor like the plague, unless you're Fred Astaire." I'm not one to always follow the rules, and I liked dancing so I tested that as well. A couple of times, I went to the center of the circle and just started dancing. It was my hope that I would just have fun and dance with everyone. Both times, the women stopped dancing and one woman came forward and said, "Pick one." Both times, I didn't pick anyone! I was upset, because women always claim that they're just "having fun." The women go to a club to meet a guy, and they have their own strategies to get him. It's just that on the surface, they act like something else is happening.

That isn't the last of the problems concerning clubs. If I don't give up, I will eventually find an attractive woman who is available. One of two things usually will happen. The first is I get her phone number. By the time we met Mr. Crying Arab, I'd lost all interest in phone numbers. I'd usually meet a woman on the street or in a bar. I won't even hint at a phone number unless I was sure that we had a solid connection <u>and</u> we already set up a date to meet. If she wasn't on the calendar, she'd have to be an incredibly memorable person. Why is this? Women will give you their number if you ask nicely. On any given night I could get at least five phone numbers. If a woman gives me her number, and she's not an amazing person, or we don't have a date, then that number would get lost in my phone; no matter how hot she is.

I've tried many things to remember the women. I've used the notes, pieces of paper, everything. If I have a hard time remembering who I'm supposed to call, even if I do get the right person, I'd be trying to remind myself who she was. I knew a guy who had a spreadsheet, with notes about where they met, what she looked like, and detailed notes about each contact. It was like he was a telemarketer and he used the phone numbers as leads. It's not hard to get thirty to fifty numbers per week, but I lose interest when it seems like a job. Even with being strict about taking a woman's number, I still had to spend time, every few weeks deleting contacts that I don't remember.

Getting a phone number in a club is worse than any place else. It's dark, loud, and women give out their number like a religious pamphlet. I hate having to try and figure out who I'm talking to when I'm calling, but it's even more annoying when the girl is trying to figure out who you are at the same time. At night clubs, I don't bother with phone numbers.

The other possibility, if I meet someone attractive and available, is that I become a part of the group. It seems nice that I found someone, and we clearly like each other. When her group of girlfriends rotates around the club, she would hold my hand and lead me from place to place. That usually leads to a phone number and a kiss on the cheek or to a late night meal with the whole group. After the meal, I'm likely just getting her phone number. I wasn't interested in joining anyone's group. I wouldn't be alone otherwise.

Thus, I developed my own strategy to separate a woman from her group and take her home that night with me. It involved standing and waiting for an opportunity. The only issue is where would the most optimal place for me to wait? Mystery prefers to hang out by the bar. That's too difficult for me. First, I was on a strict budget. Second, I'm too short to be hanging by the bar. The bar area is appealing since it's usually quietest place in a club. But a bar in a NYC club would have three to five rows of people waiting in line for a drink. Camping out by the bar, at a club, would be perfect if I were over six feet tall. I'm not so I avoid the bar. I choose a spot by the wall close to the dance floor.

Once I find a good place, I would make my pose. I stood with my feet a little bit past my shoulder level- like I'm comfortably taking up space. I'd stick my chest out and put one thumb in my back pocket. A hand in the front pocket, full or partial, seems too timid. I usually bought a Corona, as they are almost like drinking water. I don't want to be drunk. Also, Corona's have long spouts. My other hand would hold the Corona, but I held the beer at my side. Other beers slip out of my hand too easily if I keep the beer to the side. The easiest position to hold a drink is in front of my chest. But that would look like I'm shielding myself from something.

Honestly, it's hard to tell how effective the pose is. I understand why I would want to do it, but it's difficult to know for sure how good it is. But the face I used is what put it all together. In his DVD series "Double your Dating," David Deangelo recounts the story of a peg legged Count in Europe; during the time when royalty had political power. This Count shared in his memoir the secret to his ability to get women at dance parties, while only having one leg. I don't know why that face is so effective, but apparently guys have been doing it for hundreds of years to great success.

To do the face, you pucker your lips and stick them out, like you are going to kiss someone. You raise your eyebrows like you're surprised about something. Then you squint your eyes together like you are straining to read something. Doing the face always made me laugh. It's such a stupid face, but it's incredibly effective for some reason. I would've never thought to do the face, unless someone else told me to do it.

A few months ago, when I first started writing this book, while watching the show Tosh.0, I saw the face again. Tosh was highlighting the meme, called the duck face, ridiculing the dearth of female selfies posing with the duck face. "That's the face!" I said to myself. It's amazing to me that guys have been doing this face for hundreds of years, and it means something to women. A few weeks ago, my twelve year old niece was sitting next to me on the couch, and I hear a click from her phone. I saw her doing the duck face from the corner of my eye. After I wrestled the phone from her, I begged her to explain why she made that face while taking a picture, and she said, "I don't know. I was just fooling around with my phone."

The duck face itself highlights the challenge in interacting with women. It's simple enough to do the face, and you can go out right now and do it. The face means something to her 'Inner Woman'. Somehow the face means "approach this man." Sometimes women would just walk up to me and kiss me. It's crazy. But the problem comes when women are consciously aware that you are purposefully making the face. If a woman reads these pages she will see you and know what you are trying to do. Also, if the woman didn't read this book, and too many guys at a venue are doing the same face, then she will become consciously aware as well.

In any case, by about 12:30 am, I found a good spot, doing my pose, and the duck face. I wasn't scanning the crowds. I would just stare off into general areas. Sometimes when the DJ or a song would tell the single ladies to raise their hands I'd look around. If I saw anyone I liked, I'd make a move. I couldn't depend on that since those moments don't happen often enough and I'm short so I can only look at the people right in front of me.

The point of finding a good position, the pose, and the face was to take advantage of the rotations that the women all do. They say that they are just having fun, but their actions tell a different story. They rotate themselves around clubs and bars for maximum exposure to every guy. They hold hands and travel through the venue in search of a potential mate. Each girl has veto power on where to position themselves. One girl decides to move and another girl can decide to stop. It was my intention that I'd be a reason for a group to stop.

Sometimes women don't stop, but are interested. They would either kiss me on the lips or pinch me on the butt. Then they would chuckle as they continue along their trek through the venue. I make it clear to them that I'm not going to leave that spot. I had no intentions of following any more groups around the club. If a group does decide to stop, the one who's interested would usually make obvious signals. This way, I get to choose whether or not I'm interested. If I don't show any interest, they are free to get back to their rotation.

That evening, I wasn't in my position long when a rotation of a group in front of me, revealed your group. I saw Shorty, and thought to myself "I'm in the mood for Indian." I know now that she's Italian. I was just looking in a general direction, but she initiated eye contact while she was dancing. "I got her!" I said to myself.

Many years ago, when I first started out, the seduction community was a fascinating curiosity to me. I loved studying and learning, and it was just a unique topic that I thought could be useful. When I stumbled upon the seduction forum, it was like I found the holy grail of all seduction training, and it was all free! The community has a self-grading system. The lowest level is AFC, or average frustrated chump. The forum was open to anyone, but they had one rule; do the "Read First" section before posting. If you post a question already answered by the Read First section, you would at least be flamed.

I liked studying so I didn't mind doing that section. It was an immense amount of information and it took a few weeks for me to get through it all. Some of the things I learned from courses that I had purchased, but a lot was new information. One post blew my mind. I believe it was called "Deer caught in headlights." I'm not sure if that was the name, but it's irrelevant. The post described how women would have that look, especially if you did something right. I believe the poster stated something like "it's the moment when you know a woman throws all logic out the window." For me, I like to simply say that it's an indicator of a woman being in the 'Woman's State'.

The poster then went on to say, "if you've never experienced the 'deer in the headlights' look then you'd have to go out and experience it." He suggested that I go to the nearest mall and basically have staring contests with women as they walked by. It seemed like a stupid suggestion, but I was following the plan, so I decided to go with it. There were not really any malls in NYC at that time. The only one I knew of was Kings Plaza in Brooklyn. I had to take two buses just to get there; I never took the bus.

Once there, I took a seat on a bench, and attempted to make eye contact with every woman that walked by. I was totally floored with what happened next. One woman after the next gave me the blank stare of a deer caught in headlights. It was like I had a 'Matrix' moment. It felt like being in a horror movie. Women would stare at me with a weird face, while continuing to walk and talk to whomever they were with. Then as they walked pass me, they would go back to normal. For a few weeks after that, I would have staring contests with random women on public transit. I'm always amazed how women are able to last so long without blinking.

Usually, I get that face from a woman when we're on a date. I'm always caught off guard when it happens. Purposefully not blinking is tough to do. I've tried to ask women what they were thinking after the staring contest was over, but they would always deny that it ever happened. I don't bother asking why anymore. When I see that face, I only have one thought; win! I'm not sure if the post finished with this, but I'm going to finish with this statement. "If you win the staring contest with a woman, she will purr like a kitten." What's also interesting is that she usually lets you win.

So I locked eyes with Shorty and thought to myself "I got her!" I instantly recognized that familiar face, and the only thing I had on my mind was winning. We were seven to ten feet apart and I made up my mind to make my move after I win the staring contest. That's when I noticed that your entire group was staring at the both of us, from the corner of my eyes. Shorty kept inching towards me while dancing, and that's when you stepped in. It was comical watching you chase her around the dance floor, while she maintained her focus on me. I wasn't sure you guys were together until you physically grabbed her and blocked her vision of me. You were much taller than her, but her head popped up above your left shoulder. She reinitiated eye contact with her head bobbing to the music. When I saw this, I became extra cautious, because I knew that the entire situation wasn't about me.

The way that I'm describing what happened, you'd think I'd say, "I'm so sexy that she couldn't resist." But I've seen similar enough scenarios to know that it wasn't about me. Knowing this, I became defensive as not to be tooled by a woman in her complicated schemes. Women often lash out in this manner when something is wrong. For some reason, she simply can't tell you what's wrong. You have to figure it out. If you don't figure it out, then it's your fault.

Your aggressive handling of her, and her acceptance of it made me change my calculus on the situation. I now had three goals, diffuse any potential physical confrontation, isolate her from the group, and then figure out the situation. I needed to deflect any blame of aggression in order to diffuse the potential fight. So I decided to inch my way closer to your group.

Even though you were attempting to get her undivided attention, she would always return to looking at me. When I was sure that no one in your group was looking at me, I would blink a few times and take a few tiny steps forward. You chasing Shorty around was a perfect distraction for me. I admit that I was worried when a guy passing by saw your fumbling attempts with Shorty and moved in right away. I was mad at myself for being overly cautious, but used that distraction to take a solid leap forward. I was relieved when Shorty broke away from that guy and you and went back to focusing on me. I was extra concerned because you were dancing aggressively and angrily. Then another guy passing by, seeing you chase Shorty around, made his move.

After that last distraction, I leapt forward and made my final blinks. I was only a few inches away from your circle. Shorty broke away from the second guy and you as well, and focused on me again. Clearly, from the remarks she told me over a year later, she didn't realize that I had moved. At this point she was only about two steps away from me. We locked eyes again. She was dancing and I was doing my pose. When she began dancing her way towards me I wondered if she'd taken any blinks at all. Her mouth was wide open, as she danced her way towards me. It felt as if she wanted to bite me. When she got close enough, she turned around, bent over, and was preparing to grind on me right in front of your face. I knew again that the situation had nothing to do with me.

If you ask anyone in the PUA community, who has even a modicum of skill, what's the easiest set of people to approach, they will all say, hands down, groups with guys in it!! The community calls it Amogging, or routines for the Alpha Male of the Group. Newbies usually get their asses handed to them by misunderstanding why mixed sets are so easy. I usually err on the side of caution, and I'm extra polite when talking to a man.

Let me explain why it's easier to talk to a group of people, with men in it. First, all guys feel anxiety when talking to a woman. There is zero anxiety talking to another man. Second, guys don't understand that women have an expectation of overprotection in those types of social settings. A woman is used to her grizzly bear cock blocking friend protecting her from guys trying to approach her. Women incorrectly assume that guys understand that this is what she expects, and guys have no clue.

When I see a girl I want, and she's with one or more guys, I simply walk over to the guy and I'm super polite. Sometimes she won't be able to hear me, so I make sure that I act out what I'm saying with my body. I say something like "Is that your girl? Because she's beautiful." A few guys say something like "Get the fuck out of here!" I don't mind that. All the women watching just saw me walk up to one or more guys to talk to a woman. That raises my status a little. The reality is I was SUPER nice.

Many guys will admit that that he is with the woman. These guys are polite back to me as well. They appreciate that I came and asked permission before doing anything else. It's frustrating to a guy when you go out with your girl and another guy hits on her right in your face. It's like a dare to fight. Sometimes these guys would buy me a drink out of appreciation, but mostly I would just thank them and be on my way.

Then there are the vast majority of mixed sets of people. Guys show up at a venue with the woman he wants. By asking the guy if that one woman is his girl puts him on the spot. They vehemently deny any relationship, and when they do I ask, "Do you mind if I talk to her?" They have to say no, and I make my move. The women are always surprised by the lack of defense.

Then there are some idiots who tell me that I should make my move on the woman, and they live together or they are married. The woman is just as shocked as usual, except they ask me what we were talking about. After I tell her the exchange she would say something like "I can't believe my husband/boyfriend." Then when I look back at them they are giving me two thumbs up and waving me on, like it's a big joke played on his woman. If I make out with her or hook up with her later, it's his fault. I mean, I asked and he said yes.

Let's go back to our meeting at Latin Quarters. I was a few feet in front of you, and I saw the anger and disappointment on your face as

Shorty began to bend down in front of me. The club was loud, so there was no way to talk to you directly from there. So I used body language. As soon as her butt touched my crotch, I raised both hands in the air, I pointed at her, then I pointed at you, then I pointed at myself and waved my hands 'no' in the air.

I don't know if you noticed that Shorty hadn't even started dancing yet. She was bent over looking at me communicating with you. When I was done, she turned her head to see your response. You, and your four friends, all waved your hands 'No' in the air, and waved me on. You and your friends officially gave me permission to be with Shorty. I don't know if you were paying attention, but Shorty gave you a disgusted face, as if she was saying, "Oh no he didn't!"

She shrugged her shoulders in a 'fuck it' motion and commenced grinding on me. I took my left hand and placed it on her waist, and slowly began dancing backwards towards the wall. Once at the wall, I achieved the most optimal positioning, or I "locked her in."

You've got to understand why I moved away from you. It was an automatic reaction. Usually, when a girl takes a chance and leaves her circle of defense, I move her away from the group immediately. It's more palatable the instant that she decided to leave the group. I'm not hauling the woman far away. She's usually close enough for her friends to see that she's safe, and far enough that the decision to go back to the group is a significant choice.

Locking in takes many forms. Using props to lock in is the easiest to understand. For example, the girl is faced with a choice when her friends decide that it's time to rotate. If she leaves, there will be somewhat of a scene with a girl begging me to follow her and her friends dragging her away. Some other girls may see that, realize that I'm not moving from that spot, and take a chance with me. If she decides to stay, her friends 'lock her in' by giving her a cell phone or a handbag to watch. This way, the woman is still connected to the group, even if they aren't right next to her. When the friends come back to see the woman safe and sound, they usually ask for their props back. Thus freeing me to ask if it's ok to leave.

Positional locking in is somewhat different. First let's discuss a neutral position. A neutral position is you talking or dancing with a girl on the open floor. Neither of your backs is against any walls. I would only risk such a position with a woman I already know, or if the venue is too crowded for any other position. The problem with this type of position, you should be familiar with, is that you could be chasing the woman around. If you actually chase her, she could become bored of you chasing her and just start dancing with someone else. There are ways to make the neutral position effective, but in the beginning it's best to not risk it.

The worst positioning is the woman's back against the wall and you facing her. This could happen anywhere, while you are talking or dancing. The best I can say as to why this is position is bad, is that it takes away the choice away from the woman. When I learned about positioning, and I saw a man and a woman in a bad position, I would ask a random woman to talk about the situation. One hundred percent of the time, the women would say something like "He's really into her, but she's not into him." They would say all of this without knowing the relationship of the two people. Once I was at a house party, I saw a man talking to a woman, and she was trapped in a corner. I was talking with a group of girls and I interrupted the fun conversation they were having. I asked them, "What do you ladies think of that guy over there?" Their mood instantly changed and they all agreed that he was a "creep." All of the women at that house party hated that poor guy's guts before anyone even met him. Who knows what the guy and girl were talking about?

The most optimal position is my back against a wall and the woman talking or dancing with me. To the woman, she's free to go whenever she wants to, but she usually decides to stay. To the women watching, they see a woman all over me, and that is more attractive than me chasing her or pinning her against the wall.

This is why I'm always cognizant of my positioning. If a woman positions herself against a wall I give her a way to escape if she wants. Sometimes I'd just talk to her sideways until she moves. I'm not going to engage a woman against a wall, unless she explicitly asks me to.

Another excellent reason to lock in with a woman is she and all her friends know where you'll be. You could have a similar positioning if you get bottle service. But that's not necessary. If a woman, or a group of women, knows that I'm going to be at a certain spot, it frees her up to go to the bathroom, get a drink, or smoke a cigarette. The last thing a woman wants to do is to spend an hour looking for her friends in a crowded and dark club. This is why they go to the bathroom together, get drinks together, and go for smokes together. If I claim a spot, they can split up if they want. That happened with Shorty and Friend that night.

When I reached the wall, and was dancing with Shorty, I noticed that your circle was destroyed. I watched you and your friends walk closer to where I was standing. You were all standing in a semi-circle. I remember you standing, with your arms crossed, and an angry look on your face. I remember that you had a friend on the either side of you looking and pointing at us, saying something to you. I remember you shaking your head yes with a scowl on your face. At this point, I was seriously concerned. I would be hard pressed to find another club in NYC that had as many shootings, stabbings, and hospitalizations than Latin Quarters. I had to find out the situation, and that's when I said my first words to Shorty.

I stood her up straight, pulled her close to me, and said, "How do you know this guy?" She twisted her body, made a cup with her hand so I could hear her, and said, "I met that guy on the street the other day, and this is the first time we're meeting up." "Checkmate!" I thought to myself. I was already thinking of secondary locations. Latin Quarters has a bar just above it, not connected to the club. That would've been my first choice. But Shorty wasn't finished. She leaned back again and said,

"Those guys are his friends." She then waved the other girl in your group over to us. When she came over Shorty said, "This is my friend Friend. She's visiting me from college until New Year's."

"Eject!" I shouted in my mind. Sets of two girls are my kryptonite. Being solo, I've never had any success with two close friends. They are impossible to separate, and you have to entertain them both. If you just pick one, you will get an instant jealously cock block. To make matters worse, Friend was visiting Shorty; meaning she can't leave with me. That added to the already impossible circumstance of a set of two women. In addition, you were standing there mean-mugging me, with your arms crossed, and your friends egging you on. I started scanning the area for a new spot to camp out at. That's when I noticed Friend standing next to us.

Friend was standing with her arms crossed, pouting, and looking at Shorty. "I just took the life of their social circle." I thought. Friend seemed uncomfortable, but she was literally waiting for Shorty to do something about it. Also, Friend was slightly more attractive than Shorty. This is when I hatched the idea that I could finally catch that white whale of separating two friends. A friend visiting from out of town could certainly be separated from a group of two. I had to figure out how to switch to Friend, and somehow give Shorty back to you. I actually was a little greedy with my planning. Since I knew that I might have to entertain them both, I planned to have Friend that night, and add Shorty to the rotation after New Year's Eve. I knew what a White Whale meant. There was no way I'd put too much effort into making it happen. I gave myself until the end of the song to figure it out. If I couldn't devise a workable plan, then I'd eject.

While I was standing there, with Shorty grinding on me and Friend pouting at Shorty, your friend Douchebag came over to us from the right. I knew that he was a total douche as soon as I saw him. It wasn't the clothes, as they were typical club wear. It wasn't his spiked hair. If I could spike my hair like that, I would. He was wearing dark sunglasses in an already dark nightclub. That is a clear sign of douche-baggery. But if you have the slightest doubt of his douchery, please let me explain.

Douchebag leaned against the wall, only a few inches from me, and then he pulled Friend towards him. She started dancing with him. I was upset that he took Friend away before I could figure out how to attempt a switch. But I was extra livid when I notice him leaning against the wall in the same aloof manner that I was. He was holding his beer in my exact same position, and he was even mimicking the duck face!! I was concerned that Douchebag sensed how upset you were, and decided to fuck with me. All I could think was "EJECT! EJECT!! EJECT!!!"

At that time I was considering two possible exits. The first would be a polite "I have to go to the bathroom." Then never return. The other would be a shove and saying something mean. The latter option seems harsh, but sometimes you need to be mean to get the point across that it's over. The situation was completely over for me. I had to look for other opportunities and be free from any distractions. Then a miracle happened, Shorty and Friend switched!

"Hallelujah! Hallelujah! Hallelujah! Hallelujah!" Only Handel's Messiah can truly describe the joy that I experienced. The switch breathed life back into my plan. In fact, without Douchebag, I would've had no idea how to proceed. As soon as the switch happened, Douchebag showed his douchey colors. He lifted his hand way up in the air, to slap me five. He had a douche-like grin on his face as he bobbed his head 'yes' to the music. It was as if he was saying, "This is how we do it son!" Both the girls looked back at the two of us, and I felt ashamed that his hand was dangling in the air like that. I begrudgingly gave him five, as without him I'd be totally lost.

Douchebag solved two problems for me. First he made the switch possible. The second was far more important. Now he was dancing with Shorty. There was no longer any need to be concerned about my physical safety. Mr. Crying Arab, for future reference, do not go to social events with Douchebag. Clearly, he would bang your girl and tell you that it was your fault. Also, he was quick to ditch you and your other friends to become my fan boy. I'm sure that if I asked, he would've dropped you guys in a heartbeat to leave the club with me. Having a guy like that around reflects poorly on you.

I could tell that neither of the women wanted to dance with Douchebag, and they switched between us often. So I used that to my advantage. Once, right after a switch, I was dancing with Friend, so I started inching my way to the left. After a while, switching between us comfortably became a problem. For the rest of the evening, the women took turns dancing with me, going to the restroom, getting drinks, and talking to you. Eventually, I spent most of my time only with Friend.

It was close to four o'clock in the morning. Most of the people had already gone home, the lights were turned up, and they announced last call at the bar. I had achieved what I planned, I was dancing with Friend alone and you, your friends, and Shorty were about ten feet away. I usually don't stay that late at a club; I would normally have found someone and left by then. Because I had two attractive women grinding on me for over three hours, I had a mild case of blue balls. I wasn't sure if things were alright between you and Shorty, but I had to take my chance. Friend was already pressed up against me when I told her "Hey. Let's get out of here." She pulled away, shook her head yes, put her index finger up, and mouthed, "Ok, give me one second."

As she trekked over to where you were, to talk to Shorty, I was praying that Shorty would allow her to leave with me. I was planning to have Shorty call her cell using my phone, so she could feel safe about letting her friend leave, and also so I could call her later. Friend said something into Shorty's ear, and Shorty said, "Oh!" Then she downed the drink that she'd been nursing for a while. She grabbed Friend by the arm and hustled over to where I was standing. I hadn't noticed, but she left her heels and her handbag behind me. She put her handbag under one arm, picked up her high heel shoes, and shoved me in the back, while still holding Friend's arm. "Let's go!" She shouted.

My heart sank when I heard that. I was actually physically frustrated, as my balls felt like they were screaming at me. She dragged us both to the coat check line. It was lame that you and your four friends followed us. But when you pulled Shorty away I was so happy. I was really rooting for you. I think Friend was rooting for you as well. Neither of us turned back to see what was happening with you and Shorty. We simply held hands and continued waiting in line for our coats. When we got our coats, we quietly walked by you and went up the stairs.

Outside we walked and talked slowly. If you could've just held it down Mr. Crying Arab, everything would've been perfect. Friend and I waited halfway up the block for you guys to figure out what was happening between you. I don't know if you noticed that both Shorty and Friend were wearing spring jackets and almost nothing else. I unzipped my coat and embraced Friend; she was shivering. I caressed her and ran my hands across her back to keep her warm. I could've kissed her there, but I prefer to do those types of things in private. Instead, I was lightly brushing my lips across her neck when Shorty finally reached us and shouted, "Fuckin Fagot!"

The first few minutes of our car ride, the two women laughed hysterically at the thought of you crying. They were both drunk with their own feminine powers. Once that subsided, Shorty spent about twenty minutes bemoaning how you messed up by taking her to the club. She mentioned bringing sand to the beach at one point. She complained that you hoped to get in bed with her straight from the club. At one point, she exclaimed that she already had a man, and that he takes care of her when she needs him. She was talking to herself. She was the only one of us talking. At the end of her rant, she positioned herself in the backseat so that our eyes would meet in the rearview mirror, and said "I know you wouldn't take a girl to a club on the first date; right?"

I replied with political word salad. I didn't want to be associated with whatever she was thinking. Also, I didn't like going to clubs to begin with, so a club on the first date would be out of the question. I couldn't really engage her with what I was really thinking, as I tend to be long winded and technical sometimes. In case you haven't figured it out yet, Shorty really liked you a lot.

Her feelings for you were as obvious to me as how the two of you had arrived at that point. First, she was clearly upset that things didn't work out. If she weren't, she wouldn't have been talking about it for so long. It's like she had to get it out of her system. I was aware of what was happening and just allowed her to vent. What about her boyfriend? I happened to meet him the next day; the two of you were polar opposites. He was a prototypical bad boy. Although Shorty likes to act like she loves partying, she really wanted a nice guy like you, someone who she could introduce to her traditional, immigrant, Italian parents. Dude, she was totally going to switch you for him! It may look like she wasn't wearing anything that night, but I've seen her get ready to go out. If I rush her, it will take three hours for her to get ready. She was dressed up for you. Although for a nice guy like you, she probably would've made you wait a long time for sex.

No one ever told me how you guys met, or how you decided to meet up. But given the information that I had, it's easy to piece together. You met a girl on the street and you were infatuated with her. You exchange numbers and begin talking on the phone. You spend hours getting to know each other, and you just know that she's the one. You ask her to go out on a date with you. She says that she wants to, but her friend is visiting her from college. You could wait a week for the friend to leave, but you suggest a double date, and Shorty agrees. She sends you a picture of her friend and you are your friends realize that Friend is sexy. I think it may have been more of a nosebleed moment, because I'm certain Shorty would've sent you a link to Friend's photo shoot. When your friends saw Friend posing over exotic cars and bikes, in a bikini, for a car magazine, they probably lost their minds. Your friends likely fought over who gets to be on the double date with the sexy friend. When nobody would give in, I'm willing to bet 100:1 that Douchebag suggested that you all go to Latin Quarters and let Friend decide who she wanted. Douchebag probably suggested going to a nightclub thinking he'd have an advantage over the other three guys. What a douche!

Where did things go wrong? How did you mess up? You forgot that you had two women to engage! Your problem the entire night was Friend, and I don't think you realized it. Women need each other, especially in a hostile social environment. Friend was the shy and sexy one and Shorty was the fun and outgoing one. While you were dancing with Shorty, did you even pay attention to Friend? I wasn't there, but Friend must've felt trapped. On the one hand, she had the choice between three nerds and a douche. On the other hand, she would be alone in a nightclub. How do you expect her to defend herself from the guys approaching her? Honestly, I believe when Shorty originally approached me, it was because she thought I would be a good match for Friend. If you would have been chill, she would've done the switch on her own. I would not have had to worry about getting jumped, and you would likely still be with Shorty to this day.

Once I entered the picture, you and your friends performed a comedy of lame errors. I understand that Shorty wasn't just another woman for you, and I truly felt bad that you were crying. I was jealous of you actually. I would give almost anything to feel what you were feeling. Usually, I'm blank and empty. My night didn't end the way I wanted to either. We went to a diner in Brooklyn after the club. I went to the bathroom and attempted to masturbate, to alleviate my blue balls. I had to stop myself, but it felt like I was going to start screaming in that tiny bathroom. I didn't want anyone to hear me.

I went back to the table, to finish off my Reuben sandwich when Shorty said "Listen Mister, don't get it twisted. You can only have one of us. There won't be any taking turns business going on here. So you better pick which one you want." Before I could respond Friend interjected "And whoever you pick, nothing is happening tonight. Cuz we're tired." "That's right!" Shorty added. "Come on Friend, let's go to the bathroom," she continued. I was mad at myself for trying to split two friends again. My balls were in pain and all my plans failed. I was angry that they both squeezed into that tiny bathroom. I was sad that I had put so much hope in you Mr. Crying Arab.

I sincerely hope that my perspective of that night would give you a better understanding of women. I could write a lot more about this situation, but I need to be cognizant of space. By now, a great guy like you might be married. Even still, there is still much to learn, and I hope that you take that plunge.

A WORTHY MISSION

My epiphany regarding women, made me realize what I was lacking. I was forced to face the reality of my own weaknesses. The infinite dance, between men and women, has obvious purposes, outcomes, and rewards.

It's clear that men and women are polar opposites, especially when it comes to mating. The essence of a man is to find a purposeful mission and live according to that mission. This essence has strengths and weaknesses. The power of a woman is her deep connection to her inner self. There are strengths and weaknesses to this power as well.

While the idea of 'connecting with your inner self' may not make immediate sense to a man, for a woman it's a profound moment. There are countless works by women about achieving this 'inner person' state. Although, not all women achieve this state.

There is a mission that men all around the world could accept, to transform the entire planet. This mission has boundless rewards and will never lead to an emotional collapse. The mission is one of discovery. The mission is to connect with and engage your partner's 'Inner Woman'.

When you do this, a woman's body will change for you. Her body will activate hormones, and pull you in deeper. There always is something new to discover, as the 'Inner Woman' is always changing and unpredictable. This dance can continue indefinitely. At the very least, sex will become better, but the connection achieved is just as desirable.

Knowing that I was incapable of partaking in this mission, it made dating pointless. Being hyper analytical, I was always aware when the process was happening. I called it "losing brain power." I'm sure biologists have a scientific way of describing this loss of brain power. I never allowed the loss to take hold. Potentially, a woman could mentally revert me to a baby if allowed.

There was one time, when I gave it my all to allow myself to lose brain power. I wished nothing more than to spend the rest of my life with Sunshine. But allowing the loss in brain power, resulted in panic attacks. I still didn't give up. I hypnotized myself every day and did every NLP technique I knew. The panic attacks morphed into revulsion. I almost threw up on Sunshine a couple of times. After Sunshine, I thought dating lots of women would change me; it didn't.

When I realized what I was doing was meaningless, I all but gave up on dating. If I'm not able to accept what a woman has to offer me, then there is no point in sex. It will be meaningless. One of the purposes of this book is to declare to the universe that I hope that I'm finally ready for a real relationship. But if it doesn't happen, then I'm content. I've learned a lot along the way.

I had actually planned on ending the book here, and not commenting too much on anything the female writer's had written. But I feel compelled to say something to Chan's father.

NOTE TO DADDY CHAN

Hello Daddy Chan. It's a pleasant surprise for me writing this to you. It's interesting for me considering that it's totally unplanned and uncommon for me. My heart sank when your daughter wrote something about you. She said. *"My mother is a talker. A very loud talker I might add. My father, after 40 years of marriage has figured her process. Let her yell (talk) until she feels heard then retreat to the garage, grocery store, back yard, etc. If he actually did something wrong he quickly fixes it and if it was her fault she apologizes to him a few hours later. At times it seems strange and wrong but it works for them because he respects her process."*

First I'd like to thank you for allowing me to talk about what I really wished would happen within the community. I really wish that there were a place for a man like you within the community. It's quite unfortunate that it's called the pickup artist community. Most of the guys attracted to such a name, are guys who faced a tough breakup and just want to have sex. I would prefer it be called the "Men's Power" community or movement, or something similar. As time moves on, and more guys become exposed to the community, it will likely reach where I wish it to be. But I need to address the "Power" issue.

In America, we've had a long history of "White Power." It seems counterproductive to attempt to empower a group that already dominates our society. In fact, it could seem quite scary. The White Power or White Supremacy tactic has been in effect for hundreds of years, and still is alive today. When a person hears "White Power" they understand it to mean that someone is to be oppressed, disenfranchised, or worst. For me "White Power" is actually White weakness. It has always been used to do nothing but divide and distract the people.

When I say that I'd like it to be a "Men's Power" community, I don't mean that we will go out and oppress women. On the contrary, a powerful man needs a powerful woman. Men all around the world are frustrated when it comes to the topic of women. Powerless men feel threatened by a woman's salary, education level, and career. Powerless men have to kill women who have the audacity to make their own choices. I see powerless men all the time on television, yammering away about what a woman is supposed to be.

It's obvious to see those guys are powerless, and call them out on it. But it's much more difficult to tell someone like you, that you have no power. It's troubling to me that your daughter thinks that your relationship with your wife is normal. It's extra troubling to me that Chan is buying into the lie that women are somehow emotionally irrational. The fact is your wife is just emotionally irrational to you.

I'm not a therapist, and there may be something deeper going on that Chan didn't explain. If there is, by all means, seek professional help. But for me I've seen and experienced something similar many times. Your wife's 'Inner Woman' is trying to engage with you. It's amazing that she still tries after forty years. Ducking and hiding until it's over is the definition of powerless. Unfortunately, I can't tell you what to do. You are technically supposed to figure it out on your own. But, even if I could tell you something to do, it may not work. What if she discovers that you just did whatever I told you to do? Then you'll be worse off than before.

Here are some general suggestions to improve your ability to connect with a woman. Mastery of anything takes time and effort. There are only a few things to improve your abilities:

Get Help from Other Guys

It's a good idea to meet up with likeminded individuals. Chances are, your close friends may not have any interest. Fortunately there are two options available to you. You could check meetup.com and search for PUA or Seduction meetings. They have them all over the place nowadays. If there aren't any meetings nearby, you could make your own meet-up events. Next, you could connect anonymously to the many free seduction forums that are on the net. I don't know which the best forum is anymore. For sure, guys at meetings or online will give you some good advice to take your situation.

Make a Study of It

There are five different paths that one can study:

1. **Language Patterns (Ross Jeffries)**
2. **Inner Game (David Deangelo)**
3. **Physical Arousal (Venus Butterfly Technique)**
4. **Situational Routines (Mystery Method)**
5. **A Unique Personal Path**

I spoke of the different paths of the seduction community. I highly recommend that you purchase and study the thing that calls to you the most. Be forewarned, none of these things are easy and they take time and energy to achieve success. It's best to focus on one thing for a few years before choosing to move on.

'A unique personal path' is something that refers specifically to you. If you are a musician and you married a groupie, then you have to realize that you can't just retire from music! You need to keep making new songs and playing anywhere people will listen. Not only that, you should study your wife in respect to your personal path. I don't know what makes you unique or special, but it's not something that can be taught, you have to live it.

Studying Popular Works

Next I suggest studying movies and/or plays. There are many situations that can be acted out or imagined. Having an in depth study of a movie and how you can use some of the scenes in your life will be incredibly fulfilling; even at your age. Also, mimicking characters or emotional states are beneficial. Movies and plays are professionally constructed for maximum emotional effect.

You may be wondering why I didn't suggest television shows? Those programs are usually contrived and resolve on a dime. How about reality shows? Those things are all scripted. I'm mentioning this in order to expose you to a simple emotional combination.

Let's say that your wife loves a particular reality show. You watch it and attempt to understand the emotional intent behind the episode. Then you would notice that most of them have a similar pattern: anticipation/buildup of a conflict, physical or verbal fighting, making up, and then calm. That literally is the cycle of abuse. I've known many abusers of women. I asked them all why they do what they do. The universal answer is "Women like it."

The first instance, I can remember that a guy said something like this to me, was in high school. My teacher, Mr. Rogers, entered the class in a chipper mood. One of the girls in the front asked him why he was so happy. He did a jig, smiled, and exclaimed, "Me and my wife just had a big fight!" His statement perplexed the entire class, and after more questioning he said, "Listen, you guys are young. When you reach my age and been married for ten years you'll understand. Whenever me and my wife have a big fight like that, the makeup sex is sweet!" He did another little jig after he said that.

Is he right? No. This is the very same reasoning that female abusers use for beating on them. They do the entire cycle of abuse because the sex is intense. Then they incorrectly assume that the woman likes it. The fact is women usually hate the pattern, but stick around to figure it out. These women will essentially be stuck in that emotional state until the intense emotions wear off. This is the unfortunate reason why the abuse must escalate; the initial emotional intensity fades. I believe that women getting stuck in this state are men's fault. First, the men who abuse them wrongly assume that this is the way to get better sex. Second, the countless frustrated men with no power don't offer women a better alternative.

If you really want to do such a combination, you may, but with permission. Doing this emotional combination could be fun if it was planned out and you both gave each other safe words to stop whenever you'd like. You can both enjoy this combination without the negative side effects, and since the woman is a willing participant the sex will get better not worst with time. There won't be a need to escalate. The combinations are better with movies and plays. Trust me on this.

Practice Makes Perfect

I also suggest checking out online personals. Pick a woman there and create a date using your chosen path. Your wife could get jealous with you looking at personals alone. So do it together with her. The idea is to create a date, or series of dates, given the information at hand. It's intended to help you be creative. You could spend years, having your wife 'try on' different women. If you pick the woman together, then she won't be upset about you setting up three or four dates attempting to impress an Asian marine biologist. She could be the Asian marine biologist. What if she picked a Haitian Chef, or a ballerina? Each personal will take you out of your comfort zone and make you think of how you can impress different women, given what you already have.

Who knows what could happen if you do this. This is almost the same as creating your own "Mystery Method." Though it is important to have chosen a specific path of study. The more you do it, the better you'll get at it.

Romance Novels

Lastly, there are romance novels. You can of course read any book with your wife. But romance novels are written in a way to excite women. I don't know what else you can do with those books, other than read them together. It is an easy way to connect with her 'Inner Woman', without that much thought. You just have to be next to her. Romance novels have one good thing about them; the language. By reading one together, you can have a secret and play language between you. The secret language is great if she wants to tell you something, but needs plausible deniability.

Discovering your woman is a powerful and rewarding experience at any age. I hope you appreciate the things that I've shared with you. I had no intention to insult you. I hope that one day most guys see women as I do, a lifelong challenge to learn and engage with. Thank you.

FINAL CONCLUSION

It was a pleasant challenge, to attempt to do on paper what I've witness countless times in person. Women in general are dynamic and secretive about their inner parts. I'm forever grateful to the female writers, as without them I wouldn't have been able to do this book. Also, unexpectedly, I learned a few things.

A man needs to find a way to connect with the 'Inner Woman'. For all of my explanations, it usually takes no more than five minutes to connect with her. This is what surprised me about the female writers. I came into this project with my own assumptions, based on my personal interactions. I assumed that women overuse their 'Inner Woman' in general. I assumed women easily connect with their inner parts. I also assumed that I could have them recognize a state change at the end.

In retrospect, Part 1 could be considered a complete failure. On the contrary, it was even better than I had hoped. This is the way that it is with women, you put lots of effort and planning into a thing and she will change it and sometimes make things better. You should look at Part 1 for what it is, a unique and interesting experience that I made for three female writers. There are interesting points that I raised, and the women made entertaining and interesting comments. But none of that really matters. What matters is that I spent a few months attempting to create an experience that lasted three weeks for each woman.

What separates average men in the pickup artist community, and an average guy is that the pickup artist usually has about ten hours of planned material. Women are attracted to the new and unique experiences that the PUA's offer. Unfortunately, most guys in the community have nothing to offer beyond those first few hours. They are ok with that since there is always someone new.

What I've suggested is constant and consistent improvement. A man can improve his ability to connect with and engage not only the 'Inner Woman', but many other parts. It would be a mistake copying the things that I've said in this book. It's important to understand why things work or don't work. While I may have written a book to attempt to engage women, maybe that's not what you are all about. But if do you want to write a book for a woman, and that's something that's consistent with who you are, then go for it. Failure is impossible if you try and learn from your mistakes.

I had Perfecta in mind when writing this book. After weeks of communicating, I'd discovered more than any man had about her 'Inner Woman', and what excited her. Close to the end of our relationship, I posed a question to her. "Given that your husband is all that you'd ever dreamt of, and I've seemed to connect with you in a way that your husband doesn't, wouldn't it make sense to tell your husband everything that I've done and said so he could actually be the perfect husband?" She froze up and refused.

We debated about that for a long while. At the time, I didn't understand. Her husband had to discover what I had, all on his own. Otherwise, it wouldn't be the same. A book, to me, seems to bridge that gap. A woman can read this book and share it with others, with total plausible deniability.

If you liked this book or learned something valuable, please write a review on Amazon.com or Goodreads.com.

Thank you

End

www.ingramcontent.com/pod-product-compliance
Lightning Source LLC
Chambersburg PA
CBHW071858290426
44110CB00013B/1196